SCARVES &

SPACEBOOTS

A Hobo Story

BASED ON A TRUE STORY, REAL PEOPLE & REAL EVENTS

By

Michael Jesmer

This book is a fictional representation of a remarkably true story and is dedicated to not only the astounding individuals who work in such a thankless industry, but the underdogs they represent.

In my mind, this novel stands as a testament to the grand design, faith and good in human nature. Without the support I received from those standing on their last leg, this book would not exist and neither would I.

-Michael Jesmer

Table of Contents

Acknowledgments

Special thanks to Linda Norman, and my grandma Alice Tymchatyn for the initial editing. A special thanks to Camara Swap for a phenomenal job on the cover art. And a final thank you to the DI, as well as to all the folks who work and live in this reality.

Without any of you this book wouldn't be what it is and I can't thank you enough.

About the Author

Michael Jesmer is an up and coming author with over ten years of experience under his belt, as well as a history of addiction and mental illness. *Scarves & Spaceboots* is his debut novel, but you can expect more to come.

PROLOGUE

What did I know?

If I'm going to lie to you I may as well tell you the truth. When this all started, I knew I was going to write a book on the homeless condition. But what did I know? I could have been someone just like you; hell, I could have been someone just like your Grandpa. Twenty-one years old, intelligent, talented, good looking (if I do say so myself), independent, ambitious; maybe a little bit ignorant.

Unfortunately, some rightfully mistook my ambition for stupidity; what twenty-one year old starts a production company? Outsiders reassured me that even though my *company* didn't work out, all artists make mistakes- that experience leads to success. I could appreciate their helping hand of optimism, but I was faced with the weight and reality of my *mistake*. I was broke. Not only was I broke, but during my last two months living in accommodation I developed the ability to turn any possession I had into cold hard cash. All I had was my laptop. My laptop and a dream. A stupid, stupid dream.

I was watching YouTube videos about homelessness, the wealth gap, and class warfare late at night; January 2014, laying on the ash stained beige carpet where my computer chair used to be, the laptop loosely filling in the still beige rectangle that once belonged to the desk. On the floor of my cold room watching the winter bite at my window between videos, realizing there was no way out this time, I began searching for a reason my life had come to the point that it had.

That night, two nights before rent was due, I discovered something. There was a whole different scary world out there, and it wasn't hiding in the dark or behind a mask. It wasn't painted over or swept under the proverbial carpet. This world wasn't even a secret. It was right there, smack dab in the open for everyone to see and it was too God damned ugly for anyone to look at. But what did I know about it?

Viktor E. Frankl, a Jewish psychologist, was detained and deported to numerous Nazi concentration camps (Auschwitz and Dachau to name a couple) over the course of 1942 to 1945. From the beginning, Dr. Frankl smuggled a journal into camp and proceeded to take on an objective study of his Jewish comrades and the way they adapted to the extreme and abnormal conditions of the concentration camps. Long story short, a book was published (_Man's Search for Meaning_), and a field of psychology was created; _Logotherapy._

But what really caught my attention about this book was that it was not only a study of the mental and physical conditioning and adaptation of prisoners, or specifically, Nazi prisoners. It was a study of _human nature_; two words that contradict each other in modern times. An objective study of human nature became what I'd aspire my book to be, but I sure as hell wasn't any doctor.

What I was looking at on my computer screen that night was a neglected condition- a condition that has been around since the beginning of time. I mean, wasn't the Virgin Mary seeking shelter? Where did the dinosaurs sleep? I knew based on what my ego was telling me and based on the big fat zero on my bank statement that it was up to me to write a book on the homeless condition, I just never would have dreamed that I'd succumb to it.

The Drop-in Center- better known by its occupants as the _Mansion_ or the _DI_ - a six story homeless shelter in Calgary, Alberta. Home to eighteen hundred Hobos in the winter time, the largest shelter in North America. An enormous brown brick building with a big orange sign in front that features digital cartoon images of people walking around in a circle. The building itself is surrounded by a black steel gate that closes at 11:00 pm. The outside is decorated with a few dark green plastic garbage cans, some smokers, and police and/or ambulances more often than you'd think.

Immediately when you enter the building, you scan your fingers for one of the Dice (drop in center employees) who stands behind what I assume to be bullet proof glass. Once the computer gives you the ok the Dice will buzz you through. Straight ahead you'll find a security guard who sits behind another pane of bulletproof glass focusing on his phone until he gets a distressed signal over the walkie-talkie.

From there, to your left would be Intox; a room open day and night dedicated to Hobos who are too drunk or high to function in society, or even at times the DI itself, and need to sleep it off. RCMP will even drop them off to Intox if they're found sleeping somewhere they shouldn't be or intoxicated in public. The cops usually say it's because the drunk-tank is too full, but rumor among the Dice and occupants of the DI is it's because they just don't want to deal with Hobos.

To your right of the security station is the lobby, about the same size as Intox with the addition of a small hallway. It's big and occasionally features people throwing up, arguing, fighting or just conversing, but is more or less empty unless people are lining up for meal tickets or tickets for the Warehouse A.K.A 2907- a secondary male shelter where Hobos are transported to between the hours of 4:45 pm – 9:00 pm on a shuttle bus if they happen to be sober that night. It shelters an additional one-hundred and seventy. Twenty bunk beds on the top floor, sixty bunk beds crammed in the basement and ten floor mats along the walls.

On your left side of the lobby and further down the hall are a series of offices where three counselors, a doctor and two nurses work selectively through the weekdays for however many of the eighteen hundred (give or take) need their expertise. At the end of the hallway is a temporary labor office run by the DI. Another word used by those working in the temporary labor trade, or most who know what temp labor is for that matter, is *slave labor*. At this particular temp office you can line up with a minimum of fifty other men ready to work, to draw balls with numbers on them from a bingo cage. On a good day they'll send out seven guys that get paid $50.00 for an eight hour day of hard labor. So if you're lucky…

Less than two hundred kilometers away and a week after I was lying on the dirty carpet of my dingy room in Red Deer, that was about as much as I'd figured out about my new home.

PART 1

ONCE UPON A TIME THERE WAS A BEAUTIFUL PLANET

ON THAT PLANET THERE WAS A VILLAGE

IN THAT VILLAGE THERE WAS A BOY

INSIDE THE HEART OF THE BOY LAY THE BEAUTIFUL PLANET THAT NURTURED HIM

BEASTS HAD ALSO FOUND A PLACE IN THE BOY'S HEART

THE BOY'S ELDERS FOUND A PLACE FOR THE BEASTS AROUND THEIR WAISTS AND BACKS

EVERY DAY THAT FOLLOWED EVERY NIGHT, THE BOY'S ELDERS TOLD TALES OF A WISE OLD WIZARD WHO LIVED ON THE HIGHEST PEAK OF THE HIGHEST MOUNTAIN

EVERY NIGHT THAT FOLLOWED EVERY DAY, THE BOY'S ELDERS TOLD FABLES OF THE BRAVE SOULS WHO WERE BLESSED WITH ENLIGHTENMENT UPON SUMMITING THE PEAK

THEY TOLD HIM THIS EVERY SUMMER THAT FOLLOWED EVERY WINTER

THEY TOLD HIM THIS EVERY WINTER THAT FOLLOWED EVERY SUMMER

THEY TOLD HIM THIS UNTIL IT CAME HIS TIME TO TELL IT TO THEM

FOLLOWING UP ON A TIME THERE WAS A BEAUTIFUL PLANET

ON THAT PLANET THERE WAS A VILLAGE

IN THAT VILLAGE THERE WAS A MAN

INSIDE THE HEART OF THE MAN LAY THE BEAUTIFUL PLANET THAT NURTURED HIM AS DID THE TOOLS HE USED TO DESTROY IT

THE BEASTS HE HUNTED FOR FOOD AND WARMTH HAD ALSO FOUND A PLACE IN THE MAN'S HEART

TOO DID THE TOOLS HE USED TO TAKE THEIR LIVES

TOO DID HIS PEOPLE

SCARCE TIME PASSED AND THE MAN HUNTED HIS STAKE OF THE UNDERTAKING

HE HAD A BOY, AND EVERY DAY THAT FOLLOWED EVERY NIGHT, THE MAN TOLD HIM TALES OF A WISE OLD WIZARD WHO LIVED ON THE HIGHEST PEAK OF THE HIGHEST MOUNTAIN

HE HAD A SON, AND EVERY NIGHT THAT FOLLOWED EVERY DAY, THE MAN TOLD HIM FABLES OF THE BRAVE MEN WHO WERE BLESSED WITH ENLIGHTENMENT UPON SUMMITING THE PEAK

HE TOLD HIM THIS EVERY SUMMER THAT FOLLOWED EVERY WINTER

HE TOLD HIM THIS EVERY WINTER THAT FOLLOWED EVERY SUMMER

HE TOLD HIS SON THE LEGEND UNTIL IT CAME TIME FOR HIS SON TO TELL IT TO HIM

CONTINUING UPON A TIME THERE WAS A BEAUTIFUL PLANET

ON THAT PLANET THERE WAS A VILLAGE

IN THAT VILLAGE THERE WAS A MAN

INSIDE THE HEART OF THE MAN WAS HIS SON

INSIDE THE HEART OF HIS SON WERE THE TOOLS THAT GAVE HIS FATHER POWER

THE MAN WALKED THE PATH HE WAS GIVEN

HE WAS A MAN NO MORE, BUT AN ELDER

HIS SON WAS A BOY NO MORE, BUT A MAN

THE ELDER HAD SEIZED HIS MEASURE

AND IT WAS TIME TO GO

CARRYING ON A TIME THERE WAS A BEAUTIFUL PLANET

ON THAT PLANET THERE WAS AN EMINENT MOUNTAIN

ON THAT MOUNTAIN THERE WAS AN ELDER

INSIDE THE HEART OF THE ELDER WAS HOPE

INSIDE OF THE HEART OF THE ELDER WAS TRIUMPH

HE HAD REACHED THE HIGHEST PEAK OF THE HIGHEST MOUNTAIN

BUT HE WAS ALONE

THE ELDER PRAYED FOR THE WISE OLD WIZARD TO APPEAR

HE COULD NOT SEE IN THE BLINDING SNOWFALL

THE ELDER HOWLED OUT FOR ENLIGHTENMENT

DEAFENING WIND HOWLED BACK THROUGH THE MOUNTAIN CREST

GRAVER THAN THE JAW OF A BEAR IS THE DUPLICITY OF WARDENS

WAITING ON A TIME, THERE WAS A BEAUTIFUL PLANET

ON THAT PLANET THERE WAS AN EMINENT MOUNTAIN

COVERING THAT MOUNTAIN WAS SNOW

UNDER THAT SNOW SAT AN ELDER

PIERCING THE HEART OF THE ELDER WAS THE DECEIT OF HIS ELDER'S

PIERCING THE HEART OF HIS ELDERS WAS THE FEAR OF THEIRS

IT WOULD BRING ME DELIGHT TO ADVISE YOU THAT YOU ARE THE WISE OLD WIZARD ON THE PEAK OF THIS MOUNTAIN, HOWEVER, BLESSING YOU WITH ENLIGHTENMENT WOULD ONLY ENCOURAGE YOUR DEMISE

CALLING UPON A TIME, THERE WAS A BEAUTIFUL PLANET

ON THAT PLANET THERE WAS AN EMINENT MOUNTAIN

ON THAT MOUNTAIN WERE AN ELDER AND A WISE OLD WIZARD

AND THE ELDER WEPT FOR CLARITY

CAST AWAY THE BAG THAT CONFINES YOUR PROVISIONS AND TOOLS

EVERY DAY WHEN THE ELDER WAS A BOY HE WAS TOLD TALES OF A WISE OLD WIZARD WHO LIVED ON THE HIGHEST PEAK OF THE HIGHEST MOUNTAIN

THE INNOCENT SKIN YOU WEAR, THAT YOU PERMITTED YOURSELF TO DEFACE AND DISFIGURE, CAST THEM OFF NOW

EVERY NIGHT WHEN THE ELDER WAS A BOY, HE WAS TOLD FABLES OF THE BRAVE MEN WHO WERE BLESSED WITH ENLIGHTENMENT UPON SUMMITING THE PEAK

FINALLY, CAST OFF THE WHITE BUFFALO HIDE YOU'VE SO LONG USED TO SHELTER YOUR FEET FROM THE EARTH YOU LIVE UPON

THE WHITE BUFFALO WAS MORE SACRED THAN AN ELDER

THE WHITE BUFFALO WAS MORE SACRED THAN A WIZARD

THE WHITE BUFFALO BOOTS FADED INTO THE MOUNTAIN FLURRY WITH A HEAVE

YOU WILL BECOME ENLIGHTENED IF YOU ARE ABLE ENOUGH TO REACH THE FOOT OF THE MOUNTAIN WITH ONLY THAT WHICH YOU CAME INTO THIS LIFE

ONCE UPON A TIME THERE WAS A BEAUTIFUL PLANET

ON THAT PLANET WAS AN EMINENT MOUNTAIN

DESCENDING THAT MOUNTAIN WAS AN ELDER

1

IT WAS A FRIDAY

Friday, February the 7th, 2014. I was lining up for 2907 with Biker Mike, a fifty-three year old ex-biker with medium silver hair longer than his beard and a voice so gruff and accented I could tell it was from Louisiana before he spoke more than a word. His puffy black and blue jacket always looked brand new, leading me to believe it had been a gift. We were at the back of the line of about forty of the most sober people the DI could offer. Standing in this already too familiar lobby I found it hard to believe it had only been a week since I'd arrived.

***

Skipping a hospitable train ticket courtesy of the RCMP, followed by the pleasantries of getting lost in downtown Calgary amongst high rises that were foreign to me as a result of living an isolated life in Red Deer, I finally made it to the DI.

Walking through the gate I could see a line of people up to the door smoking. I stood at the back of the line and lit one up myself, looking up along the sides of the building to see brick upon brick six stories high. When I Googled the DI before coming to Calgary I'd imagined it as more of a hotelesque establishment. It became very clear very fast that this was no hotel, but a fortress.

Letting my backpack down I felt the divots in my strap embroidered shoulders. The muscles in my legs felt tight from the backpack I was carrying and it had only been about four hours walking with the damn thing. I felt as though perhaps I took too much, figuring the pack must have been between sixty and seventy pounds, but realistically people travel carrying much more than that; I'd just have to get used to it. Not that I had much choice.

The man ahead of me in line seemed to be growing more and more impatient with me, his dilated pupils inspecting me from the corner of his eye behind his long dark hair. He looked back and away again until I finished my cigarette. I assumed he was going to ask me for one, but he stood questioning himself about me until he realized I wasn't just there to smoke.

"Who the fuck are you?"

"Sorry?"

"Who the fuck are you?" Confusion overwhelmed me. "Why are you standing here?"

"Isn't this the line to get in?"

"No, the door's over there," he pointed beyond the wave of smokers.

As I walked past them I noticed that most of these smokers were seniors or soon to be. One man who was collecting cigarette butts from the ground caught my eye and I was shocked. I mean, in my time I had rolled tobacco from *my* cigarette butts and even considered *that* greasy; but *other peoples*?

Reaching in my pocket to give the man a real cigarette I looked around to have sense made. All these old folks were smoking rolled cigarettes, seemingly rolled from the cigarette butts dropped outside the building. Most avoided eye contact. They weren't lining up or sitting out front to smoke and they weren't about to ask for anything either. They were just waiting for more to be stomped out so they could salvage enough tobacco to roll. I was pretty put off by this to tell you the truth.

After walking through the doors, I was officially signed in with the DI - the process took all of ten minutes. They said it would have taken a bit longer had I not had ID, I thought it slightly unnerving that *anyone* could be in there. They had me scan my fingerprints at the door and assured me in a rehearsed manner that they do not work with the RCMP and that the fingerprints are strictly to get into the building. Through the doors a security table was set up for bag checks and they waved me through because my bag was so large; this I also found unnerving.

Intimidation stopped me in my tracks when I got into the lobby. Before me was a hoard of Hobos. Some were sleeping on the ground with fleece blankets that didn't cover their body, some were talking in groups and a few were waiting outside the counselor offices, not to forget the old guy puking beside the vending machine. *They have vending machines here?* One Dice rushed up and escorted him over to a nearby garbage can while another came promptly with a mop and bucket to clean up the mess.

As soon as I entered the lobby I could hear music, but it was only now that I realized it was live, and coming from upstairs. Reaching the top of the bastardly stairs I would later learn to despise, my eyes were unwrapped by a hamlet inside the DI.

There were easily eight hundred people gathered around tables drinking juice and eating pretzels and it seemed like everyone and their Grandma had a laptop. There were live performers playing off to the side and everyone seemed to be having a blast. Some Dice were walking around handing out the bags of pretzels and cartons of juice that were in the hands of almost everyone I could see.

What surprised me wasn't the scenario itself but how perfect of a place this was to come in search of a study of Logotherapy in the homeless condition. *This is the place,* I thought to myself. Though surrounded by freezing cold weather, homeless and most likely facing very hard financial and social crisis, they all learned how to cope and celebrate and just enjoy time spent. *This is what I was looking for*, I thought, lacking the insight to tell myself that I couldn't even fathom what I was attempting to accomplish.

After a couple songs, the scene was getting to be too much for me. Besides the eyes jumping at me and my backpack, the crowds in every direction and the boisterous echoes of amps and drums and voices, I began questioning myself. *What am I doing here? Is anyone here younger than me? What am I doing here?? Why doesn't anyone else have a big backpack like mine? What the fuck am I doing here?* Before I knew it I was downstairs and out the front doors smoking with the seniors.

Fighting to get his backpack on was Biker Mike, his backpack was presumably the same load as mine and, because of the pity I had for myself, I was empathetic to his plight. He grunted after I offered a hand and stumbled away, continuing to fight his backpack onto his shoulders. I dropped my backpack to the ground and smoked, watching the stubborn old man as he came to terms with the fact that he'd need to accept my help.

Whether it was because I helped him, because I was young, or simply because we had the same name is anyone's guess, but after that Biker Mike had my back. I suspected he saw a little bit of himself in me. He told me about 2907 and we went back into the DI to get me a ticket to the place.

When we walked in and lined up, the old man who had been puking beside the vending machine was on the ground convulsing. There were so many faces around us, so calm, like it happens every day. There were some Dice by his side but in the end there is nothing you can do when you are by-standing an overdose, especially in a place like the DI. All you can do is wait for the ambulance to arrive. Watching this old man's eyes roll into the back of his head, twitching as he took his final breaths, I had witnessed not only the first death of the story, but my life.

***

Standing in that already too familiar lobby, I found it hard to believe it had only been a week since I'd arrived. Brad and Lyle, two of the few living at the DI who were my age, mobbed up behind us.

Brad was twenty years old, 6'4 and as obnoxious and as conversationally aggressive as all hell, though I am sure if he channelled it right he could be quite charismatic; a world-class salesman perhaps. Upon meeting him, judging by his shoulder length hair and nipple length beard, I assumed that he'd been living at the DI for some time now.

Lyle on the other hand was clean cut and quiet, almost too quiet, always wearing his hard hat even though his day consisted of following Brad around; a bodyguard no doubt. They'd taken to calling me Red Deer, I'm sure you can imagine why.

They were standing behind Biker Mike and I, Brad boasting their presence "And he was like 'It's not that bad, it's just gonorrhoea, it's not like it's permanent.' And I was like 'well yeah but it's still a green discharge comin' out yer dick!'"

Biker Mike was startled and looked back in an elderly fashion, it reminded me of something an old gentleman would do if he heard a youngun' belting out in public. I looked back too and Brad was already smiling at me with pearly yellows. "Red Deer, we've been lookin' for you buddy." He put his arm around me and tried to walk me away but I didn't move, Lyle stood in front of me grinning. Biker Mike was keeping our place in line, checking out the scene to see if he needed to get involved.

"We noticed you don't get fucked up like these other bums." He announced unbelievably loud before looking around to make sure at least a few people heard him. "We wanna know if you wanna get involved in what we got goin' on." His yellows gleamed neon in the fluorescent light as he gave a conspiring nod to Lyle, who looked like he had no idea what they had going on.

"I'm good man." I replied before looking over at Biker Mike to give him a smirk, letting him know all was good. Brad took his arm off my shoulder and backed up, spreading his arms out, acting offended like we'd been friends forever even though this was the third time I'd met him.

"Alright, I see how it is Red Deer, I see how it is. I know when I'm not wanted." He walked back up to me, looking at me with medicated eyes. "You got a cigarette?" Giving him a smoke was probably what made him think we were friends in the first place.

"Sorry man I don't." Brad turned his attention to Biker Mike.

"Don't look at me partner." Biker Mike objected, getting all puffed up like he was about to enter some sort of uncomfortable confrontation.

"Alright, Red Deer," Brad mimicked himself, "I see how it is. I see how it is. I know when I'm not wanted."

Lyle smiled at me with a nod and walked off following Brad. They never stayed at 2907. Well, Brad wasn't allowed because he got caught smoking pot there; Lyle just didn't go because Brad couldn't. 2907 in my opinion was the best place to gain a foothold on this new found lifestyle.

"Don't get involved with those two," Biker Mike's sandpaper voice rubbed into the sound barrier. "they don't got nothin' goin' on." I grinned and agreed and the line started moving.

The first Friday night when Biker Mike showed me 2907, he swiped a jug of juice out of the kitchen for our table to make me feel more welcome. Then the next day he took me around the downtown core of Calgary, explaining the grid system of their streets and showing me the *better* temp labor offices around the area to work at. I was baffled that he was able to teach me all this stuff, later learning that night had been his first night in Calgary in twenty five years. With the effort he was putting into teaching me how and what way to get out of the DI the fastest, I didn't have it in me to tell him I intended to stay a while.

Now, a week later, Biker Mike landed a contract job through a temp office meaning he was going to have steady work with a company and quite possibly a permanent position. I think he was counting on me to do the same, but I, however, was still passionate about sinking my roots into my new habitat. I'd come to Calgary with a little over a hundred bucks in my pocket, cash that was long gone by now.

We got our tickets and headed out to wait for the shuttle bus. Biker Mike popped a cigarette in his mouth "You got smokes?" He asked me, and I nodded with a smile.

The cold Alberta wind was scratching our faces, the lot of us all lined up beside a frosted chain linked fence close to the DI across the street from under the bridge. It was quiet, and it wasn't because the herd had nothing to complain about, it was because our jaws were all frozen shut. One man seemed to have been outside the entire day, his beard frosted and a giant boogsicle dangling from his nose. I later took to calling this guy Nomad because I never saw him go inside, save 2907, and I never saw him stop moving; saw him all over Calgary. Even when we'd wait for the bus he'd pace the length of the fence. Arabian I think, with long hair and an even longer beard and he was always carrying a way larger backpack than anyone I saw around the DI.

A very drunk, dark man came staggering over yelling nonsense about the government, then stopped to inspect me and my cigarette. Biker Mike was already staring him down. "Problem here partner?" The man did his best to see who he was talking to.

"I'm just saying that if shit hits the fan here I'll be the first one fighting!" his psychosis bellowed out before he continued staggering.

"I doubt that!" Biker Mike grunted in return.

The man turned around "What!?"

"I said 'I *doubt* that!"

The guy looked shocked at the old man barking at him and took a step closer.

"If shit hits the fan here *I'll* be the first one fighting. You won't be able to do a *damn* thing."

"I can fight!" The guy was already backing up.

"And when you trip over yerself I'll go in and finish it for you!" Biker Mike really didn't want to be involved in this, he wasn't making eye contact with the guy and I could almost feel the uneasiness in his breath.

It may have been a need to have the last word or just his way of being protective, but something very similar to this happened a few days earlier; only in that instance a man just walked up to me before Biker Mike got between us with his chest puffed out. Somehow on both occasions he got them to walk away without a fight. It was touching that this old man was looking out for me, but feelings of guilt were persevering because I thought my position was disingenuous.

One Dice would take the tickets at the front of the bus and off we'd go - half of us standing, most of us squished with our name-sake-backpacks jammed into each other. Imagine something like a Tokyo subway cart only smaller and filled with Hobos.

When we got off, half the crowd ran to the front of 2907 to sign in and line up for dinner, the other half went to the back of 2907 where the semi-gated smoke pit was; knowing there would be more food when they got in. Biker Mike and I were still in the group rushing to sign in because we didn't have *designated* beds yet. You sign in right at the door where you get ambushed by three Dice. One to sign you in, one to determine your sobriety and the other to make sure the guys heading in for food were only grabbing a couple pieces of bread and not the entire loaf.

Lockers ran the walls around the perimeter; in the corner of the room was a makeshift dining room and there was always a large garbage bag full of buns waiting on a table in the middle of a lobby a lot like the lobby at the DI. Meals at 2907 were the same meals as the rest of the DI, usually some kind of rice, pasta or pizza and some kind of meat; always a lot of bread. All carbs, anything that will put meat on your bones.

This day Biker Mike and I barely spoke until we got our food and sat down, indicating to me that he wanted to ask me something because usually he was full of stories and advice. We sat with Greg, another old fellow Biker Mike and I had been sitting with since night one. Maybe a bit younger than Biker Mike with a wicked sheriff's moustache and deep blue eyes, Greg said he'd been there since too long.

I managed to swipe Biker Mike an extra couple buns while he was getting us towels for a shower before they were out before we sat down with our chili. Ripping one of the buns in half I dug in.

"You work today kid?" Greg asked as Biker Mike sat down.

"Not today, sat at the office until eleven but no luck." A lie.

Biker Mike grunted and ate a bite of chili. Could have burned his tongue but I assumed it was because he didn't believe me.

"Ah, that's alright kid, your time'll come. Someone'd be stupid not to hire a strong kid like you," he said with a wink. Greg gave me the same impression Biker Mike did, that he thought he saw a little of himself in me.

"My boss" Biker Mike said between sipping hot chili off of his lips, "really likes me. He knows I'm hard workin' and if you want I could put in a word for ya'." He drew his attention from the chili to me. "But you gotta be hard workin' too."

I was nervous to tell him that I wasn't planning to work, at least not until I'd dove deeper into poverty. "It's all good Mike I'll get a good job."

"Atta' boy!" Greg joined in.

"Don't say I didn't offer!" He looked down at his bowl, then at my empty bowl of chili that I ate savagely through the brief conversation. "Here, you want this?"

"You don't?"

"Naw it's not good for me I got one of them ah, ulcer things," he claimed before scraping his meal into my bowl. "Had A&W with the boss for lunch anyways." Because of that I wondered if he actually had an ulcer or if he just wanted to make sure *my* belly was full.

After dinner Biker Mike went to shower and I watched his stuff. Usually I'd shower after and he'd watch my stuff, then we'd go out for a smoke but this Friday night one of the Dice, Trent, walked up to me with eyes that said he already knew me. Trent was a little bigger than me and wore the Dice uniform including the optional hat; a real trooper.

"What are you doing here?"

"What do you mean?"

"I mean, what are you doing here?" I was confused. "How'd you end up here?"

This was the first time someone asked since I became homeless and I realized that I myself hadn't even asked anyone else. Actually, I realized how dazed and confused I'd truly been since I decided to try and martyr myself in the wonderful world of woe.

"I started a company that went south."

He stood with his left arm crossed and supporting his right arm which was supporting his chin.

"Uh-huh."

"And I'm an alcoholic." Trent's eyes rolled and I looked back at Biker Mike's bags. They remained idle.

"Ok. So what are you *doing* here?" There was a sarcastic friendliness to his voice.

"Trying to write a book on the homeless." Wasn't the answer he was looking for but it was good enough.

"What's your name?"

"Michael."

"Alright Michael, do you have an assigned bed here?"

"No."

"Well ya do now." He held up his index finger then turned towards the 2907 office, right next to the room with the twenty beds. Having an assigned bed at 2907 meant that I was now going to have a bed guaranteed to me at the Warehouse and a big container that's kept underneath the bunk for storage, as well as my own locker. This to me was bliss; not having to carry around a seventy pound sack on my back twenty-four-seven.

I wondered if this was shirking off some of the responsibilities of writing a book about the homeless, but I had also noticed by the first week that a good portion of the other Hobos walked around without a giant backpack like mine. Most everyone else either had nothing but what they carried on their back or they had a place to stash their stuff.

Trevor came back to me with bed 207 and locker 37. Didn't make sense to me but Hell I'd have taken bed 666 and locker Pluto. When Biker Mike came back I let him know about this new development.

"Ya get me designated?"

"No."

"Why the hell not!"

"You weren't here." Like his jacket, he seemed kind of puffed up, it was hard not to laugh but I could tell he wasn't mad. "You can use my locker until you're designated."

"I was plannin' on it!" he said with a nod and I showed him to our locker.

We found my locker, number 37 under locker 258 and in between lockers 10 and 67. It was clear that these lockers must've been donated, in fact none of them looked the same. They were all different colors from mismatched sets. But it didn't matter, now all that mattered was that Biker Mike and I could get unpacked. He made fun of me for bringing all the body wash and hair product I had and I made fun of him for not having any at all. We both unpacked our hard hats, vests, work gloves and our steel toed boots. Well, he did, my steel toed boots were all I had for footwear. Biker Mike had a pair of extra shoes that he had dangling off of his backpack for the last week while he walked around in steel toes.

"Gonna need these if yer plannin' on bein' here a while," he asserted while tying on his runners.

"I'll tough it out."

"Tell me that when yer cryin' of blisters. Trust me."

"Think the DI has a pair for me?"

"Had *these* for *me*."

And that was it. Biker Mike joined sixty other guys to watch the movie of the night on 2907's 32' TV that was propped in the top corner of the *dining room* parallel to a surveillance camera, and I went to shower. The shower was what you'd expect from a swimming pool change room, only more dead skin cells and *I hope that's not sperm* all over the place.

After my shower I went downstairs to dress bed 207 with what reminded me of hospital sheets. I was getting ready for an early night sleep knowing I was going to be crammed in a basement with a hundred and thirty other guys on chili night. Unfortunately my bunk buddy, a ginormous Native man with long gray hair and a pair of stretched out, crying sweat pants, had the same idea. Called him the Bear God, I felt it suited him because of his size and the serious look had on his face at all times. *That man can speak to bears*, was the initial thought.

Fighting with a ratty blanket about half the size of me turned out to be the least of my worries once an ungodly smell seeped up from the bottom bunk. The night for me was already starting but I wasn't going to be defeated! Not yet. I hopped off my bed and stuffed a sweater in my pillow case to make the plastic pillow a little more comfortable and pulled the collar of my shirt over my nose. Trent came into the basement and began looking around; I wondered if he was looking for me. He was.

"Michael, you want a new blanket?" Of course I did; I wanted a new *anything*.

I followed him to a storage room where he handed me a blanket, still wrapped in its package. Blue fleece, it was a nice blanket but I couldn't assess the quality until I knew if it covered my body or not. Trent was giving me a more serious look when I looked back up at him, holding another packaged blanket out to me. "Take this one too."

"Thanks."

"You know," he started, and I knew he was going to try to lay into me with some advice so I tried to hide my arrogance and took on a more serious look- "most of these old guys are Veteran's."

I nodded at him because I thought I understood, thinking he meant Veterans of the street. My mind started to wander, wondered if he meant real Veteran's. Heroes. Post-traumatic stress jockeys.

He must have seen my mind trail off because he added: "And *all* of them are tired. They're survivors. You..." Gloomy eyes tried to find the words he wanted to say to the dumb kid standing in front of him. "You're one of the few." He didn't continue. *What do you mean? One of the few that have a chance? One of the few that shouldn't be here? One of the few that are indubitably screwed if they don't run for the hills?*

"I really appreciate it, but I went to rehab. Been sober for five months; I'm not going to relapse as long as I stay focused on my book." He shook his head.

"Volunteer in the laundry room, say Trent sent you. You need to put in ten volunteer hours a month if you want to keep your bed at the Warehouse, twenty if you want to get onto the for fifth floor. Sign up for our EST program, they'll get you your tickets and everything you need to start working; your forklift ticket, first aid, you name it."

Maybe I was a *little* interested in what he was saying, but at the same time I couldn't help but think *I want to submerse myself, this is where the story is.*

"Listen, I know you want to do what you want to do, but… No one plans to be out on the street. You get mixed up with the wrong guys in a place like this you can kiss your life good-bye, I've seen it happen."

The honesty was appreciated but more importantly he just gave me a lead; volunteering. Still, I had to keep him appeased.

"EST?"

"Yeah I'll write it down for you." Trent began writing a list of helpful information out for me with a look of dedication in his eyes, making sure he wasn't forgetting anything.

Within the first week at the DI I'd found more kindness in complete strangers than I had in friends and family. Unrelenting sympathy and pity were something I expected to find in the homeless condition, but not genuine kindness. As much as I didn't want their efforts to be in vain, the idea of an objective study consumed me.

Trent handed me the list with a smile. "Have a good night Michael, I'll catch up with you tomorrow."

As I lay in the midst of a hundred and thirty men on chili night with my ambition to get to sleep before they all came down crushed, other ambitions sheltered me from my surroundings. The amount of support I'd already come across, though somewhat comforting, stood as a symbol of things to come. I knew as well then as I do now that the intention to protect habitually originates from the appeal of redemption for prior calamities experienced.

Where I thought initially those such as Biker Mike and Trent saw hope, what they really saw was a chance to prevent tragedy. Concern from complete strangers was telling me I was treading very dangerous territory, it had me shamefully excited. This was no place to be playing games and I knew it. However, in many ways, laying in my bed that night dissecting every piece of information I'd come across since the day this all began, focusing on my book and not giving work or EST a second thought, it has become very obvious that I was under a spell of denial and under the impression that I still had the power of choice; and it was intoxicating.

2

YELLOW TEETH

To my surprise, it was the best sleep I had in a while, but I also woke up the earliest I had since I got to the DI because someone nearby got an early wakeup - too early. My phone, really more of a pocket watch without service said it was 4:00 am.

I grabbed the Ziploc bag with my tooth brush and tooth paste out of my backpack and made my way to the washroom. My sore arms didn't feel so sore. I took my shirt off and in only a week I had built a substantial amount of muscle just from lugging my backpack around. *Most Hobos*, I thought, *must be in fairly good shape. At least until they're passed their prime.* Putting my shirt back on, I reconsidered leaving my backpack in my locker. With all the food at your disposal when living in shelter you need to find *some* way to wear it off.

As I pushed toothpaste onto the brush, I found a new appreciation in this everyday act, or what *should* be an everyday act. One thing I *had* noticed in my short time in the condition, was that every person besides staff here had awful teeth. If they weren't rotting, falling out or already gone, they were yellow. My teeth were still white and I planned to keep it that way. Perhaps it may be demeaning to brush your teeth in a public place but as long as I had access to a working washroom in the shelter, I would brush my teeth religiously.

After getting dressed I made my way upstairs where there were around thirty other guys watching TV. *Do they even sleep?* The garbage bag in the middle of the lobby that usually contained loaves of bread and buns contained doughnuts instead. *Score.* Turns out they were a frequent generous donation from Tim Horton's. Most of the guys had stacks of doughnuts on their plates so I grabbed a plate and helped myself.

When I originally went homeless, I expected to struggle. I expected to go hungry, but at the DI it seemed easier to find food than a glass of water. Lack of privacy, and by lack of I mean zero, was the major issue I could find at this point. The curfews of a shelter would be annoying I'd imagine, especially to the older more independent generation, but the exchange for security and your immediate needs being met is out of the question. It baffled me that a person would choose the streets over shelter - much to learn.

The morning news featured a story about a group of teenagers in Calgary taking embarrassing pictures of the homeless and posting them on Facebook under a degrading group name and questioning myself became the theme of the morning; why did I want to write a book on the homeless condition? What was my aim? I certainly didn't want to create entertainment at their expense, though, the story had to be objective, and in the wake of all of this, it was clear that there was a lot to take in that was far worse than rough around the edges. After beating the dead horse that was my brain for about an hour, my solution came to be: *go with the wind.*

Biker Mike came up at second last wake up, 6:00 am, and snuck a cup of coffee that was left out for the volunteers.

"Apparently they have doughnuts here really early in the morning. I think they all get eaten before everyone's awake," I told him.

"Doughnuts!? You get me any?"

"No."

"Why not? I would've gotten *you* some."

"Didn't think of it. Sorry, I don't really have a container."

He started going through his pockets, then pulled out an old bread bag. "Here, if you wake up early again git me some."

I smiled and put the bag in my backpack.

"Why're you still carryin' that bag around?" he wanted to know. Couldn't bring myself to tell him.

Shortly after, Biker Mike and I were on the first bus from the Warehouse to the downtown core. Biker Mike insisted we get off a stop earlier than usual. "I've never tried Tim Horton's," he explained.

I was appalled. He reminded me that he was from the U.S and he hadn't been to Canada in twenty five years. Wasn't about to ask him why, even though I was dying to know.

Biker Mike offered to buy me a coffee but I declined and used my last toonie to avoid becoming a burden. We posted up at a booth in the corner, I connected my phone to the Tim Horton's Wi-fi and Biker Mike pulled out an Android tablet to do the same. He began playing around on it, then put on a pair of reading glasses and continued on. For some reason I saw him in a new light, like he was a *normal* person.

How conceited I've been! I had been so arrogant towards the condition that I failed to remember that underneath the dust of time and grime of struggle, all of us were still the people we grew up looking at in the mirror, with the same values and quirky character traits that come with our very essence; myself included. Biker Mike caught me staring.

"Ever seen one of these?" Referring to his tablet.

"Yeah! They're cool. Never had one."

"Me either, it was a gift. I'm still trying to figure out how to work the damn thing. Someone told me I could download movies with it and now it has a mind of its own."

"Can I see it?"

Sorry folks, but this is the part where I taught Biker Mike how to torrent movies. File sharing is legal in Canada, don't worry. I taught him a few tricks on his tablet and he was bewildered because I said I'd never had one. When I told him it worked just like a computer, we got into a conversation about the difference between his generation and mine. We both agreed that his generation was better. Actually, we both agreed that my generation is the plague of the Earth.

Walking down the street and continuing the conversation an hour or so later we came across an air vent that opened on the sidewalk. The air flow was warm and provided so much relief from the cold that we stopped right there in the middle of the sidewalk for a smoke. I pulled my last one out and Biker Mike took note of it.

"What're you gonna do once you git workin?"

"Not sure."

"Git a place?"

"Yeah. Definitely."

"Whatsay you get a place with me?" *That what's been on your mind this whole time?* "Just temporary. Then you can git a girlfriend."

"Get a girlfriend?"

"Yeah, then you two can git your own place and *I* can have my own." Honestly the offer would have been enticing if I truly had just fallen on my ass and needed to get back up. *The story. The story.*

"I don't know, maybe. Gotta get working first!"

"Well..." Biker Mike looked at me expectedly. "Git at 'er! There's a lot of money in the world, we just need to find out how to git it."

We finished our smoke in silence after I responded with only a grin. Knowing that what he'd asked me could probably help him out a lot had me feeling guilty, and I knew he didn't want to push me too hard because part of him was depending on me to come through. There's a chance that if he pushed harder, my guilty conscience would have taken over and led me back into society's arms, left to tell the story of the condition of our apartment.

We continued on our trek, I *think* Biker Mike knew where we were going. We wound up at the TD Mall on 3rd street; another Wi-fi location located on the third floor. Biker Mike never ceased to amaze me. Only God knows where he found the time to gather information, considering I was with him most of the time. He always knew all the tricks. Wi-fi spots, places we could let off our backpacks and loiter without having to pay, and almost everything I knew about the DI at this point was thanks to Biker Mike.

We sat at the table in silence for an hour. Biker Mike was on a downloading frenzy, on a quest to find every movie he'd wanted to see in who knows how long. After a while he left and came back with a couple burgers and tossed one in front of me.

"Are you sure?"

"Already bought it." He started unwrapping his while watching me. "It was two for five bucks." He took a bite and wiped some cheese from his beard. "We can't go hungry."

"Thanks Mike." Guilt doesn't taste too bad when you eat it with a burger.

If he wanted to get a place as soon as possible, why would he spend his money on fast food? *Could be a bribe.* Maybe he just wanted a burger and didn't want to eat in front of me. Hell, he could've simply been bad with money. But someone like Biker Mike? I figure he was keeping a foothold on his independence. The way he saw things, he probably saw taking food from the shelter as a form of institutionalization. *Maybe.*

"Eatin' the food they got at the DI is like twistin' a knife in my guts, I don't know how them guys do it. Apparently there's a guy that's lived there for twenty five years!"

"Crazy." Taking a large bite of his burger his eyebrow raised as he looked away from me.

"I hear some stupid kid *at* the DI is tryin' to write a book."

Busted. There were only two obvious routes I could see in the pursuit of my goal; tell people I'm writing a book on the homeless condition or 'pretend' to be homeless. Before I came, I decided I was going to do both. Pretend to be homeless while selectively telling people that were more reserved around me that I was a writer to get them to open up a little more; Biker Mike hadn't been one of them. I swear he had psychic powers. He wasn't making eye contact, I grinned.

"Oh yeah?"

"DI's no place to write a book." He warned while shaking his head, a mouthful of burger.

Watching me as I ate for a minute he decided to pull his wallet out, then solemnly slid his old ID to me across the table.

"How old were you in this picture?"

"Thirty five." The man looked happy and well kempt, even had a gentleman's moustache.

I looked back at him and smiled, and he slid another piece of ID over. *This* man was bald, depressed, worn out with a beard more than twice as long as the man sitting across from me. The man in *this* photo looked like it could be Biker Mike in ten years if he wasn't careful. "Forty eight."

"Your beard was a lot longer."

"Yeah. Mom made me trim it when I came to visit her."

"She live here?"

"Vancouver Island. I was there for two weeks before I come out here."

"Is she the one that gave you the tablet?" He nodded.

"Jacket too." *Called it.*

"That's good that you're still in touch with your mom."

"Yeah well, it'd been twenty five years."

"What happened?"

"Met my second wife and moved to Louisiana. We started a business together. Owned a house, a Harley, a dowg." Staring at me he waited for acknowledgment.

"Then what?" His eyes widened and his shoulders tensed up like he grabbed his knees or something.

"Well then she tried to kill me!"

I couldn't help but laugh. "You serious?"

"Shotgun. Missed me by four inches! Crazy fuckin' broad."

"Then you came here?"

"No. That was years ago. Then I moved into a swamp east of there with a buddy. We'd just get messed up all day it was no way to live."

"On what if you don't mind me asking?"

"You name it we did it."

"What about the house?"

"Gave it to her! Left her with everything. Just packed up and got out of there."

"Why?"

"Two kids. They're fully grown but they're out *there* so..." He shook his head in disbelief.

Bringing the memories back hurt him a little. This was Biker Mike's story, his cautionary tale. His eyes did the talking, I didn't even need to hear it. *This could be you* he wanted me to know. I think his intention was to try and scare me but it was too hard for him to open up more than that. Who knows, maybe we were just friends and he was confiding in me.

When he began to pack up I took it as a cue that we were leaving. Before we left I had to use the washroom.

This may be too much information, but this was my second week at the DI and only the second poop I'd taken. There was a popular opinion amongst the Hobos that it was a hard tossup between going hungry by not eating the bread and pasta, and constipation, as well as persistent rumours of expired 'still good' meat being used in the meals; understandable given the amount of bodies they feed, but the combination is brutal and my intestines weren't as understanding as I was.

I sat on the toilet for about fifteen minutes in a writhing pain I hadn't experienced before, however, during this time I learned something valuable, and this wasn't just regular toilet thinking. This was lighters being clicked, cans being cracked, sniffing, smoke rising over the stalls and the smell of plastic.

Public washrooms, I concluded, are a sanctuary for some Hobos, most likely the introverts. They're a safe place to use substances alone in privacy. Given my luck, of course, my stall was out of toilet paper. *Do I ask the guy on the left that's presumably smoking meth or do I ask the guy on the right drinking beer?*

I knocked on the wall to the right.

"Yeah?"

"Um. Sorry I'm out of toilet paper." He began pulling the entire length of toilet paper out of the dispenser before an armload of toilet paper hiding his hand appeared under the stall. There was so much that a lot of it overflowed and got wet from what *hopefully* was water on the ground

"Thanks!"

"Let me know if you need more." Another can cracked open. "I'll be here a while."

Returning to Biker Mike, I couldn't keep the smile off my face. "There's a bunch of guys in the stalls of the bathroom doing drugs and drinking."

"Drugs!? You should've come and got me!"

Next stop was the library. I hadn't been there yet even though it was only a few blocks from the DI. We took the train, usually we just walked. Learning that the train was free from Centre Street all the way to 9th I couldn't help but wonder why we didn't take it before. *Is all this walking an attempt to discourage, or educate me?*

Looking out the window, covering most of the free fare area, I noticed quite a lot of familiar faces from the DI. This nine block radius was Hobo Central during the day, and it was just as obvious that the cops knew it too.

Some graffiti caught my eye. Spray painted on the base of a high-rise beside the entrance in blood red: EAT THE RICH! The homeless condition in Red Deer had been so minute compared to Calgary. I'd *worked* with a lot of them without even knowing it through temp labor; that was how I found out about the DI in the first place. Having only visited Calgary fewer times than I could count on my one hand, it was still hard to believe that this was a reality.

A reality? No, this was *my* reality. This *is* reality. An inevitable struggle between classes, inevitably created through, and to put it as blunt and simple as possible; failure and success.

Years ago, in a time when I would have laughed in your face if you'd told me I had a *possibility* of succumbing to the condition, I never gave any of it a second thought. I wasn't blind to it, but I figured if I minded my business and they minded theirs, we'd all be happy - or at least *I* wouldn't have any problems. You could say I considered it a lifestyle choice. *Anyone can get a job.*

Now, I could see my old perspective on the faces of all the 'normal' people. There's really no way of saying it without sounding ignorant, trust me I've tried. Normal people, regular people, *every day* people. The public. Society. *Them.*

Plebs was the most suitable label I could find for the working class masses. They're not bad people with ill will towards the condition, they just don't understand it. We fear that which we do not understand, this instinct of fear is one of the things that separates us. On one side of the spectrum we have ignorance, avoidance, fear and ego, then, on the other we have addiction, mental illness, denial, entitlement, pride and ego. Hey at least we all have ego in common.

Red Deer's barren wasteland of a library almost got shut down, so I expected something similar from Calgary, but it was packed. Biker Mike and I walked around the entire first floor without finding a table. There were probably about fifty tables on the floor and all of them were taken by Hobos. Plebs didn't need to stop and sit at the library, I thought. They were on the move; they had places to go and homes to get to. Eventually we pulled a couple chairs up beside an electrical socket, Biker Mike plugging in his tablet, me my phone.

"You haven't been here yet huh?" I shook my head.

"No need. Don't have a library card."

"Well git one! You can use mine if you want. I only need it for the Wi-fi."

"Yeah?" He handed it to me and nodded and I left my belongings in good hands as I made my way to the second floor.

Since I went homeless, I hadn't spoken to any friends or family nor had I checked my email to see if they'd tried to contact me. Following up on those thoughts is what I had in mind, unfortunately all the computers were taken; but it was beautiful. Hobos and Plebs, sitting together, side by side.

Funny how the internet brings people together.

I took myself on a tour of the library; five floors, two of them have forty computers. There were more Hobos than I thought and they were taking up most tables on every floor. A lot of them were, to my ignorant surprise, reading.

My new objective was to find out what the majority of them were reading and, as you probably guessed, there was a substantial variety; everyone has different interests. The most common genre though happened to be fantasy. *Interesting* I thought, thinking back to rehab where I learned that children who are lonely at a young age are intrigued by fantasy. They develop 'fantasy worlds' as an escape from their reality, obviously leading into isolation and, in extreme cases, psychosis. These same lonely kids grow up and often turn out to be addicts.

You see, there is a difference between being an addict and having an addiction. Anyone can have an addiction, but addicts are born with different brain chemistry. We're not born with an addiction but we are more susceptible to develop addictions and struggle to break them. This isn't a theory either, it's science. Look it up.

Once my tour was over I returned to Biker Mike, who was still sitting with my giant backpack, watching a movie with his reading glasses on. "Done already?"

"All the computers are taken." Instantly he took his glasses off and began packing up. "Alright let's git out of here."

"You sure?"

"All my movies are done downloading already!"

On our way out Biker Mike continued on about how good his tablet is for movies and how he used to have to *pay* for movies. When we were almost at the train stop, a Native man in his early thirties jumped out from beside us.

"Yo! Yo!"

"Holy shit!" Biker Mike saw before I did, a second Native man lying on the ground convulsing and throwing up and a third standing beside him.

"You got a smoke?" Genuine concern swiped Biker Mike's face and he promptly drew a smoke out.

"Are you sure he should be smoking?" The man lit the smoke and took on a look of content and Biker Mike's concern transformed into irritated confusion. "Is he alright?"

"He'll be fine, he's just gacking out."

Biker Mike shook his head angrily and we walked towards the DI to line up for 2907.

"What-a-piece-a- " Biker Mike looked back in disgust. "That really fuckin' pisses me off. His friend's ODing on the ground and he asks me for a fuckin' *smoke*."

On the 2907 bus, a man caught my eye. He was dressed the way I'd always envisioned the *traditional* Hobo. Dressed in hiking boots, khaki pants, a dress shirt, a plaid green padded medium length trench coat, fingerless gloves and a toque that stuck up in the air a bit. The man had long blonde hair but was more or less cleanly shaven, his teeth were white too but he was missing one of his front chompers. I gauged him to be early to mid-thirties. One of the reasons he caught my attention was because he was the only one on the bus I could say looked happy *and* sober.

His name was Lee and he was talking to Greg when I heard him say "We as Hobos depend on the generosity of the good people."

Lee didn't sit with us at dinner like I was hoping he would, but he did come and ask Biker Mike for a smoke and, when he did, Biker Mike offered me one. He was ready to guard my stuff but with a wink I reminded him we had a locker. Regardless, he said he was going to shower before he smoked, but I had a feeling Greg was his go-to man on what he should do about me.

I followed Lee out for a cigarette and lit up, watching him whistle cheerfully to himself as he puffed away. There was a book in his off-hand.

"Dark Tower," I said, startling him.

He looked over at me. "Erm. Yes! Yes."

"Never read Stephan King, more of a George Orwell guy myself."

"I love all of em'! Stephan King! Orwell! Kafka! Twain! Keats! Dickenson! Lovecraft! Poe!" His accent was a heavy shade of French, but his voice sounded worn out the same way Biker Mike's was.

"You like reading eh?"

"Love reading! Reading's what I do."

"Cool! I'm a writer."

Letting out a grunt of skepticism he gave me a prejudice inspection. "You? You're just a kid."

"I'm young, but I've been writing for four years. Right now I'm working on a book on the homeless."

"Don't say homeless, it's insulting."

"Sorry."

Anticipation emitted from him as he took a long puff off of his cigarette, his interest piqued once he understood he had something to offer me. The wheels in his head were turning as he waited for me to resume.

"I couldn't think of a term that *wasn't* insulting to be honest."

"Hmm. Hobos! Call us Hobos. Yes."

"Yeah? I probably will."

"Go to school!" He ordered.

I responded with a smile. "I'm *pretty* good man. I can let you read one of my short stories if you'd be interested."

"Sure! Anytime!" He stomped his cigarette out. "You can never read too much! Nope!" And inside he went.

Stars in the night sky kept me company for the remainder of my smoke, my eyes being drawn to Orion's Belt, and I wondered what I was doing the last time I looked at this constellation.

When I got in I saw Nomad was at a table laying out containers upon containers of food as he often did, and my mind reacted with a routine thought, *where does he get it all?* It was 8:05 pm and I had signed up for the 8:00 pm slot for the computer on the far right;

immediately when I got to the Warehouse family and friends still on my mind.

When I got to the computer there was someone sitting in my seat, he turned around to see who was tapping him on the shoulder.

"Sorry man it's eight o'clock, I got this computer booked."

"No."

"Um, yeah."

"Check again."

"Alright, but I'm pretty sure-"

"Check again." Waving me off, he returned his attention to the computer.

After reading the sheet over I saw that even though I'd signed for the far right computer, the sign-up sheet was a mirrored image and it was actually the left computer I was signed up for.

According to the sign-up sheet, *Dorian* was the name of the guy I just met. I went back to Dorian and apologized, explaining the confusion. He seemed shocked that I actually went out of my way to apologize and when I offered to give him my computer time for the following day he looked at me like I was an alien and took on a more cautious air.

By the time my half hour computer time was over, Biker Mike was getting ready to go to sleep.

"What you doin' tomorrow?" he asked as I walked up.

"Volunteering in the laundry room."

His eyes widened. "*Volunteering* in the *laundry room*!? Why?"

"Gotta get my hours in if we want to keep our locker. You wanna come? It'll probably get you a designated bed."

He shook his head. "Don't need one. I'm gittin' out of here."

"Alright!"

It was morning before I knew it and I was already on the bus leaving 2907 with the intention of seeing one of the counselors for a free library card and a pair of shoes. The weight of the boots wasn't bothering me as much as my bleeding ankles were, the heels were wearing out. My socks had been fused to my feet for the last day, though I wasn't aware until I attempted to change my socks that morning.

The counselors didn't start until 8:00 am, and it was 7:30 am. I sat down beside one of the counselors offices and watched as some of the Dice blocked the stairs to the second floor, continually repeating to the same people as they'd try to go up, variations of 'They're serving breakfast right now, we'll let you up for the next round when we get the OK.'

The impression I got was that some of them thought it fun to try and sneak upstairs, some kind of short sighted achievable victory that also goes against the man. Others were concerned about their backpacks or other things they'd left up there. Some just plain seemed like they felt like they were missing out on something if they weren't where the action was or that they wouldn't get breakfast before work.

"Fuckin' nut house this place is, I tell ya!" Parallel to my side of the door frame was a middle aged man dressed in a baggy hoody and a toque, sitting in a chair. He leaned toward me and I noticed he had the worst posture I've ever seen. "Can't wait to get out of this fuckin' shit hole."

"When you getting out?"

"Hopefully at the end of the month, I'm just waiting for a cheque."

"Congratulations man." He had no intention of letting the conversation stop there. Then again, neither did I.

"Yup. I'll get out of here and go back to my house on the island."

"Vancouver Island?"

"Yup." Folding his hands behind his head he leaned back, closing his eyes and sighing in reminiscence. After about half a minute he sighed again. "Can't wait."

"No doubt. You have work out there?"

"Yeeaahh, own my own business."

"Doing what?"

"I own a warehouse that makes pool tables."

"No way!" *No way.*

"Oh yeah! I have a very impressive clientele too!"

"Oh yeah?"

"Eminem?" He lifted his eyebrows twice and a tricky smirk crept across his face. "Rihanna?"

"You sold pool tables to Eminem and Rihanna?"

"They're my friends!"

"That's *really* cool, I'm *pretty* jealous."

"You know the song 'I love the way you lie'?"

I nodded.

"Well they wrote that for me! Know the song 'Monster'?"

I nodded again.

"They wrote that *about* me."

For about twenty minutes he continued on about his successful pool table making business and his pals in the limelight. Of course, I could find humor in this, but it was also sad to me that someone would just come up with such an outrageous unprovoked lie. As he went on I could tell that to some extent he believed every word he was saying, or at least he thought *I* did.

Two weeks ago I would have asked: *What kind of person would just make up a lie like that?* Answer: someone who's very lonely. Someone who is very unsatisfied with their life. Someone that is *probably* mentally ill.

Finally counselor Sean showed up. "Which one of you was here first?"

Eminem's friend nodded at me with a smile, I knew he appreciated me listening to him even though everything he said was a bold faced lie. I followed counselor Sean into his office and he sat down and looked at me wide eyed.

Grinning, I had to tell him; "That guy out there just told me he's friends with Eminem."

"*Everyone* here is friends with Eminem. What can I do for you?"

Counselor Sean hooked me up with a voucher for a free library card that was good for one month, said I'd have to come back for the shoes though.

Afterword, I made my way to the library and got my card, then checked out <u>Haunted</u> by Chuck Palahniuk. On my way back from the library, under the bridge beside the DI there was a small posse huddled up.

As I was walking up, one who was sitting away from the rest waved me over. "Need any food?"

"No I'm not hungry, thanks though!" *What a nice guy.*

"No, food."

"Huh?"

"Food." I tilted my head. "Rock." *Crack.*

"No thank you!" Thus, new terminology was learned.

There was an older woman staggering close by, maybe in her forties. Because of her attire I believed she was a prostitute, I never saw her *inside* the DI but you could always find her under that bridge.

Finally, I got into the DI and then ate a meal on the second floor for the first time. There was virtually nowhere to sit, so I found a little place in the corner to make myself comfortable. The behavior and atmosphere reminded me of a high school cafeteria, taking into consideration the amount of people and rowdiness, only the cliques here seemed to be divided into young and old, working and drug dealing. After lunch I let staff know I wanted to volunteer in the laundry room. They seemed reluctant at first, but I was down there seconds after dropping Trent's name.

The laundry folk seemed to be having a fun conversation until I was escorted into the room. There was only one staff member down there, the rest were volunteers living at the DI. Usually there was a limit of about six people at a time because it would get too crowded otherwise.

Every sheet, pillow case and blanket that is used at the DI goes through here at least once a day. They have three of the most industrial looking washers and dryers I've ever seen, and a rectangular hole in the ground for water displacement behind it all that they called the moat.

The only one who introduced himself to me was Homer, the Dice. A skinny man with a short beard and glasses who always looked like he had something on his mind, he always wore blue work overalls with the Dice vest over top. Homer was friendly enough and even let me take a new wallet and some sun glasses from the lost and found, but age discrimination hung strong in the air with the rest of them. I was the youngest by at least twenty years.

A woman, whose name I gathered was Ester, was in charge of teaching me the proper way to fold 'bundles', which consisted of one fitted sheet, one flat sheet and a pillowcase. We folded for about two hours while listening to Ralph, a small, older man with long hair, stubble and an accent I couldn't put my finger on, talk about his reputation at the DI. He spoke about how much respect he had among the staff and occupants, the outrageous amount of volunteer hours he puts in and how he should have a job there. Ralph went on without encouragement until there was nothing left to fold and everyone was reading in silence. No one was listening to him so he left, wishing us all a good day. No one was listening to him, except for me. I cracked my book.

After learning the premise of my library book wherein all the characters are writers who go on a retreat to seclude themselves for three months to complete their masterpieces, I couldn't concentrate on reading any further. If choosing not to lug my backpack around was fringing on shirking my responsibilities, staying in contact with my friends and family was unquestionably negligent. I had to be alone. *I have to know what it's really like... Three months*, I told myself, *until I talk to anyone again.*

3

FEAR OF RODENTS

Standing beside the sleeping Bear God, I silently tried on my new steel toed boots. Before I left for the warehouse that night, counselor Sean came through for me. Unfortunately they were size fourteen, four sizes too big. I'd like to say something witty about someone that might have needed them but come on, who wears size *fourteen* boots? Me.

I waddled upstairs and threw some doughnuts onto a plate, then some into Biker Mike's bread bag. While we all watched the morning news I discovered new and exciting ways to tie a size fourteen boot onto a size ten foot. When it was time for me to leave for work my feet were locked into the boots for good, but at least I wasn't waddling.

Staff gave me a couple sandwiches in exchange for a promise to return with proof of work. Today I was determined to get some cash, I didn't want Biker Mike to have to support my cigarette addiction and knowing him he would have. Biker Mike wasn't awake when I left, he'd have to wait for his doughnut fix.

When I walked into the temp agency that Biker Mike had showed me, the lobby was already full of people ready to work. It was 5:40 am and they'd only been open for ten minutes.

Greg looked up from his newspaper and smiled wide. "There he is!" *Great, he's probably been here every day I lied about trying to get work.*

"How ya doin' Greg?" I shook his hand.

"Ah can't complain." He motioned his head to the desk and I went over to sign in. The front desk guy, Tim, pulled up my file from Red Deer and made a little small talk to make sure I was sober enough for a day of work.

It wasn't long before they called my name with a job and I felt bad for all the guys that had beat me there that morning. A lot of times at these temp agencies they won't send people out because they have liquor on their breath or are clearly intoxicated in some other way; understandable, but they don't let them know they're not getting sent out either. Also, they often just send the young guys or their favorites out; the guys they know will get the job done. This leaves good old men waiting hopefully in the lobby with the rest of them until around eleven when they know no more calls are coming in. I felt bad, but I guess I really *did* need the money. Greg patted me on the shoulder proudly as I walked out the door.

The job was at an unfinished old folk's home on the outskirts of the city. We were driven there for the cost of seven dollars from our cheque and given bus tickets to get home; an additional three bucks. *There goes an hour of work.* The entire ride out there old man Willy was cracking jokes and telling stories to the irritated driver who was humoring him. Willy looked to be realistically in his eighties. He looked so small, even just sitting next to me, I pegged him for 5'3. His hair was long, white and wiry from under his hard hat and he had a giant curly moustache - it didn't look like hair even grew anywhere else on his face. His jaw shook while he spoke and his fingers looked like bones wearing peach latex gloves.

We were dropped off around 7:30 am, our shift didn't start until 8:30 am. Willy pulled out a handful of cigarette butts from his pocket and emptied the tobacco from them into a rolling paper, then rolled it up and smoked it.

"I'm Willy," he said in a soft, friendly, rattling voice while extending a shaky hand. He was smiling at me with gums and a handful of scraggly teeth.

Willy was dressed neck to ankle in one-piece construction overalls and the top of his hard hat only reached the middle of my chest. Looking at this shaky old man I set my mind to be patient with him and work twice as hard for his sake.

Another car from the temp agency pulled up and let two more of us out. One was a very large, very bald old man named Denton who had a dead look in his eyes like he was half asleep all the time, the other was an African guy a few years older than me; Malcolm. The four of us waited in the cold for the next half hour or so until the site crew showed up. We sat in the trailer while the crew talked to each other, each of them checking us out to see if we'd suffice.

An hour and a safety orientation later we got to work, easy. Malcolm and old man Willy were sweeping the floors while I was given a vacuum and told to get the dust out of the corners and in between walls before the drywall got installed. Denton just walked around and told the three of us what to do but we all ignored him because he was the only one that wasn't do anything.

We were left alone for the most part, the only other guys we saw were people from other crews. Malcolm and Willy were working, but at a very *modest* pace while they swept together. There were so many heaters in the building that it made the boots on my feet feel like I was walking with two lit cigarettes. All of us were in our T shirts except poor old Willy, shaking and sweating while he pushed the broom in his construction overalls.

When noon arrived our boss came and told us to take lunch, then Denton had the audacity to tell Malcolm and Willy they should keep sweeping.

"Man if that guy tells me what to do one more time…" Malcolm murmured with a clenched fist, shaking his head with anger in his eyes.

On the way back to the trailer where I left my lunch, I saw a guy light up a cigarette and then get called in by his boss. He dropped the cigarette on the pavement and went inside. I rushed up and grabbed the cigarette and put it out for later.

It was only Malcolm and I having lunch in the trailer, he was telling me about Montreal and his chance to become an actor back when he was a teenager. The moment I pulled out my sandwich with a sticker sealing the saran wrap with *Mon* written on it, Malcolm smiled big.

"You from the DI boy! How long?"

"A week or so."

"Ah ok, ok. I lived at the Mansion before!"

"How long were you there?"

"Too long brotha too long." Malcolm gestured towards me and sat back nonchalantly in his chair. "How old you think I am? For real."

"Twenty four, twenty five," I guessed. Swallowing what he was chewing the last time he spoke, he managed to get a laugh out.

"Thirty two brotha." He nodded his head a few times. "I was there a long time. Two years ago now, but I got me some little bit of money, paid me some little bit of rent. It's not perfect but its home!"

While I ate my sandwich he told me about how he ran away to Calgary from Montreal when he was my age. Held a job for the first few years but got mixed up with the wrong crowd and got evicted as a result. It wasn't until his sister had found him almost ten years after he'd left that he remembered who he was and began to value his life once again. *Maybe that's what everyone needs.*

At a wild party of about twenty close friends during high school, I shared an interesting observation I made with a friend; everyone at the party had single parents. I'm not one that believes in coincidences and, even back then, I speculated loose family bonds had a large role to play in addiction, but I was just a kid and it wasn't a thought that I'd taken too seriously. Now, seeing how strong of a role addiction plays in the condition, it was a thought I'd have to pay attention to.

Once I was finished my sandwich I went outside to smoke the cigarette I found. Malcolm said he was going to go back to work early. Outside, Willy was collecting cigarette butts, I watched him walk around the trailers picking them out of the snow and throwing them back down because they were wet. I gave him the smoke I found, telling him I'm not a smoker.

Back inside the trailer I put my spinning head down. Was I running away? *Is all of this a masquerade of my failure?* The addict mind has a funny way of playing tricks on you.

Willy came in and thanked me again for the cigarette, sat down and opened his backpack. He pulled out a snack pack of tuna and crackers, a specialty from the dollar store I used to call cat food crunch. I knew what it was because I used to pack cat food crunch in *my* lunches, right before I went homeless; when I started struggling and tried to save money on food. He seemed to chew his food with the help of little invisible men using a series of pulleys and wires as his loose jaw dropped down and forced its shaky way back up. The one snack pack was all he had, I wondered if he had ever been homeless, or if he was just out of money in his old age.

We had five minutes to get back to work and we had a bit of a walk and a few flights of stairs to go up. I looked at Willy reading the newspaper and I didn't have the heart to tell him we needed to get back to work.

Willy came back a half hour late from lunch, about half an hour earlier than Denton came back who came back saying "No one told me to take a lunch, so I took it a half hour ago."

A little while after that, the guy that led the safety orientation showed up and walked up to Willy. "Who's taking care of you?"

Willy postured up and shakily held his broom proudly. "Well, I take care of myself!" The words rattled from his throat.

A look of annoyance shot across the guys face. "That's not what I meant." He inspected the shaky old man standing in front of him and grunted in disgust, then came over my way. "Are you doing anything right now?"

"Vacuuming, why what's up?"

"I need you to come help me with something."

For the remainder of the day I was moving extremely heavy packages of porcelain showers from the basement onto zoom-booms with a guy named Bruce who was triple my muscle mass and age. At first I thought the man worked for the company, but the way he'd lay down between loading the zoom-booms and the excruciating pain his back was causing him told me otherwise.

When the shift was finally over, the four of us from the agency plus Bruce waited at the bus stop for the only bus that came to that section of Calgary. I was right, Bruce had been from the agency as well and after relaying a story about how the guy he showed up with today walked off site he began complaining about working for this particular temp agency. Denton and Willy were quick to agree.

"I don't know," Malcolm objected with a smile. "If you're good wit them they good wit you."

"*If* you're *young*," Willy piped up. "There's no place in the world for an old fella like me. Just look at this great big home for old people they're building. You can bet your bottom dollar *I'll* never be living in a place like that. No money. And with all these people getting older and older and being kept alive longer and longer they just have to keep building and building! Eventually…"

We were all paying attention to what he was saying and God dammit it was all true, but that was where he left it. "Oh well I'll be long dead before then anyway," he said defeated, losing the spunk in his voice. *What do you say to that?*

We all went back to the temp agency together to hand in our time cards, I was the second to do so, but Tim asked me to stay back. Malcolm waited with me; I guess he wanted to talk to me about something. Tim told me that the company called in and asked if I could work the next day.

"For sure."

"What about me?" Malcolm walked up to the counter.

"They only asked for him, sorry."

Malcolm patted me on the back and went to stand by the front door. Tim gave me a new timecard for the next day and I left with

Malcolm. We walked a couple blocks while he told me a few cautionary tales of street people he'd let into his life that he believed had a part to play in his previous downfall. Then he told me the Mansion was a rough place and I could crash at his place if I needed to.

"I'm good," I told him. "It's not that bad."

Ripping a piece of paper from his copy of the days' timecard he wrote his info on it. "Okay!"

He gave me the piece of paper. "Here's my number. Give me a call brotha. For real. For real."

"I will." *Maybe.* I had to get going though, it was almost 4:30 pm and I wanted to make sure I got to the Warehouse. At least that's what I told Malcolm. Having a designated bed meant that I wouldn't have to worry about making it back too early, but I really wasn't looking for friends. *I'm at work* I told myself.

***

Biker Mike, Greg and I were eating spaghetti at our usual table at 2907.

"How was work today kid?" Greg asked.

"Oh, you worked today?" Biker Mike asked casually. *Greg already told him.*

"You bet! It was alright. They got me working again tomorrow." Biker Mike nodded at me with a look of approval, Greg patted me on the shoulder.

"There ya go!!" His sheriff moustache always put a smile on my face. When we were done eating, Greg went out for a smoke. Biker Mike pulled out a box of dollar store cookies and took a few out;

sliding the open box into the middle of the table, looking at me trying to fight back a smile of self-satisfaction in treating me.

"Dessert?" he invited.

"Sure, thanks."

"Yeah, help yourself!" And he turned around to focus on the T.V.

I only ate the two cookies he saw me grab. I really wasn't that hungry – couldn't shake the guilt of letting Biker Mike try so hard. He knew I was a writer, I'm sure of it, but he didn't want to let me stay at the DI. In his mind, what I was doing was a mistake. Upon meeting him I believed that I reminded him of himself, but I realized now that his protectiveness over me must have been parental instinct. Biker Mike missed his kids, it all started to make sense. Following up on the thoughts of loose family bonds, I toyed with the thought of it being a blessing and a curse. The laws of physics, every action has an equal opposite reaction. You don't know warmth before you've felt the cold, the light before you've seen darkness. You can't feel love without pain. Vice versa all around.

Once the evening news was over, Biker Mike rolled a cigarette over to me and I followed him outside. Valentine's Day was coming up and that was mostly what the news was about (go figure) so most of the guys outside were making a fuss about what a sham Valentine's Day is. Biker Mike and I didn't talk much, he mostly just mean mugged drunk people who shouldn't have been there for almost bumping into us, and I was probably thinking about things. I went to bed early and actually slept through the whole night, waking up at 6:00 am; the standard wake up time.

"GOOOOOOOOD MORNING EVERYONE!" Arwin yelled. "IT'S SIX A.M. TIME TO GET UP, TIME TO GET UP!"

At once, a symphony of coughing, grunting and moaning began. Upstairs I showed Arwin my timecard for work and he gave me a few sandwiches, then I asked if I could have some coffee and was denied. Arwin, a small Native Dice, had a look of bravery in his eye and a voice that boomed to the Gods, I guess that's why they had him on wake up duty. Biker Mike came into the office and got a few sandwiches. He tried to get some coffee but was also denied by Arwin. I walked out with him while he was in a huff.

"This is fuckin' bullshit, half of the guys in here don't do a fuckin' thing all day and they won't even give a workin' man a fuckin' cup of coffee cause he don't do chores for em'." Biker Mike wasn't a morning person. I followed him to the empty bag of doughnuts.

"And they eat all the fuckin' doughnuts so none of the rest of us can eat in the morning." Then I remembered the doughnuts I saved for him the morning before and pulled the greasy bread bag they were squished in out of my backpack. All the sugar and icing had melted and gathered at the bottom of the bag.

"Got these for you yesterday but I left before you got up." Biker Mike looked over, pissed off, then almost started laughing when he saw what I was talking about.

"At least you tried."

***

My ride was supposed to leave at 7:00 am and I got there just in time. They sent eight of us out today, Malcolm and Bruce made the second cut, but old man Willy and dead-eyes Denton would have to wait until they got put on another job. In the temp agencies eyes it's better to send old timers out once a week than not at all. There's only so much work available and they need to keep their clientele happy, otherwise there won't be any work for anyone.

The company had me and Malcolm and a couple other guys cleaning up the third floor of the old folks home, I was vacuuming and the rest were sweeping. I spent the morning thinking about what it's going to be like getting old. What it would have been like to face the condition for the first time in late adulthood or old age.

Right before lunch one of the guys from the agency asked if I had a phone, he told me he had to call the temp agency for an advance.

"You can do that?" In Red Deer you couldn't, strictly paid every Friday.

"Yeah but you need to call before noon."

"Sorry my phone's out of service."

"Fuck!" He took off to go find someone with a working phone.

I checked the time; I had ten minutes to find one. No one on the third or second floor was willing to let me use their phone but finally right at noon an electrician handed his to me without question. When I finally got through to the temp agency the lady said I was too late.

"Come on it's like twelve oh one."

"Sorry there's nothing I can do, you missed the dead line."

"It was twelve when I called!"

"No. Sorry sir, there's nothing I can do."

"Please?"

"The system shuts down after noon." *Yeah right.*

I hung up and called again, told the guy I called on time for an advance and was denied and I'd like to report whoever it was that spoke to me to the manager because she was very rude, that's how much a pack of cigarettes was worth to me. It turned out the system doesn't shut down after noon, and I'd have an $80.00 advance to pick up when I was done work.

After lunch they had me moving the showers and tubs with Bruce again. He was getting more and more aggressive with them and I thought it was because I wasn't performing to his satisfaction but it became apparent that he was thinking about something that was pissing him off.

One of the showers wasn't lining up properly and he began shaking it as hard as he could, cracking it against the zoom-boom. The driver of it yelled at him and told him to be careful with the showers and drove off to unload them. Bruce walked over and dropped himself onto a pallet and laid there staring at the roof. I sat down on a pallet farther away and watched him as he tried to get comfortable. The boss walked in and told him he could go do something else on the forth floor, then told me one of his staff would be in to help me with the rest of the showers.

Rest of the day flew by, me and the new guy found a much easier way to carry the showers than the way Bruce and I had been doing it and we talked to make the day go by faster. By the end of the shift he encouraged me to apply for a job with the company and said he'd put in a good word for me. Told him I'd think about it.

Malcolm talked his way onto the bus for free and I sat with him on the ride to the train stop. I asked if he knew of a place I'd be able to cash my advance without having it held and he said he'd take me somewhere after we handed in our timecards. When we got to the train stop he was adamant about sitting at the front of the train so we could keep an eye out for transit officers.

"Always sit at the front if you free riding. I'm telling you!" Malcolm advised before we got on the train.

He told me that transit officers have a thing for Hobos because Hobos generally don't have the money to pay for transit services, made sense. Also told me the police in the downtown core 'pick on the homeless'. *That can't be true.* He told me to watch for it, then continued on with a few stories of social injustice that I would have to see to believe.

"Trust me," he said. "If you down there long enough they'll start recognizing you, and once they recognize you, they pay attention to every little ting you do." Then he pointed to a sign on the train that informs you that the train has audio and video recording and is monitored at all times.

We both got time cards to work the next day from the temp agency and made our way to a cash store a few blocks away. Malcolm asked if I knew where I could get my taxes done and I told him I didn't. He said he'd show me, he had to go anyway. I walked all the way to his tax firm smoking and listening while he told me about all the pussy he'd been getting since he got his own place. More of a one woman man myself, so I just listened.

We got to the firm and sat with Mac, an incredibly slow genius of an old man and his gorgeous young assistant. It was an excruciating forty minutes but by the end of it Malcolm was ecstatic because he was getting around $1800.00 back. He asked Mac to deposit it into his bank account and then introduced me. Took another half hour or so to get me into Mac's system before he told me according to my file I owed the revue agency money unless I was expecting more than one T4 - I was expecting a lot.

We left and made our way to the mall, it was after five and this would be the first night since I got to the DI that I didn't eat dinner with Biker Mike. Malcolm told me he'd show me a few other cool places but all he did was walk me to the TD mall on 3rd street.

"I wish *I* had someone to show *me* around when I first got here." He credited himself like he'd done me some tremendous deed. I suppose he had been nice, but thinking back to Biker Mike, I just felt more guilt.

When we got to the mall he was drooling over the nearest A&W in the food court and asked me to buy him a burger.

"I don't know man this is all the money I got."

"Pay you back Friday."

I was hesitant.

"I'll hook you up when I get my tax return."

"Alright man." He ordered the most expensive meal on the menu and upgraded to onion rings and a large drink.

Pissed off, I got the same thing not wanting to buy him a better meal than I bought myself. Neither one of us spoke while we ate. I was a little choked, he knew it too, but couldn't care less. After we ate he asked to borrow $20.00. "I can't." He pulled out his timecard for the next day and held it up.

"I'm workin' wit you! You'll see me. You saw my tax return; you know I'm good for it." What held my body together is beyond me, but it obviously wasn't a backbone. I gave him $20.00 and shortly after we went our separate ways.

Walking back to the DI I looked in my wallet. I had $19.00. *How?* $4.00 to cash the cheque, $10.25 for smokes, $13.35 for each meal and $20.00 for Malcolm. *Damn, that happened fast.*

By the time I got back to the DI it was after eight. I scanned my fingers at the front door and went in to see a few Dice doing bag checks, one holding a clip board.

"Second floor?" the one with the clipboard asked me.

"Naw, I have a bed at twenty-nine-oh-seven."

She pulled out her walkie-talkie. "Warehouse we have one more, says he has a bed." A few seconds of silence.

"We're full," said the inanimate object in her hand.

Of course she relayed the message I already heard, I was flustered. "I have a designated bed though. Two oh seven."

She raised the walkie-talkie to her lips. "Says he has a designated bed, bed two oh seven."

Silence. Then "Yeah, sorry we're full."

They said I could come back later. They said if I proved I was working they'd hold my bed until nine. My unconsciously high expectations of the shelter had not been lived up to.

"Second floor?" she asked.

"No." Instead I sulked into the lobby before I sat down on the ground against the wall.

The lobby at this time of night wasn't so empty. A lot of Hobos going in and out, trying to get comfortable or arguing over electrical outlets they're posted up at. Buying liquor and drinking the night away was a tempting idea while I watched my brethren stew in the lobby of Hell, or what my mind was conditioned to believe was Hell. *Get ahold of yourself,* I thought. *This is where you would have slept anyway if it wasn't for Biker Mike.*

Someone walked in front of my line of site and I looked up at Ross. Ross was the first of the Dice that I'd spoken to about my writing in general, come to think of it. He couldn't have been much older than me and told me he respected what I was doing and encouraged me to pursue my dreams. Told me he understood because he was a musician in a band that broke up when he decided to go to college and he regretted not pursuing music. Also, I knew that he was the driver of the van that took the Hobos that have designated beds and arrive late to the Warehouse because our conversation was cut off when he had people to pick up.

"Sup man?"

"Apparently my bed at the Warehouse got taken."

"Shitty." He jingled his keys. "Ready to go?"

Following him out to the Dicmobile, I hopped into the passenger seat. He jumped in and twisted the keys in the ignition.

"I thought you guys were full."

"We are. Kind of. We don't like saying we have beds over the walkie-talkie because people we turn down that don't have designated beds get mad."

"Ross we have another one at the front," the walkie-talkie said.

"Hold on." Ross said to me before he got out, leaving the keys in the ignition and the window rolled down.

"No bed's, sorry," he said into the walkie-talkie before leaning into the window. "If anyone tries to steal the van, punch em' in the face!"

We laughed, then he ran inside. Keeping a good sense of humor, when living or even working in the condition, is fundamental to your sanity. After all, that's what Logotherapy's all about; adaptation. Ross came back with another lucky Hobo and we drove to 2907. Biker Mike wasn't up when I got there so I decided to get another early night after smoking a cigarette.

When I got up Biker Mike was still sleeping, it was the first time I'd seen him sleeping in the basement; he was one of the guys on the floor mats. Before I left for work I went about what was becoming a routine and even mopped the floor for a cup of coffee.

Malcolm wasn't there that day and at the end of the shift I told the company I wasn't going to be able to return. Decided to quit working for *this* temp agency all together. Malcolm wasn't worth the concern whether he was candid or not. I spent a majority of the day angry about the situation but I tried not to think about it. *All you wanted was a pack of smokes* I reminded myself.

"Where've you been?" Biker Mike asked as we waited for the shuttle to the Warehouse.

"You were asleep by the time I got back last night."

"I thought you gat the Hell outta here!" He didn't say much else, even at dinner.

His face was red and he was acting a bit different, I assumed he'd been drinking. I'd given him the benefit of the doubt until a segment of the news featuring a story about an animal shelter letting the public choose a puppy's name. The dog on the screen jumped over a small fence and ran away from the shelter workers. Biker Mike started giggling.

"Hehehehe, look at that puppy. He's like: 'I can't live my life behind bars, I gotsta go!'." *Either drunk or he really loves animals.*

Someone came up from downstairs hollering about a mouse he saw.

"Oh shut up." Biker Mike mumbled so only I could hear. "I've seen lots of mice down stairs - they ain't gonna hurt anyone."

My stomach turned. Mice. Rats. *Rodents.* Just the word is fucking disgusting. There was a fear of rodents I developed out of the blue in adolescence. Dirty, cagey, crafty, disease ridden, intelligent, short, fair haired, warped, ugly cats with thumbs. *Shoot me now.* I needed a smoke.

Outside it was too cloudy to see Orion's Belt, or any other constellation for that matter, just a rainbow circle from the dark clouds wearing the moonlight. I looked down. Mice. Rats. *Rodents.* Just the word was fucking disgusting, but the animal itself is worse and there was one standing right in front of me!

I guess it's not so different from me, it's just trying to keep warm, keep from starving. Ironic it should find itself at a homeless shelter. Watching as it licked its bony little fingers, I thought back to old man Willy and all the other good old boys who will struggle to the very end to support themselves. I thought about how rodents could find their way into anything and get whatever they want and the way they can sense food from a mile away and I compared that with addiction and the craftiness and sly manipulation that comes with it. A newfound respect emerged for this relatively harmless critter sharing the smoke pit with me. *We're all struggling,* I thought. *Doing what we need to do to survive.* Plebs and Hobos, humans and animals, we all have that in common. A Pleb no better than a Hobo and a Hobo is no better than a mouse. The world belongs to all of us. *There's got to be a better way.*

Startled by a noise, the mouse ran into the Warehouse. *I'm rooting for you buddy* I thought, for now, in my mind, mice would always stand as a symbol of survival; beating the odds as prey to damn near everything in the world and doing it without making a sound; scavenging crumbs. I finished my smoke and made my way inside.

When I got in the door I saw my symbol of survival lying on the ground, skull crushed and bleeding onto the stairs to the basement.

4

VALENTINE'S DAY

Biker Mike left before I woke up and I didn't have time to volunteer for coffee. I hopped onto the morning bus to the DI with the intention of finishing my volunteer hours in the laundry room. When I told one of the Dice about my plans for the day, I was pointed to Ralph. Very friendly, as usual, but that just seemed to be his way. While I followed him to the elevator I noticed he walked with a fairly severe limp, but besides the limping itself, it didn't seem to faze him. "Yestaday I was up hya and saw a gal *you* probably could have dated crying and I walked up to ha and says 'hunny what's wrong? You shouldn't be in a place like this!' And she tells me she doesn't know whea to go so I says 'hunny come with me.'"

Guess the staff gave him an access card to the elevators because he used it to open the otherwise locked elevator door. He didn't continue his story. *Hope that's not where it ends.*

"Where'd you take her?"

"I took ha to the YWCA down the road. Gals can't stay in a place like this, aw you kidding me?"

It made sense, there only seemed to be a few dozen women at the DI and most of them were old or were only there for a few days with their boyfriends between places. Statistics showed that people struggling in the condition were more or less divided right down the middle between males and females, so I'd been wondering where all the females were. *Surely they don't sleep outside.*

A lot of Hobos with blue balls gave credit to the lack of females for them using sex for a place to stay or for money to get one, and perhaps there was some truth to that; but it should have been as obvious as a flying rhino smoking a blunt with Richard Nixon that there were female shelters.

"Anyway theya all mad at me down theh because I left them hangin' yestaday. But *you* know *me*, well actually ya *don't,* but I put moah houwas in than the staff so *I'm* not feelin' sorry for *them*!"

The elevator door opened and I walked to the laundry room, Ralph went back up.

Us volunteers were left by ourselves for a majority of the mornings. The staff person's job was to run around the shelter and collect the bins of dirty laundry and bring them back down and bring the clean laundry up to Intox or Day-sleep and coordinate everything he was doing and everything *we* were doing with whatever flow worked best with the shelter that particular day. Even though there was only one Dice that worked in laundry at a time, their job may have been one of the most important. Hell. I'd even be as bold as to say there would probably be a riot on the DI's hands if the job wasn't done right.

Our job was to fold bundles. Unlike my first day in laundry they opened up a little more around me but only to each other. Must have figured if I wasn't going anywhere they may as well not kill themselves with boredom. Al, the Dice in the morning was a friendly old man who reminded me of a science teacher with his glasses, moustache and hazmat suit; his Walter White response to Homer's overalls. He made a point of telling me he has a son my age every time he saw me.

Over the course of the day, I noticed most of the laundry folk reminded me of teachers. Ester was a painter; the art teacher of course. She'd put so much emphasis and passion into her well spoken words as she spoke either of paintings she was working on or the book she was reading.

Wade was the guy she seemed closest with, he kept to himself but listened intuitively and would jump in here and there if he thought what he had to say was witty enough. He had medium grey hair that he wore in a ponytail and a goatee and looked sad most of the time unless he thought something was funny. Sported a pair of glasses and most times a sweater vest. A poet; the patient English teacher.

Donald also sported glasses and always wore something colorful, he had a look of ambition in his eye that I'd found rare in a majority of old folks, let alone the ones living at the DI. Balding, but he had a rough, gruff voice that told you he wasn't slowing down anytime soon. Like Wade, he was funny and witty, however he spent a lot of time thinking about what he was going to say and it seemed he didn't pay much attention to conversation unless he was involved or wanted to be. There was a touch of envy of Wade I picked up on. The way he looked, more than his behavior reminded me of a mad scientist; the one Al probably replaced.

The only one who didn't remind me of a teacher was Ray, a kind hearted Native guy with a bushy moustache and a baseball cap. Folding beside each other, Ray and I listened in silence and usually laughed at the same peaks in conversation between the rest. At one point Wade walked over to where we were with a blank stare like he forgot why he came over there.

"Alzheimer's?" Ray asked Wade with a smile.

The three of us thought it was hilarious and, once Ray was under the impression I thought he was funny, he started to pay attention to me and join in on the conversation with the rest of them more often.

The day flew by without me saying a word. By the time it was 2:00 pm, and Al was clocking out and Homer was clocking in, I felt like I knew all of them pretty well. Ralph came down conveniently when Al left.

"Come down when all the bundles are folded!" Donald joked.

"I got caught up doing stuff! Had to help out on Second and then they needed me to run the elevatahs. Well actually between you and *me* I just didn't want to be down hya with Al workin'. He's a nice guy but whenevah *I'm* workin' he takes advantage of me and just leaves me down hya in chawge of you guys! It's not fair!"

"No it's not." Homer joined in while putting his staff vest on over his work overalls. "You're a hard workin' guy Ralph you deserve some time off eh, don't push yourself too hard." He walked up to me. "Michael how was it today?"

"Painless!"

"It wasn't bad eh? Good! Oh uh," he walked over to a table in the corner supporting a few boxes of crackers, granola bars and bread. "You hungry? You can eat this eh."

"Yeah?"

"Yeah take as much as you want. You're a growing man eh, you need lots of food to keep you goin'."

"Thanks!"

"No problem. There should be juice in the fridge if you're thirsty and peanut butter and jam if you want to make a sandwich. And uh, margarine and a few packets of ketchup, two containers of mayonnaise three apples and a few sandwiches."

I opened the mini fridge and saw everything he listed and not a thing more or less, except the sandwiches.

"Oh the sandwiches are gone eh?" Homer said peering into the fridge with me to make sure his inventory was correct.

"Yeah," Ray said, smiling with playful guilt. "I ate em' all."

"Oh that's alright." Homer looked back at me. "Ray's a good guy eh." Then he looked around at everyone. "All of you are, you all work really hard. We really appreciate the help eh; it really makes a huge difference."

He asked me about how long I'd been at the DI and how I ended up there if I didn't mind him asking. Once I mentioned I started my own company I seemed to have everyone's attention, but after I mentioned I was writing a book everyone shrugged me off and went back to reading, except Ester.

"Oh you're a writer eh?" Homer asked.

"Yeah I've been writing for a few years now."

"What kind of writing do you do?"

"A lot of different things. Screenplays, short stories. Usually tragedy. Mostly fiction."

"Oh ok. I really like William Faulkner eh. And Joseph Conrad, William Blake. Anything by Franz Kafka is *always* good. Jane Austin, you ever read her work?" I shook my head impressed.

"Female author. Emily Dickinson is good too eh. Oh and Virginia Woolf." Kafka and Emily Dickinson rang a bell.

"As a writer I don't read as much as I should, I don't know a lot of authors. George Orwell, Philip K. Dyck and Chuck Palahniuk are a few of my favorites though."

"Oh Chuck Palahniuk eh, *Fight Club* is one of my favorites. You ever hear of Hunter S. Thompson? He's good too. What's your favorite book?"

"Probably *1984*." Homer nodded.

"Yeah George Orwell was neat eh." When I asked if he'd ever heard of *Man's Search for Meaning* he was caught off guard and ready to absorb any word I said. After explaining who Viktor E. Frankl was, I went into detail what his book was about. While I was speaking I noticed that the few that were listening were impressed by what I had to say and were taking me more seriously as a writer. I took it as an invitation to, and only to a point, reveal what I was trying to accomplish in coming to the DI.

By the time we'd finished our conversation it was almost time to catch the bus to 2907. Homer and I thanked each other for the good conversation and he told me to come back anytime, I was always welcome. The laundry folk; the circle of friends that worked down there, they were different than the rest of the DI. They were sober, sophisticated, happy, but yet they were here. *Why?*

Biker Mike was nowhere to be seen when I caught the bus to 2907, I ate dinner watching the news with Greg and Lee who reminded me I was supposed to give him a story. *Didn't think you were that interested*, I thought, *at least not enough to follow up with me*. I couldn't help wondering if Biker Mike had gone drinking after work. Wasn't until I was getting ready for bed that Biker Mike showed up.

"Where you been?"

"Went and put my damage deposit down on a place."

"I thought you got the Hell outta here!" *Wait, what?* "Damage deposit on a place? Congratulations Mike!"

"Yeah! Movin' in tomorrow after I get paid."

"Right on." Mixed emotions on both sides I think.

"Thanks! Take my number down." Handing him my phone I watched him struggle to punch everything in, then he handed the phone to me and I made sure it all saved.

We called 'er a night and shook hands. I thanked him and told him I didn't know what I would have done over the last two weeks if it wasn't for him; true, then I let him into our locker and went downstairs while he packed up all his things.

That night as I lay on the top bed of a bunk that felt more like an earthquake thanks to the Bear God's tossing and turning, I felt like I was facing the condition all over again. In all reality, I hadn't been by myself yet, nor had I struggled, I'd been coddled in the shelters arms by the best of the people in it. *It's not fair*, I thought, *that I'm shown so much kindness because of my age.* Questioning the authenticity of my quest, I thought, *who's going to listen to a kid? Who's going to listen to a Hobo?*

Maybe I should have taken Biker Mike up on his offer, maybe this is a mistake. But it was too late. Hours later I finally convinced myself the story was worth the sacrifice and was able to get some sleep.

Valentine's Day; Biker Mike was gone before I left. *I'll see him tonight when he picks up his things. There's no way he took it all to work.* Volunteering in the laundry room crossed my mind but instead

I decided to go for a walk around Calgary; I had only really been around with Biker Mike, being stuck at the warehouse from 5:00 pm - 6:30 am. I was yet to dip my dick in destiny's dirty dumpster.

Hobo Central was more or less empty when I began my walk, it was too late in the morning to see anyone sleeping outside. Notably, most of the people I suspected were Hobos who were out at the time were also on their way to work with hard hats and steel toed boots along with the rest of society's laborers. There were a few suits out, but the rest would come out later. Professionals work later in the day, but not too late because they're fucking professionals. That's why I assumed I didn't see any buskers or pan handlers yet, although come to think of it, I hadn't seen many pan handlers or *any* buskers in the time I'd spent in Hobo Central with Biker Mike.

Trying to gain a handle on my surroundings I began walking a perimeter of downtown. *Where would I go if I was homeless?* I contemplated while sporting a ridiculously heavy backpack, no home to my name. *I'd want to sit down.*

During my walk I recognized that the passing looks I got from people were something that I'd have to get used to if I was going to do this for a while. This in mind, I figured it probably wasn't something most Hobos were fond of. Rather than taking any scenic route or going across any bridges or up any hills I chose to walk to another section of downtown through the alleys.

Smoking a cigarette, I spotted a Native guy sitting on a step behind some kind of shop garage staring at me. Wearing a black bandana, a winter jacket with a leather jacket underneath, fingerless gloves and black boots, he sat playing with one of the many piercings in his face, he also had a backpack similar to mine sitting on the ground beside him which is why I assume I acknowledged him when he asked "Hey, you got a cigarette?"

As I got closer I saw that he had a tear drop tattoo, I heard they meant you'd killed a motherfucker so I was a little on edge.

"Yeah man." After I gave him a cigarette he held his hand out for a light, he asked for the time and I checked my phone. "Half past noon. Mind if I sit down?"

"Sure." He watched as I took my backpack off and carefully propped it up against the wood railing.

"Streets?"

"Yeah. You?"

"Yeah." I cracked my back and it popped loud.

"Heavy?"

"Yeah. How did you end up on the streets if you don't mind me asking?" Thought it was natural enough conversation.

"How did I *end up* on the streets? I've always been on the streets."

"Since you were a kid?" The look he gave me said what I asked was a step too far.

"Something like that." He took a long puff off his smoke. "Why?" *Do I tell him?*

"I'm writing a book on the homeless." His face grew more serious.

"Oh yeah?"

"Yeah." When it fell quiet for too long I stood to leave. "Well I should probably get going."

"Wait, tell me about your book. Maybe I can be in it."

Telling him about Viktor Frankl and the other pieces of my master plan that hadn't been glued together yet turned out to be a mistake when he stood up with his backpack and gave someone behind me a nod of the chin.

"Ever been jacked before?"

My heart sank. "No."

Two friends of his walked up beside him, I could tell they didn't know what was up but they were going to go along with it anyway. *Must've already been waiting for them when I showed up.* Homer let me take a wallet from the laundry room the first time I volunteered, believe it or not I took it for an occasion such as this but it happened to be nicer than mine. So I pulled my old wallet out and opened it up to show him the empty void contained inside.

"I don't have any money man."

"No shit you don't have any money," he said, "you're fucking homeless. What's in your backpack?"

Shaking like old man Willy, I opened it up and stepped aside. Rooting through my backpack, he tossed all of my work gear out while his friends watched casually. He pulled my laptop bag out and looked at it like 'Ehhh, it *could* be valuable.' Not knowing it had every piece of writing I'd ever done on it, everything valuable to me.

He tipped the backpack towards me letting it fall to the ground then held his hand out. "Phone."

I reached in my pocket and handed it over and they walked away. *Fuck.*

It all happened so fast. Why didn't I do anything? What would have happened if I did? My writing.. These thoughts ran through my head as I marched to the liquor store. Bought a mickey of whiskey and a big gulp from 7/11. $3.35 is what I had left and I used $2.00 to buy headphones from the dollar store to listen to music on the phone I forgot I didn't have anymore before I made my way to the third floor of the TD mall on 3rd street.

***

It didn't smell *that* bad *most* of the time. After all, it was a party of sorts. I'd been in the washroom for about twenty minutes and polished off half the mickey in a sulk when the janitor came in. He mopped right into my stall and the stalls on each side of me before leaving and I noticed once I heard him leave some of the Hobos got up and left, some of them throwing their cans out before washing their hands.

Fuck my book. Fuck the homeless. Fuck the world. Count your fucking blessings man. I told myself. *I'm done.* I didn't want to think. I didn't want to live. Without my laptop, without my writing, what was I? A Hobo chasing a dream. That was the same reason I *couldn't* give up, I really didn't have anything else. *I have to give up. What's going to happen if I don't?* The janitor started knocking on the doors of the bathroom stalls, I pulled my pants down around my ankles and when he got to my stall I told him I was taking a shit.

A new rotation of Hobos were in the bathroom by the time I finished my mickey. My pants were still around my ankles and my head was resting in my hands. *Biker Mike.* His contact information was on my phone and nowhere else. Even if he was going to the Warehouse tonight I was way too drunk to get in.

This is the only spoiler I'll give you, but I never saw Biker Mike again. While face-palmed on the toilet of the public washroom on the third floor of TD mall on 3rd street with my pants around my ankles I recognized that Biker Mike was more than I gave him credit for. He was the bait at the end of societies fishing line, a mechanic that could have helped me get my train back on track; an opportunity for me to have a normal life, and a missed one at that; a guardian. Over time as I kept an eye out for him I often concluded that I took him for granted as a false beacon of hope.

The janitor came back in to mop and I realized he must have done this every half hour. Standing up and pulling my pants back on I left the stall, throwing the mickey in the garbage. I threw my backpack back over my shoulders and left without washing my hands. The janitor inspected me and most likely took a mental photograph as I came out of the bathroom because man was I ever wasted; my five month sobriety binge took my tolerance down a notch. I was finished drinking, but the wallowing continued.

It was still the middle of the day and I was wobbling around the mall like it was 3:00 am on New Year's Eve. The faces that got under my skin when I was sober were tearing my hair out while drunk. People tried not to look at me but the ones that did stared. Eyes of an old French woman eating dinner with her husband caught me and he looked over as if she pointed me out to him. Outraged, I walked up and sat at the table directly beside them, pulling out a journal and pretending to write things about them.

They started talking to each other in French and this *really* pissed me off. For a few moments I considered telling them in French that I knew exactly what they were saying, but I don't know French. Instead of doing anything, I kind of forgot where I was and drifted off thinking about what the situation would have been like if I *did* know French. *Fuck would they ever be sorry.*

When the couple decided to get up and move I snapped back into reality. Once they were out of sight I decided to leave too, I didn't want to make a spectacle of myself.

Outside the mall I was enjoying the first cigarette I'd had in a while and the first *drunk* cigarette I'd had in months. Two mall security guards came out and lit up cigarettes and I watched as they pointed out Hobos and laughed together. When I was finished my cigarette I pulled out another one and walked over to them.

"You guys got a light?" I slurred. They looked at each other and fought back smiles, one of them handed me a lighter. "Thanks."

Lighting my smoke I continued on. "How you guys doin'?" They looked at each other again.

"Good," the one said.

"Right on, right on." I said back and took a puff off of my cigarette. "You guys are security guards right?" The one that was doing all the talking nodded at me. "How do you like it?" Looking at each other awkwardly they attempted to communicate mentally for a solution to me.

"It's good."

"Yeah, it's good man," the other one said.

"Cool! Hey I'm just wondering like, how *badly* do you need to do at the academy to become one step *lower* than a peace officer?"

Instantly the quiet guy walked up and shoved me and I laughed at him. He looked like he was going to hit me but his partner pulled him back.

"You better get out of here!"

"Why?"

"Get the fuck out of here man!"

"I'm just curious." His friend pulled him in another direction and they put their smokes out and went inside.

Walking around starting shit with ignorant Plebs had me feeling like the patron vigilante of the homeless condition. Sobering up hours later I realized that what I had just done was the typical kind of thing that gives Hobos a bad name, this was all the more verification that I was just as fucked up and vulnerable as anyone else.

By the time I got to the DI I was out of smokes; I don't know what time it was when I stumbled into the doors. As I waited in the entrance I noticed Donald ahead of me in the line through the reflection of the bullet proof glass. His face was red and eyes were crazed and I presumed he'd been drinking too. When I got through the second set of doors the Dice working the front told me it was too late for me to go to the Warehouse, not that they'd let me anyway in my current state. She asked if I wanted to sleep in Intox or second floor; I wasn't ready for Intox yet.

Before I went upstairs they asked to search my bag. "Don't worry, you won't find a laptop in there." One of them gave me a puzzled look but the rest shrugged it off. "You can bet your bottom dollar." I said with a tear in my eye.

This would be the first night I actually stayed at the DI. When I got onto Second, my vision was flooded with a sea of blue floor mats and bodies. To give an accurate estimate would be nearly impossible, but if I were to guess, I'd say somewhere between five and eight hundred. Walking through row after row of floor mats squished together, it seemed there were no empty ones. When I told one of the Dice that I couldn't find a place he told me to follow him, we came across an empty mat dressed in sheets and he ripped them off.

"Are you sure?" I asked.

"Yeah, whoever had this mat hasn't been here in a while, I've been watching." He walked away. Looking around it was impossible not to notice he put me in the middle of a few drunken Native guys and I was obviously responsible for their friend's bed being taken away. They didn't say a word to me and stopped talking to each other while I laid myself down and slid a toque over my eyes to shield from the florescent lights. Tried to go right to sleep and I may have drifted off a few times but I really don't think so. The guy beside me kept hitting me and telling me to stay off his mat but as far as I knew I was laying straight as a pencil. After five times of this I purposely kept myself awake to see if he'd do it again without me moving and he did.

"Don't fuck with me man." My toque still covering my eyes. "I'll fucking kill you, I swear to God."

He mumbled something back but I didn't catch it. It was a little while until I finally started drifting off to sleep again and the guy kicked me in the leg. His leg didn't move from my mat and I took the toque off of my eyes and looked over at the sleeping man beside me. Kicking him in the shin as hard as I could sprung him awake with a look of fury in his eyes.

"What the fuck?"

"You keep telling me to stay off *your* mat, stay off *mine!*" I barked back still laying on my back.

Punch after punch connected to my face, I thought he was going to stop, but he didn't until I sat up and had a slightly bloody nose and a small cut on the bridge of it - but nothing serious. Luckily even though I was drunk I recognized the consequences of beating the Hell out of him, and it scared me to death. *I can't get kicked out of here, I'm not ready for the streets. I'm not even ready for this!*

The moment I saw two Dice rushing over, memories and thoughts from the last two weeks began drowning me. When the Dice got there all the guys friends pointed at me and said it was my fault and was the one causing problems. One of the Dice offered the guy a cigarette and they made way to the smoke deck on the floor.

"This guy punches me in the face and you give *him* a cigarette?" The Dice didn't know what to say and just continued to the smoke deck.

Not having smokes was what infuriated me about the situation more than anything. The remaining Dice stood in front of me and asked me what happened. Tears fell out of the corners of my eyes and I just shook my head in anger and disappointment.

Lloyd, the Dice dealing with me, took me into a room in the back to talk about what happened. While sobbing I explained my side of the story and ended up bursting into tears, telling him about my book and the faith I'd lost in people and society and told him I was going to end my life.

"I can't even *afford* to end my life! How sad is that?" I remember saying.

At one point he accidently dropped the name of the guy that hit me and I took note of it; *Casey*.

My mental breakdown lasted around four hours, though half of that was time spent convincing them that they didn't need to call the police on me. Lloyd made me promise that I'd go see him the next day on the second floor to let him know I was alright but in reality nothing had changed by the end of our conversation.

When walking to my newly assigned mat for the night the Dice that offered Casey the cigarette offered me one but I walked passed him like he didn't exist. *That'll show him.*

Wake up on Second is 4:30 am and I got less than two hours of sleep. It was the worst hangover of my life, I was sure I was going to die of dehydration. Dizzy, I searched for a water fountain and when I found one I drank from it for at least a week. Lloyd told me that if I needed he could put in a word to Day-sleep and I could take the day to get some rest; I took him up on it. Day-sleep didn't open until 8:30 am and, as tempted as I was to volunteer to stack the floor mats and set up the tables and chairs in exchange for a cup of coffee, I realized I hadn't gotten a very good look at Casey. *He could be anyone of these guys.* Reading my book in a Tim Horton's public washroom is how I ended up spending the morning because I didn't want to walk the streets either.

***

Day-sleep is on the third floor, it has a couple hundred beds and at night it's divided into male and female sides. With the amount of energy I had, that was all I was able to figure out about it before I passed out. Waking up starving I realized I didn't eat the day before, nor had I eaten today and there was just enough time to catch the bus to 2907. Food being the only thing on mind I hopped on the bus without giving Lloyd a second thought.

Even though Biker Mike was gone, Greg was still there, so I hung in the back of the room to avoid relaying the story of my nose to him. Nomad was the closest and stillest I had ever seen him and I actually got a look at the food he hoarded in his containers. Before, I'd assumed he was a kitchen volunteer and just scored extra portions as a perk. *That's not DI food.* Most of what he had looked gourmet and the meat he had looked like real meat. *Where the hell do you get it!?*

When I was done eating I remembered my promise to Lloyd and decided it was probably best to follow up on my word. The only Dice I could see was a girl, who didn't look like she could be much older than me, standing in the middle of the room observing everyone.

Kelsey was her name, I could see it written on her nametag as I approached her to ask if there was any way I'd be able to get back to the shelter.

She stared at my nose for a few seconds. "We can probably figure something out if you need to go back. Why what's up?"

I touched the nose she was staring at. "Got beat up last night."

Kelsey nodded while still looking at my nose, then my eyes. "Yeah it looks like your nose has seen better days."

"Yeah."

She still didn't understand why I had to go back to shelter. Once I told her the tale of the night before, her empathy seemed to foster strong pity for me. It was more than pity though, she was truly concerned about me; more than Lloyd, more than *anyone*. Said she would figure something out for me and, with a tilt of her head, told me I looked tired and I should get some sleep. Though I already slept the whole day away I agreed and went down to bed 207 to fall asleep in my own embrace.

Kelsey was supposed to wake me up when she found a way to get me back to the DI but I slept through the entire night. "GOOOOOOOOOOOOD MORNING EVERYONE!" Arwin boomed. "TIME TO GET UP! TIME TO GET UP! GOOD MORNING GOOD MORNING!"

"Who says, Arwin?" a tall Caucasian man groaned as he sat up in bed still wearing his yellow and blue winter coat.

Spent the entire day at the library gathering every piece of writing I could find through emails I had sent over time and tried to organize them somewhere online. *I need a USB stick or something.* Once I found every major and most minor project I'd started or finished I could relax, but I still lost all my poetry and storyboards - also spent a good part of the day trying to start my book on the condition to no avail; the daze was overpowering me.

After losing track of time watching YouTube videos and not doing much of anything else, I realized I missed lunch and remembered about 'snack time' at the DI between lunch and dinner. Just heard about it from Ester in laundry the other day who thought adults enjoying *snack time* was the funniest thing in the world. I logged off of the computer and made my way for the elevator as Dorian walked up to me and looked me in the eyes.. With eyes that said *I've seen some shit man*, I said "Hey man, sorry I haven't given you my computer time yet, I kind of forgot."

"Don't worry about it, you got any smokes?" His skin looked mostly white but he had a very deep Native accent.

"No sorry man. Give you some when I do though."

"It's alright, let's go find one." We walked over to the elevator.

"There's a free barbecue across the street," he said as we walked to the front doors of the library.

"Is there?"

"Yeah, it's a church thing. They do it every Sunday."

When we got outside he pointed to a lineup of around forty Hobos at a barbecue with a guy talking on a megaphone.

"See. Oh there's a good one." Dorian picked up a cigarette butt with a drag or two left on it. "You got fire?" I handed him my lighter and he lit it up, handing the lighter back. "Let's go find you one."

"I'm good man."

"Here have this one." He insisted, handing me the lit butt. Half tempted was all I could be looking at the thing.

Picking up a better butt he turned to me with a smile. "You got fire?"

I handed him my lighter again, and while he lit up, I started smoking the butt and looked back over to the barbecue.

"Here." He handed me my lighter. "They got burgers and hot dogs and coffee. Go over there."

When I thanked him we went our separate ways. As I lined up I heard the guy yelling in the megaphone.

"Yo yo yo! What do ya know!? Jesus Christ is the star of the show!!"

"Shut the fuck up!" a woman ahead of me in line yelled.

"*You* shut the fuck up!" the woman behind me retorted.

The man with the megaphone began walking up to everyone in line individually, when he was four people ahead of me I could hear what he was saying.

"Jesus loves you," he assured the pleasant woman.

"Jesus doesn't exist, get the fuck away from me you creep!"

With a smile he continued to the next guy.

"I'm with her man, don't fucking talk to me."

"Why are you so angry?"

"Because I'm starving so I come here to get a free barbecue and you're throwing all this Jesus garbage down my throat!!"

Megaphone man nodded and made his way to the next guy and put his hand on his shoulder.

"Jesus loves you."

The small man was shaking in the cold. "Oh thank you, thank you, thank you, sir."

The next guy shook his hand but raised his other as if to say he didn't want to hear it.

"Jesus loves you man," Megaphone man said with a big smile on his face to the guy in front of me. The man grinned back and nodded his head in thanks.

Then he got to me and we shook hands. "Jesus loves you."

"Thank you. Jesus loves *you* I'm sure. I really respect what you're doing." He nodded his head in thanks the way the last guy did to him then walked to the woman behind me.

"Jesus loves you."

"Give me a hug, you're such a sweet heart," the woman said crushing him in her arms.

***

On the second floor of the DI I saw Kelsey watching everyone. She hadn't seen me yet. Staring at the ground I attempted walk past her undetected but she swooped her head down and caught my eyes before I made it.

"Hi!" she said smiling a big smile.

"Hey." I forced a smile back.

"Sorry I didn't wake you up, I called over here and Lloyd wasn't even working last night. You were sleeping so…"

"Oh strange, he definitely told me to talk to him. No problem."

Again I tried to walk away but she continued. "Hey so, you don't have to talk to me if you don't want, but *why* did you want to kill yourself?"

"Because I'm a failure."

A look of concern returned to her face and she touched her lip while the wheels turned in her head. "Hm. How so?"

"I've been writing screenplays and short stories for four years but I'm not published and I haven't sold anything, I started a company and it failed so I decided I was going to write a book on the homeless condition but…" I shook my head in discouragement.

Her eyes lit up. "That's all really impressive."

It is?

"Yeah, well I'm also an alcoholic with a criminal record." I admitted in self-disgust. "Well, *recovering* alcoholic." That was more or less true; *I only drank once in the last six months.*

"How long have you been sober for?"

"Six months." Alright I lied.

"Congratulations! That's great, you should be proud of yourself."

Not really, because I just lied to your face. I shrugged. She asked me about my reasoning for wanting to write a book on the condition, and how I came to be homeless – and she listened to me explain. While I was talking to her, I felt like she was genuinely interested in what I had to say, she was talking to me like I was a person. We talked for over an hour until it was time for me to catch the 2907 bus. Apparently she wasn't working over there tonight; she normally works on Second.

"Do you feel better? At least a little bit?"

It was a refreshing conversation but in the end I was still homeless and I still didn't know what I was doing. "A little. I'm just still worried, ya know?"

"About what?"

"That I'll never be happy. Especially after all this." I gestured all around us and she smiled big again.

"Well maybe you're not looking for the right things." She said with a smile before swaying her shoulders; intentionally I believed. Was I seeing things? She was looking at me. She was *looking* at me. Was she? *Is she? Probably not, I'm homeless and she works at the shelter I live at.* Until now I didn't notice how beautiful she was. Her great big white smile, hazel eyes, perky nose, eyebrows that made her emotions easy to read. As I wondered if she could see the heart-fletched arrow fatally impaling my skull, I decided it was time for me to move along.

"I should go," I said, pushing my feelings away. *There's no way she is interested in you, don't make yourself look like a jackass. You're working.*

"Did you get my note?"

"Your note?" Internal panting ensued. "No I didn't."

"Oh that's okay it was just…" She waved her hand as if it didn't matter.

Thanking her for the talk, I began to take my leave and she told me to come talk to her tomorrow - she'd be working.

Through Kelsey I found new determination to accomplish the mission I'd set out for, and I wish I could say it wasn't because I'd fallen for her like the world trade centres. If I didn't know myself I'd probably assume that I was just lonely and clinging to delusions, but as an introvert, loneliness is something I had experience dealing with quite effectively. Delusions? Maybe, but delusions are fascinations you see and think. Not something you feel. *Kelsey.*

When I got to 2907 I rushed to the office and asked if I had any messages or notes. After double checking my name the Dice began fumbling through messages from God knows how long ago and I noticed a video camera sitting on the desk before he handed me a folded piece of paper with my name on it.

I ate dinner, showered and smoked three cigarettes before I worked up the courage to read it.

Silly really - I don't know what I was expecting it to say. All it said was 'Michael, I know things may be dark right now, but I promise things will get better for you, you have a bright future. The DI staff is always here to support you. – Kelsey'

Even though the note had no correlation with romance, I was twitter-pated; it meant a lot. After reading it over a few times and memorizing it I put it in the breast pocket of my leather jacket for safe keeping with the company of the memory card I swiped from the camera.

5

TUKAHOOT

4:40 am I woke up to an eruption as the Bear God rolled over to his side. After I strapped my boots on, I went upstairs and tried to sign up for a chore for some coffee but there was no room left on the sign-up sheet - a cup of water would have to do. Crushed and defeated I sat down at a nearby table to sulk. It felt like my world was ending, I needed a cigarette and happened to see a guy a bit older than me with a wild goatee, a mohawk ponytail and a smoke in his mouth as he was getting things out of his locker for the day.

He shut his locker and started walking in my direction to the smoke pit and his friend with a black eye walked up and asked for a smoke - both punk rockers. I'd seen them around in a group of five of them, but there was only one other guy these two were usually with. He pulled out a full pack of smokes and handed one to his friend with the black eye, then caught me staring at the smokes.

I approached him with a guilty smile on my face holding out my last dollar. "Can I buy a smoke off you?"

His black-eyed friend looked at him, said "Sorry man," then made his way outside.

"Sure." He said, distractedly scratching the back of his head before he grabbed one and held it out to me. "Don't worry about buying it off me just give me a smoke when you have some."

"Thanks." We started walking to the door. "What's your name?"

"Dave," came the half-hearted response. "You?"

"Michael."

Dave nodded but he didn't care much. Dave's friend was already outside sitting down on a piece of cardboard covering the snow on his chair. It was too cold not to be wearing my jacket and it was still dark out, but grey and brown clouds were covering the stars. *Never too early to pollute the air.*

"You remember that chick I was telling you about?" Dave's friend asked as we got outside. Dave nodded as he lit his smoke. "I was fuckin' her in the living room and her husband came home and he told me to get the fuck out, so then I told him to hold on cause I needed to get my clothes on and he punched me in the face."

Thought I'd have to ask, but Dave beat me to it. "Did you get your clothes on?"

His friend laughed. "Yeah. It was awkward though. I thought he was gonna kill her after I left." He laughed again. "Then I went to my girlfriends and she asked about my eye and I told her I got mugged and then I fucked *her*!"

"Nice!" Dave said. I didn't agree with anything he just said, but in an objective study I couldn't let morality concern me.

"How do you get laid so much when you're…" *Homeless*, I wasn't going to say it, they were watching me too intently. "Living in a shelter?" They thought it was pretty funny.

"Well ya don't tell em' *that!*"

"Wouldn't they find out eventually?"

"Well ya, but ya dump em' before that happens." *Wow.*

"That's brutal."

"Most of the money I make goes to my bitch baby-mama for child support; I can't afford a girlfriend or another kid! All I want is sex." *Maybe a sex addict, maybe a sociopath. Maybe neither. Probably both.*

"Yeah he's kind of a dick-head, his name's Dave too." *Black-eye Dave.*

"Our other buddy's named Dave too!" Black-eye Dave said. *The Dave's.*

I put the smoke out halfway and went inside to watch the news. It was featuring a story of stabbings that had been happening near the downtown area of Calgary. All the victims were homeless, the suspect had not yet been caught. *Go figure.*

The Dave's and I caught the bus to the DI and, on the way in, Brad and Lyle approached me.

"Red Deer! We missed you." Brad shouted before running up and hugging me.

The Dave's continued into the DI, unimpressed that I was 'friends' with Brad. Pushing him away I glanced over at Lyle, clean-cut wearing his hard hat.

"Yeah it's been a while," I said.

"Yeah we got kicked out for a week for getting caught blazing on Second. You wanna blaze one? I got a roach I found it over there by the gate!"

"I'm good, man."

"Hey you wanna smoke this?" Brad asked as he pulled out a thin twisted up piece of paper that I thought could have been a joint but it smelled like tobacco once he lit it up. "You got any money?"

"I have a dollar twenty-five to my name."

"A dollar!? That can get us four smokes!"

"Really?"

"Yeah hand it over."

Curious, I gave him the dollar then he turned and started walking to the doors of the DI and I followed, Lyle watching our backs. He dropped his rolled smoke in front of the seniors. "I'll leave that for some *Hobo*!"

We got to the second floor and it was packed as usual.

"Grandma!" Brad yelled across the hoard. He ran through holding the dollar in the air and I followed him through the crowd, Lyle stood guard in the invisible gated walkway all the way down the middle of Second.

We made it to Grandma and Brad gave her a big hug. "I love you, Grandma!"

She was a very old woman, a little over weight with a big nose. She hugged him back.

"I love you too, you're such a sweet kid."

"Can I by four smokes?"

"Of course you can." Four smokes were exchanged for a dollar and we walked back out to Lyle. Brad handed me two smokes and put the other two in his pocket.

"Hey give *me* one, Brad!" Lyle yelled.

"I'll give you deuce!" looking over at me for some sort of approval, he smiled wide showing his teeth, they reminded me of a banana, "Oon *one* of them!"

He started laughing and then began walking down the walkway, then; like a dog, he noticed someone he knew and zeroed in on them. "Dave!" He ran through the crowd and found a Dave I'd never seen before. "Can you hook me up man? You know I'm good for it."

"I dunno dude, you still owe me fifteen dollars."

"You know I'm good for it! Wednesday's welfare Wednesday!"

"Aight." The new Dave looked over at me. "Who's this?"

"I can't remember." Brad turned to me. "I call him Red Deer 'cause he's from Red Deer."

"Michael." I shook Dave the Dealer's hand and he motioned his head towards the bathrooms. Brad followed waving his arm at me to follow. Lyle stood guard where we met Dave with a big smile on his face, knowing he was going to get high soon.

Surrounded by everything wet and the smell of shit and vomit, Dave pulled out a sandwich container full of weed and a few little baggies. He filled one up a little. "Now you owe me twenty-five."

"Alright, alright," Brad said snatching the bag from Dave. "Let's go get high, Red Deer!" and he ran out of the bathroom. I started to follow.

"Hold on," Dave called me back. "You smoke weed right?"

"Sometimes."

"If you ever need weed come to me."

"Alright."

"Don't ever go to anybody else, aight?" He looked me up and down.

"Alright." I looked around and saw a sink overflowing and I also noticed all the stalls were taken. *I wonder if they party in the stalls here too.*

"You're cool right?"

"Yeah."

"I can trust you?"

"Yeah man."

"Ah?"

"For sure."

"Aight, man, aight." Throwing his hand in the air. I felt it'd be disrespectful to leave him hanging, so I took it and he pulled me in for a half hug. "You're good shit man, you're good shit."

"Thanks man, you're good shit too. I should probably get going though."

"Aight man, peace. See you around."

Holding up the peace sign I took my leave.

When I got out of the bathroom, Brad and Lyle were beckoning me over to the smoke deck.

"You're not going to smoke weed out there are you? You just got kicked out for that."

"So? We're not gonna get caught! We never get caught!" declared Brad as he looked over at Lyle who was holding the door open already.

"I'm not down man, I got things I need to do at the library anyway."

"Well just come out for a smoke."

"Yeah man we barely get to see you now!" Lyle joined in. *This is the forth brief moment I've spent with you guys.*

They joined a big circle of misfits when we got outside, some of them old, some young. I lit up my smoke and Brad introduced me to a kid named Andy who looked like he still could have been in high school, and an old man named Rod, who was tall like a lightning rod and looked very unhealthy; he was nice though.

"Grandma!" Brad shouted before running over to see the old woman that sold him the smokes. Lyle, Andy and Rod followed and so did I. "You want to blaze Grandma?"

"Sure!"

Shouldn't have been surprised Grandma smoked weed, but I was.

"Alright!" Brad packed some weed into a pipe and started smoking it with the crowd of people and I left. Getting suspended from the DI was not an option for me. *Not here, not now. Not like this.*

***

After getting all of my writing onto my new memory card, courtesy of the DI, I avoided taking on any possible task and, once my computer time was up, went down to the first floor of the library to read. *Maybe I'll see Biker Mike.*

It must have been around noon, a young Native guy holding a rolled up poster wearing a bright blue winter jacket and a toque missing one of his front teeth approached me urgently. An apparent friend was standing nearby watching me. "Hey sorry man but do you have a *quarter*?"

"Like, money?"

"Yeah." I reached in my pocket. "Please come through please come through please come through." His face lit up as soon as I pulled one out and he grabbed it right away. "You came through! You're fucking awesome man I can blaze you up if you can wait for a minute I just need to use the pay phone."

"Sure."

"Cool. Let's go Fats."

Instead of following his friend, Fats approached me. "You got a smoke?"

"Do I look like I have a smoke? I'm not even smoking and I'm homeless." I shot back agitated because I didn't have any smokes for myself, he laughed and walked away. They came back about five minutes later and we left, walking up Hobo Central.

"How'd you end up homeless?" the guy in the blue jacket asked me.

"I started a company that failed. You?"

"Same thing, sort of. Guess that's what happens when you chase a dream." He unfolded the poster to reveal a remarkably drawn eagle with depth and vibrant colors.

"You paint that?"

"Mhmm! And I'm gonna sell it!"

"How much you think you can get for it?"

"Usually I get anywhere between forty and eighty, but yesterday I met this guy who's really interested in my art, bought one off me for two hundred bucks! That's why I needed the quarter, he wants to meet me again today, but I don't have a phone."

"Congratulations!"

"Thanks man, if all goes well I'll get out of Calgary by the end of the week!"

"Where you gonna go?"

"Vancouver, that's where the art scene is."

"Nice! I hope it works out." We walked until we saw someone he knew waiting at the train stop, maybe someone he was looking for. Immediately when I saw the guy I thought he looked like a bulldog.

"This is Bulldog," the guy in the blue jacket said. Tried to shake his hand but he put his fist out to pound it.

"What's *your* name?" I asked the guy in the blue coat.

"Eric," he replied while trying to get a joint lit. "But my Indian name is 'Tukahoot'." Laughing before he exhaled a large cloud of smoke he passed the joint to Fats. Bulldog laughed too and nodded his head like he never heard it before.

"*My* Indian name is big-white-smoke-cloud." Fats included himself before trying to take a big haul off the joint. Tukahoot snickered.

"No it's not, they just call you Fats." Fats passed the joint to Bulldog and he hit the joint while I put my backpack on the ground.

"You guys hear about that guy that's stabbing homeless guys?" Bulldog asked while passing me the joint.

"No," Tukahoot answered. "I don't pay attention to that bullshit. *Fear mongering* is what it is! Where's all the *good* stuff going on in the world? All the art? All the happiness?"

Without taking any, I passed him the joint. He took a hoot then looked at it. "Like, where's the weed at!? Fucking smoke a joint already people, Christ." Tukahoot looked down the train line at an approaching train. "That's my train, but if you're at the library same time tomorrow, I'll blaze you up!" He passed me the joint. "You can finish that."

The train pulled up and the three got on after swarms of people flew out from the doors. Walking down the train line towards the DI, I decided to smoke the rest, even though I was anticipating my upcoming meeting with Kelsey.

I got back to the DI around snack time, but there was something happening in the main lobby so a few of us were stuck beside the security station. There was a small Irish man with an accent as heavy as his backpack introducing himself and talking to everyone half-tense. Patrick was the name. Sober, as far as I could tell, with a worldly air about him; most likely an out-of-luck traveler. I introduced myself.

"Now tell me Michael, how's a nice young lad like you wind up at the place like the DI?"

"Started a company."

"Ah! A company!? Really? I suppose congratulations *aren't* in order though, are they."

"Nope, they sure aren't."

"Any plans to get out?"

"Well I'm kind of trying to write a book on the-" *Always check first,* I thought to myself as I inspected the area around me. *"Homeless."*

"Well that's fairly ambitious, in't it? You've sure come to the right place haven't you?"

"Absolutely."

"Have you ever heard of the documentary 'Streets of plenty'?"

"No."

"It's a YouChube documentary about a regular guy that just decides to go live on the streets of Vancouver for a month. At first he begins by staying in shelters and then moves to the street and does heroin and crack and all these other crazy things for the documentary too and he's never done hard drugs before, he's a crazy guy." *That sounds bigger and better. Dammit.*

"I'll have to check it out for sure. What about you, how'd you end up here?"

"Came from Toronto; a friend of mine got me a job out here painting houses."

"Plan on staying in Calgary?"

"Maybe."

"How long you think you'll be at the DI?"

"I'm hoping two weeks at the very *most*."

"If you want a designated bed here you need to do volunteer hours. I can show you a good place to do them, it's out of the way of all this."

"Sure that'd be wonderful!" Once the commotion in the main lobby was settled I took him to one of the Dice and told him I wanted to show Patrick to the laundry room so he could volunteer. We followed the Dice to the elevator. "Which floor do you sleep on then?"

"I go to twenty-nine-oh-seven, you should too. Stayed on Second *once* and got punched in the face." I touched my nose with my thumb.

"Is *that* what happened? Jesus. Yeh, yeh, I was going to go to the Warehouse. Four thirty right?"

"Four thirty." We got down to the basement and I led Patrick to the laundry room. Homer, Ester, Donald and Wade were there. Homer walked over and greeted us. "Hey Homer this is Patrick." They shook hands.

"Nice to meet you Patrick, Michael's a good kid eh. Are you coming to volunteer for a bit?"

Patrick looked at me then back to Homer. "Yeh! I suppose for a little while!"

"Cool. There's not much to do *now* eh, you can just sit down and enjoy the peace and quiet. There's food if you want some, help yourself."

After they were acquainted I told Homer I was just there to show Patrick and asked if he could let me back up to Second. We walked to the elevator together. "Come down anytime we really like having you eh. Ray's been taking a break from laundry too so we could use the help. It's a lot better than being up there on Second. I live on Forth eh, I know."

"You live on Forth?"

"Yeah. I've lived here for three years but I should be getting out soon." He scanned the elevator open and I got in. As the door started to close he stuck his arm in. "Oh, uh Michael, you got smokes?"

"No I don't." Pulling a couple out for me, he handed them over with a smile. "Thanks Homer I'll pay you back when I get some."

"Don't worry about *me* eh, just pay it forward to someone on Second, they can use it more than I can." The elevator closed and we waved to each other.

When I got in from my smoke Kelsey was on shift. When I got close to her she gave me a big smile and got one back inadvertently. "Hey! Are you feeling better at all?"

"Not really."

Her eyebrows crunched and her smile went away. "Oh." She looked into my eyes. "Are you still feeling like you still want to..?"

"I don't know, kind of. Like, I won't; I just think about it all the time."

She held her gaze on me as I looked away and pondered what our dynamic would look like if I met her when I had my life together. Neither of us said anything for a few seconds.

"Can you do something for me?"

"What's that?"

"Can you tell me three positive traits about yourself?"

I smirked. "I know what you're doing."

A guilty grin crept into the corner of her mouth. "What?"

"You're trying to get me to give you positive things about me to work with. Before I was homeless, I tried to help suicidal people online."

"You did?"

"Yeah it was another one of my *projects*. That's part of the problem, I can't focus on anything. I feel like I'm going crazy. I met a guy that thought he was friends with Eminem the other day. I just keep thinking 'what if I'm just like *that* guy?'"

Hazel eyes and crunched eyebrows. "I don't think you're just like *that* guy."

Brad walked up almost right in the middle of us and we backed up. "Red Deer! What's going on? Why'd you ditch earlier?"

Kelsey looked at me and smiled. "Brad we're having a private conversation, can you please leave?" She asked nicely.

"Why? Do you guys have a crush on each other?"

"Brad that's inappropriate."

"*I* have a girlfriend. She's cheating on me though I think. Fuckin' bitch. I should probably go call her."

"Yeah go call her man," I encouraged, and he walked away to the public phone.

"Is he a friend of yours?"

"Hah! No, not really. Pretty sure he's going to be in my book if I ever write it though."

She looked over at him. "Oh yeah? Why?"

"I think he's the epitome of what people think *all* Hobos are like. Obnoxious, rude, usually intoxicated."

She laughed. "But there's so much more to everyone. Most Hobos I've met aren't just smart but *generous*. It's insane that, while all of this is going on all day, everyone's just out there living normal lives, working normal jobs." Her eyes told me she was also passionate on the subject. "How did you get into helping the homeless?"

"Volunteered during a class trip and I thought it was a good fit."

"Class trip?" *Should I tell him?* She thought.

"I'm a sociology student. Actually, a lot of the staff here are students."

"Are they?" A lot of the Dice, I'd half-ass noticed, were young. But I thought they were undoubtedly post-secondary graduates. "I thought you had to graduate and like, work for the government or something to get a job here."

"No. The DI isn't even run by the government, we run solely on donations." *What!?*

"That's a lot of donations."

"Millions of dollars-worth a year."

"That doesn't surprise me, this place is huge - and the amount of people you guys feed!"

Brad walked up again. "Her Mom wouldn't let me talk to her. She hates me!"

"Brad we're still talking."

"I need to talk too! Do you think it's weird that I've been dating my girlfriend for three months and I still haven't fucked her?"

"Brad that's enough."

"My friend fucked *his* girlfriend and he started pissin' green and I was like 'That's fuckin' gross dude.' And he was like 'It's not that bad, it's just gonorrhoea.' And I was like 'Well yeah, but it's still a green discharge coming out yer dick!"

Kelsey wasn't impressed that I laughed, but the only reason I did was because I'd heard him tell the story before and I thought back to Biker Mike looking back at him in an elderly fashion.

"I think you need to go take a walk."

"Alright. You comin' Red Deer?"

"No man."

"Why doesn't *he* need to take a walk?"

"You wouldn't either if you weren't saying inappropriate things." *The three of us are the same age.*

"Okay, no more no more! I'll stop."

"We're still having a private conversation. You need to leave."

"That's alright I need to find a smoke anyway." Finally he walked away. Kelsey and I looked at each other.

"See?" We laughed.

"I can see it." I apologized to her for laughing and explained why; telling her about Biker Mike and a few of the other people I'd met so far and about how I wanted to follow in Viktor Frankl's footsteps.

"See, that's why you can't kill yourself. It sounds like you're going to swoop into the homeless condition and blow the roof off the scene."

"That's *why* I want to kill myself though. Even if I write the book, what's going to stop it from turning out like the rest of my work? I don't have any money. Feels like if I kill myself my writing has a better chance of being known. Kind of like the way Amanda Todd got all that attention for her video."

Kelsey looked at the ground seriously for a few seconds considering what she should say. "I went through a hard time once too. It wasn't really anything compared to what you're going through, but do you know J.K Rowling?"

"Harry Potter?"

She nodded. "Well when I was going through my darkest time I was reading <u>*Harry Potter and the Goblet of Fire*</u>. That book really helped get me through. If I would have read it knowing she killed herself -" she said, shaking her head while still giving the floor her attention. Then she lifted those hazel eyes and looked back at me intently. "I don't think it would have meant as much to me."

"Yeah." *That's different.* The clock said it was almost time to catch the bus to 2907, it was about time I crashed the pity party anyway. "I should go though, I don't want to get you in trouble."

"I'm doing my job."

"The twenty-nine-oh-seven bus is leaving right away too."

"Oh right, you stay at the warehouse! Well come see me on Friday, that's when I'm working next."

"Alright. Thanks for everything."

"You don't need to thank me." She smiled. "Just remember that you're not alone."

"Well…" *I am.* "Thank you." I started walking away.

"Hey!" When I turned she was right in front of me. "Can you promise me one thing?"

"Probably."

"Please don't kill yourself, even if you want to. Just give it two weeks, I promise things will be better."

"I can do that."

She let out a breath of relief. "Thank you."

"You don't need to thank me." We looked into each other's eyes smiling for a moment before I left. The walls of my stomach were being tickled by the wings of a thousand cliché insects, maybe more. *Blow the roof off the scene.* I liked the sound of that.

***

Greg found a new table to sit at and it was full so I found my own place by the sink not too far off from Nomad. I wanted to make conversation but I didn't want to disturb him; he was always so focused on what he was doing, or just angry while he was doing it.

A smiley, chubby old man walked over to me and looked into my eyes. "Mind if I sit with you?"

"Sure."

"I'm Harold," he said as he sat down. The man seemed nice enough but I got the feeling if I'd have been about ten years younger someone would need to supervise our visit.

"Michael."

He asked me how I ended up there and I told him about my company.

"Really, your own company? *Wow*. I have my own company too! I'm a web designer!"

"Oh, right on."

"It's really neat! I can make *you* a website if you want! Would you have any use for a website?"

"I'm a writer so maybe."

"Really, a writer? *Wow*." He looked over to some random guy. "Did you know this young man is a writer?"

"Really?"

"Yes!" Harold said with a creepy stare. The new guy walked over and stood awkwardly beside me while I was sitting; he was small with brown skin and always looked like he was on the verge of crying.

"If you want me to make you a website all I need is a credit card number."

"Man, even if I had a credit card, I wouldn't give you the number."

"Are you insinuating I'm not genuine?"

"Yes."

Harold got up with glossy eyes and walked away with a shameful smile.

"I'm Andre," this new man said.

"Michael."

"So you're a writer!"

"Yes sir."

"I'm a teacher."

"Really? Are you working?"

He shook his head. "I'm not a teacher *here*. I'm a teacher back home.

"Where's home?"

"Columbia."

"Are you waiting for your permanent residency?"

He nodded.

"How long you been here?"

"Three years."

"How long at the DI?"

"*Almost* three years."

"Why don't you go back if you could be a teacher there?"

Andre shuddered at the thought. "It's not safe in my country. I'd rather be on the streets here than in a home there."

"It's that bad eh?"

"People dying every day, stealing from each other-" He shook his head then put a hand on my shoulder. "*You* should become a teacher." *Um, okay.*

"Maybe one day Andre. Far off from that though."

"I can give you some information on some programs if you want, to help you to become a teacher in one year." *A year huh?*

"No, it's really alright, I don't want to trouble you."

"It's no trouble!" He insisted, putting a piece of paper and pen in front of me.

Patrick walked up as I was writing my email address down. "Michael! Do you smoke cigarettes?"

"Of course."

"Would you like to go for one?

"I'd love to, but I don't have any."

He held one out for me. "That's alright."

As I stood to go smoke with Patrick, Andre looked at me, distraught, like we'd never see each other again.

"It was nice to meet you Andre." We started for the door.

"Oh, okay. Bye Michael. Michael! I'll email you!"

There were a lot of us in the smoke pit, it reminded me of a zoo cage. "I didn't think you smoked," I said to Patrick.

"You know, I quit for six months before I came here."

"It's that bad?" He nodded like there was no doubt about it and I was stupid for even asking. "Have you been homeless in any other places?"

Sighing in remembrance, he chose to stay reserved. "I've been travelin' a lot of years Michael. Well, since I was your age come to think of it! I've been all over the place."

"How old are you now?"

"Guess!"

"Twenty six." Only now that I saw him smile could I see the wrinkles on the sides of his eyes.

"Ah I wish! I'm not a young man anymore." He unzipped his jacket and, maintaining his youthful smile, let his belly hang out, farther than I expected. "I'm thirty four. Thirty five this June."

"You hold it in well!"

"I do don't I?"

When we were done our smoke we went back inside. Trent spotted me when I got in the doors and walked over, touching the bridge of his unmarked nose. Patrick sat down at a nearby table to listen in.

"I got beat up," I said to Trent.

"I know I heard. I check up on you now and then, everything that happens is in the system. You look into EST yet?"

Completely forgot about it. "Not yet."

"Figured," he grinned. "You better be signed up for EST the next time I see you Michael, or *I'm* gonna beat you up!"

***

Tukahoot found me at the library the next morning, I'd been reading over the same line in my book for at least a half hour. He was carrying a normal sized backpack with a rolled poster sticking out.

"Sup man?"

"Nothin' much, what about you?" he replied as he sat down. "Reading?"

"Kind of. You sell that guy the eagle?"

"Yeah he didn't buy it for as much as the other one though only eighty bucks."

"Ah, that's not too bad though."

"For a days work?" He shook his head and stood up and I followed him outside the library. We started walking up Hobo Central to a spot he said he knew.

"Where's Fats?"

"I don't know. I kind of ditched him, man, he just kind of uses me for my money. He's not a real friend. That's why I want to get out of here, get away from all the fake people. Start new, ya know?"

"You think it's that easy?"

"I *know* it's that easy, I just need the money."

"Fair enough. You meeting that guy again today?"

"No, but I'm gonna spend the whole day making a new picture." We walked up some stairs and sat down in the courtyard of some government building. "Don't worry man, this place is abandoned. It's like a…. Where you from again?"

"Red Deer."

"Where's a place they smoke a lot of weed in Red Deer?"

"I dunno, Faces."

"This is like the Faces of Calgary." He pulled out a toothpick of a joint. "Sorry this is all I have left."

"It's all good man, I don't have *anything*."

"It's all good man." He sparked the joint. "It's aallllll gooooood."

"Do you stay at the DI?" I took a hoot after he passed me the joint.

"Sometimes. Sometimes I stay at the Mustard Seed. Usually I just stay outside though man, to be honest," he admitted as I passed the joint to him.

"Fair enough man. I'm actually writing a book on homelessness, but I've only been to the DI so far." He hit the joint almost to the end and I passed on the rest.

"That's the place to *be* if you're writing a book on the homeless."

"True, but I've been thinking that there's probably a huge difference between sheltered homeless and street homeless."

"Homeless is homeless to me, man. It's the lack of human connection and touch. When you're homeless man, everything is just so hopeless and lonely, you'd die just to shake someone's hand half the time." *Deep.*

"It's sad but it's true. And then they all get so fucked up over it that people don't even want to push them away." He stood up and we started heading towards the library again. "Once you are or have been homeless it's like everyone knows. Like there's a stink that comes with it. That's why I do what I do. It keeps my mind occupied and *me* happy. Fuck the hater's man." *Is that the answer to my question? Why the laundry folk live at the DI? A stink of poverty that discourages them?*

"Good call."

"You don't say much, eh? That's alright. You gonna come to the library and watch me draw? It's gonna be my best picture yet!"

"I have to do some volunteer hours at the DI."

"You're gonna blaze and run? Shitty, man."

I only watched Tukahoot draw in the library for an hour before heading back to the DI and down into the laundry room. When I got down there it was only Donald, Ralph and Wade.

"Now ya show up!" Donald grunted in good humor.

"Boy, were these guys glad *I* showed up! You should have seen it in hya!" Ralph exclaimed.

Wade sat in the corner reading his book, glancing up in slight annoyance at Ralph for a moment.

"I was upstas tryin' to enjoy my breakfast, when alluvasudden Al comes up an' says, 'Ralph I need you in the laundry room!' We coulda really used you! Then maybe *I* wouldn't have to work so hard all the time."

Ralph limped over to me and slapped my shoulder as he walked past. "I'm just kidding. Well actually I'm *not* - we really could have used you. If Al doesn't stop taking advantage of me, I'm gonna have to stop coming down hya! I'm going upstas!"

He turned around and almost bumped into Al's bin full of dirty laundry. "Oh, hi Al!" And then he continued on. Donald slapped the air in Ralph's direction.

"Michael, how are you?"

"Good Al, how you doin'?"

"Good, good."

"Weather check!" Wade ordered, putting his book down then walking towards the elevators.

Weather check is the laundry folks term for smoke break.

Donald followed and Al smiled at me. "Do you smoke?"

"Yeah." He held one out to me, continuing to smile. "Thanks a lot Al!"

"You're welcome. I know how it is. I have a son your age."

On the third floor smoke deck Wade stared out into the distance while Donald fought the temptation to sit down.

Al was still smiling at me "So Michael did you graduate?"

"I did actually."

"Are you going to go to college?"

"Depends."

"Gotta go to college if you're gonna be a writer!" Donald interjected.

"I guess."

"When I was your age, I'd been all over the world and spoke three languages!"

"School?"

"Navy!" He grunted back.

"What languages do you speak?"

"*Now* I speak Thai, Korean, French, Spanish, Cantonese and a little Mandarin." Remembering all the languages he spoke I think he decided he earned the right to sit down because that's what he did. "And English."

"You didn't learn *any* of them in school?"

"When you port in a country that doesn't speak your language you *have* to learn it."

"How long were you in the Navy for?"

"Twenty five years!"

"That's a long time, longer than I've been alive!" He stood back up as soon as I said that.

"Yeah, I'm an old fucker!" Then he put out his cigarette a little less than half way and opened the door. "Well, that's halfer!"

Thought I may have hurt his feelings but when we got back into the laundry room he gave me a Japanese comic book that was written right to left. I'd never seen anything like it. He told me that was the way all Japanese literature was. Before I could read it we had to fold the rest of the laundry. "After the Navy," Donald continued, "I came back to Canada and got my bachelors in English."

"You ever teach?"

"Yeah I taught for years in a university, but the pay's shit so I got into iron working."

"Doing what?"

"Building bridges."

We all folded in silence for a minute, no one in the room agreed with what they knew he was about to say.

"I still build bridges."

Looking at Donald while he told me about which bridges he's worked on in Calgary, and the new higher paying job he was taking in Vancouver, I couldn't see a shred of old man Willy in him; although I didn't think it would be long until I could. There comes a time when your body can't handle hard labor anymore, and you need to slow down; stop maybe. But when that's the life you're used to, what do you do when it comes time to live like a mouse, and you need to feed the monkey on your back?

6

THE BEAR GOD

The DI's temp agency opens at 6:45 am. I was there at 6:15 am and I was around the twentieth person in line and drew ball 44 from the bingo cage.

"That's good!" claimed the lady running the show. Judging by her list of names beside numbers 1-100, I imagined it wasn't *too* bad, but among the Hobos I'd heard that the DI rarely sent more than a handful workers out. I stepped aside to a free space in hopes that the woman would get a call and just give the job to me to avoid the hassle of finding the rightful person on the list. There's a rule of thumb at temp agencies to make your presence known and hang around within sight if you want to get sent out.

After a couple minutes, I saw the Bear God in action for the first time. Though he was a very large, approximately fifty year old Native man, he was wearing a baseball jersey and backwards baseball cap. He walked in following a short angry looking man with a forwards cap, long hair, aviators and a handlebar moustache. They both drew balls from the bingo cage, and they too must have known the rule of thumb because they stood to the side close to me.

"Does anyone know what was for breakfast?" the Bear God asked. It was the first time I heard him speak and his voice was shockingly high pitched.

"Eggs with cut up green onions and bacon," a man yet to draw from the bingo cage replied.

"You're not kiddin'?'" the Bear God asked.

"I'm serious! Some school kids are doin' it for us."

The Bear God looked at the angry man with a look of desperation. "We probably have time for some breakfast huh?"

The angry man stood statuesque with his arms crossed, the Bear God continued, with that same desperate look on his face, "They probably won't send us out for a little while, ya think?" The angry man still did not move. "Come on Mikey it's eggs and bacon! Name one time we've had eggs and bacon this month!"

I had to leave - not only was my image of the Bear God shattered but I could go for some eggs and bacon.

While eating breakfast on Second, I noticed some familiar faces that I'd come to recognize as DI regulars, though I think it would be safe to say a majority were regulars. There was Twitch, quite possibly the youngest person living at the DI. Heard his nickname and description before I even saw him. "The young guy that makes funny faces and twitches." It was very obvious to me that he suffered from brain damage that he was born with.

Jib's brain damage on the other hand was very clearly drug induced, as he picked at his arms and made sounds of farm animals while scratching himself and laughing. I felt very strongly that these two, more than the rest, should be in the hands of the government.

There was also a group of thirty young*er* people ranging from twenty to thirty that I'd seen around all over the place. They all looked to the youngest in their crowd, a large young man with slicked back red hair and piercings all over his face; I called him Bowser. I assumed most of them were dealers.

There was also an old bearded man who wore duct-tape over every inch of his shoes, a sketchy guy who looked like a pirate and wore pants that were twenty sizes too big for him and hung around his knees, and quite a few old folks with walkers and canes, not many wheelchairs.

Once everyone was served, the DI made an announcement asking us to give our *guests* a round of applause for the breakfast they served and got a half mediocre response at best. I sat watching people for a little while longer until Al walked by with a cart full of laundry.

"Michael. How are you doing?"

"Alright, you?"

"Good. Yeah. Yeah. Do you have some free time today? I was looking for someone up here to volunteer but I don't think he's around."

"Yeah I can help out."

Al led me down to laundry where Donald, Ester and Wade were already folding heaps of clean sheets. I got to folding and looked over at Ester.

"Where were you yesterday?"

"Painting!"

"Nice!"

"Yes!" And she passionately told me about all the paintings she was working on.

"Where do you do all this?"

"I have a studio!"

"Your own studio?"

"Yes! Well it's the *DI's* studio but they're letting me use it. There are a few of us in there! I'm the only woman but they all give me my space!"

"They have anything for writers?"

"Maybe but you have to be a senior to get in there."

"Ouch!" Donald yelled.

"What?" Ester asked.

"I bent over to grab a damn pillow case and my back didn't like it. My old fucker pills haven't kicked in yet!" I laughed and he looked over at me, then at Wade. "What do you think? Time for a weather check yet?"

"Let's wait until Al brings the coffee down."

Al came down with two more guys that Ester called the Twins, even though they weren't related and looked nothing alike. The six of us folded until 8:15 am, coffee time, and Al came down with a thermos of coffee the size of my torso that in my experience never ran out. Afterwards we went out for a smoke, Donald gave me one. When we got back down Al got a call over the walkie-talkie and went upstairs.

You ready to go now?" one of the Twins asked Ester.

"If we leave now it'll only be Donald, Wade and Michael left to fold all these sheets!" she replied. One of the Twins looked around while the other observed all of us.

"We already have one rolled you know," one of them said.

"Let's at least wait until ten!"

Al came down with a young Native woman and introduced her to everyone, apparently she was there to do community service hours. Once she got the hang of folding bundles, Ester and the Twins left. We folded until lunch while the woman talked non-stop about her piece of shit baby daddy, her new man who's awesome, how awesome *she* is, how you can still be a good mother and have a good time - oh and her kid and how the government has no right to take him.

For lunch, instead of going to Second, we all got to go up to the fifth floor. We watched the news while we ate lunch then Donald gave me another smoke and we all went outside. Donald and Wade had initiated an interesting conversation about one of the news items we'd just seen and she found a way to make it relate to her and then proceeded to bum a smoke from Donald.

Ester ended up coming back down to laundry about a half hour after we did and told us the Twins bought her lunch. Her eyes were bloodshot and I said "I didn't know you smoke weed."

"When you're in a place like the DI you have to do *something*."

Al came back down and told the woman he was getting off work soon and filled out her time sheet. As soon as she left Donald pointed at me with wild eyes.

"Diagnoses!?" I grinned.

"I don't know, I guess I'd say she's pretty self-centred and loud." Donald let out a scoff. *Guess that wasn't what he meant.*

"F.A.S. Fetal alcohol syndrome. Lots of Natives have it."

"Donald!" Ester shouted.

"It's not racist Ester, it's a fact!" he retorted.

"I know about it, but I don't think I've ever knowingly seen it before."

He pointed at the door she walked out of. "Well *that* was it!"

"She didn't seem that bad."

"Well like anything, there are varying degrees and everyone experiences it differently. but it can get them in a lot of trouble, especially when liquor is involved." While Donald filled me in on some fun facts about fetal alcohol syndrome, Al switched out with Homer, whose walkie-talkie said there was someone who would like to volunteer.

"Send em' down." Homer responded.

About two minutes later, in walked a pair of steel toed boots, blue jeans, a black sleeveless shirt and a bandana. He had sleeve tattoos on both arms, one red one blue, and he had *two* teardrop tattoos; one under each eye.

"Hi." The man said sociably.

Silence told me I wasn't the only one that was weary of teardrop tattoos.

Homer walked up and shook his hand nervously. "I'm Homer."

"David," he said, shaking Homer's hand.

Other than the five minutes it took Ester to show David how to fold bundles, he got the same silent treatment I did the first time I came down. Seemed like a normal enough guy, pointing out some of the good oldies on the radio and tapping his foot to the tunes. When it was time for a weather check he apologized before asking Wade for a cigarette. Wade said he didn't have many left, but Homer was quick to offer, Ester stayed downstairs because she didn't smoke.

On the third floor smoke deck, Wade stood off by himself watching the clouds as he usually did while Donald, Homer and I stood closer to the door; David standing nearby waiting for a chance to jump into the conversation.

"Movin' on Friday," Donald groaned.

"Oh that's right eh? Good for you Donald," Homer replied.

"We'll see."

"Do you have your own place out there?" I asked.

"Brother's letting me stay at his place until I get a couple cheques."

"We'll sure miss you eh, you're a good guy, Donald."

"Hah!"

"Where ya movin' to if ya don't mind me askin'?" David timidly joined in.

"Vancouver." Donald answered, reluctant to get into a conversation with him

"It's nice out that way - I just came here from out east!"

"Ah!" Donald put his smoke out halfway. "That's a halfer!" Then went inside.

Where out east?" I invited his story.

"P.E.I., Nova Scotia. All over really, I did a bit of travelin' when I moved back from Thailand."

"How long did you live in Thailand for?"

"Twenty years or so."

"Donald, the guy that just went inside speaks Thai. I think he said he spent a lot of time there."

"Hmm. I'll have to ask him."

When I eyed the tattoos up his arms I spotted a Harley Davidson. "You a biker?"

David looked at the tattoo I was looking at with a friendly smile.

"Nah I just like bikes. And tattoos." He slapped his red arm. "Fire." Then the blue arm. "Water."

When we got back down to laundry we went to reading our books, except Homer who said he read the newspaper at work because he 'never could put a good book down'. David found a random book from a shelf in the laundry room and tried to make small talk about it but no one really bit. A load of blankets came out of the drier and David was the first to go over and help fold, followed by me, then Donald, then Ester, Wade didn't see.

"Ester, you sit down and enjoy your book eh, we have enough people over here," Homer said. Ester smiled and turned around as we folded blankets and put them into carts.

"So Michael here was tellin' me you might have spent some time in Thailand," David said to Donald.

"Spent five years there once. I went to Thailand a *few* times, Korea, all over the fuckin' place."

"I lived in Thailand for twenty years; it's like home to me."

Donald challenged David's Thai and they broke into a brief conversation I believe they were both fluent in, but honestly who knows. I think they switched back to English because Homer and I were trying to paying attention.

"*I* thought about settling down there, but there was too much work to be done. The women though, hwoah!"

"I know what you mean. My second wife was Thai."

"Divorced?"

"Widowed." David clarified as he nervously scratched one of the tear drops. "That's why I got the tattoos eh, the tear drops. For each of my wives."

"Oh pff, I thought you fuckin' killed somebody!" Donald admitted, smacking the top of his head.

David laughed. "Yeah a lot of people think that. I didn't know that was what they meant when I got em' I just thought it was symbolic." *What a reason to be misjudged.* David and Donald continued their conversation about Thailand and then figured out other places they both travelled until there was nothing left to fold and Homer told us we could go. As I was leaving Donald called my name.

"I'm leaving on Friday and I have to get all my things from my storage unit to the Greyhound station. I'd really appreciate it if you could help me out. I'll pay you."

"Yeah I can do that. Friday?"

"Meet me down here in the morning, then we'll head out after lunch. How does twenty dollars an hour sound?"

"Sounds pretty good. You don't need to pay me Friday if I can have a few smokes now," I suggested with a grin.

He smiled and pulled out a handful of smokes. "I'll give you these *and* I'll pay you, how's that sound?"

"You got a deal!" I didn't really want him to pay me, considering his situation in addition to the fact he was moving. Donald stayed in laundry and I walked out of the garage leading to the front of the building. Lighting a smoke while walking up to the gate, I saw Lyle, wearing his hard hat, of course, but without Brad for the first time. He had a cut on his nose similar to mine. He was looking at the ground, and at first I thought he was tripping out, but he may have been looking for cigarette butts.

"What's up Lyle?"

With pupils that looked like they could swallow me if they tried, Lyle looked at me in awe. "Hey what's up man!? Long time no see!"

"I guess. Where's Brad?"

"Brad's a fucking dick man, I hate Brad! Can I have some of that?" He pointed at my smoke and I gave him one of the ones Donald gave me.

"What happened to your nose?"

"Last night I was trying to buy some weed and I saw this guy smoking weed over there by the gate. so I walked over to him and held out twenty dollars and asked if I could buy some weed off him.

He took my twenty dollars, punched me in my nose and he said, 'Don't you ever ask me for weed again!'"

"Shitty deal, man." As I was telling the story of what happened to my nose he was looking around at everything in amazement and wonder. I had a hunch. "Are you on acid?"

He looked at me like I knew something he didn't. "Yeah, how'd you know?"

"Because you look like you're trippin'."

It looked like his stomach turned. "Do I?"

"Yeah." I laughed, "It's all good though man, don't worry about it *too* much; you'll give yourself a bad trip. Who'd you do acid with?"

"Brad. We were just at the library reading for a while - it was crazy. I was looking at this book with all these colorful designs and Brad was reading the bible. He looked like Jesus I was tripping out for a while I was like 'Is that Jesus?'" He laughed to himself. "Man I miss Brad."

"How'd he go from Jesus to being a dick?"

"Because man! I just feel like he doesn't appreciate me, ya know? And whenever I get money I spend it on *both* of us and when he gets money he spends it on *himself.*"

"Yeah man, don't follow Brad around if you want to get out of here."

"Alright." After studying me he said, "I'll follow *you* around!"

"That's not what I meant. What do *you* want to do? You want to work right?"

Seemed he had never given it much thought. "I guess so. Yeah!"

"Well, you've been wearing a hard hat every time I've seen you." He touched his hard hat and looked at me confused. "You need to make your own way in life, think for yourself."

"I don't know how to do that though!"

"It's easy once you get the hang of it. There's a program at the DI called EST that will get you your tickets to get working."

He looked to the side and his face lit up. "Brad!"

Brad was walking over with a nutty look in his eyes, sweating with his long hair stuck to his face and sweat dripping off his greasy beard.

"Lyle, I'm sorry buddy!" He walked up and they hugged each other.

"Aw, it's okay Brad, I forgive you."

"Sup, Red Deer?"

I gave him a chin nod.

"He knows we're on acid!" Lyle divulged..

Brad smiled. "You wanna go get high?"

"I'm good man."

"Come on, I got kicked out of the DI again! I'll give you a smoke. That's a good deal right? I *give* you a smoke to smoke *my* weed?"

"It's a good deal, but I'm alright man."

"I'll go with you Brad."

"Only if you come with me to the Mustard Seed!"

"Okay."

"Red Deer you should come too."

"Nope, I got a bed here."

"Come on! We're friends aren't we? That's what friends do, when one of us struggles we all struggle!"

"I'm not going to the Mustard Seed. Sorry."

"I'm not either!" Lyle shouted.

"If you don't come, I'll stay on the streets and I could die on the streets! You don't want that do you?"

Lyle experienced a split second of guilt. "If you decide not to go to the Mustard Seed and sleep on the streets, that's *your* decision! I need to look after myself. I'm staying here with Red Deer."

"Can I have some of your smoke at least?"

Lyle handed it to him and while he exhaled smoke, Brad started nodding to himself. "Fine, I see how it is. I don't have any friends, no one loves me. I'll just go be by myself. I thought you guys were my hommies, but if this is the way it's gonna be, then I don't need you anyway because this isn't the way hommies treat hommies." He turned around and started walking away with Lyle's smoke then turned around. "If you change your mind I'll be at the Mustard Seed!"

"Give me back my smoke Brad!" Brad looked at the smoke then back at Lyle and smiled, then left.

"Don't worry, I'm not gonna go with you," Lyle said in a down tone. "I know you don't want me around. I was just sayin' that so

Brad would leave. I can't go inside the DI right now anyway. Can I just have a one more smoke?" After I handed him a cigarette he walked off in the same direction as Brad, though I doubted he was going the same place.

When I got inside I went to the security station to sign up for EST. While the security guard was going to get an application I heard someone say "How's your nose?" And it sounded directed towards me.

"Good." I replied before glancing over at a tall Native man with long hair four feet away looking at me behind shades with a serious look on his face.

"Good." He said without moving or removing the look.

"Yeah…" *Most likely not a friend.*

"You better watch yourself." And with that he withdrew to the shelter.

"Here." The security officer said holding the EST application to me.

"Thanks."

The Native man was already a few steps up the stairs to Second when I caught up to him.

"Hey!"

Slowly, he turned around and came towards me, stopping on the bottom step. "Can you take me to Casey?"

"Why do you want to talk to Casey?"

"Want to apologize," I shrugged. "I really don't want any enemies here."

For a few moments he reflected on my request. "I don't think Casey wants to talk to you."

While he walked up the stairs I made an executive decision to stay off Second for the day. I found a chair in the lobby and sat there with my backpack propped up beside me until it was almost time to get tickets to 2907.

"Michael!" Patrick greeted. We shook hands and I noticed he was covered in paint.

"Patrick, how was work?"

"It was awrigh, the boss really wants me to do things *his* way and it's frustrating because it's like 'Man, I know what I'm doing.'"

"Gotta do it their way sometimes though."

"I suppose so. Are you working?"

"Sometimes." I pulled out my hardhat and vest from my backpack because he didn't seem to believe me.

He looked surprised and slapped my shoulder. "Good for you!"

I noticed he'd been eying the empty chair through the conversation. "You want to sit down?" Made his day I think because it painted a smile on his face, it was hard to tell if it was the consideration or the chair.

"I really would, thank you. I'm not a young man like you anymore, carrying a backpack like this does a number on your back." He groaned while putting his backpack on the ground and easing into the chair. "I want to keep my backpack in storage at the Warehouse but they won't let me access any of it until I leave for good so I need to separate all my things. I'd just leave the whole lot of it there during the day but I have a-" He stopped to study me. "Well a laptop. I can trust you righ?"

"Yeah man. I'd take care of that right away though. I had a laptop when I first came here too. You can probably bring it around if you want to, everyone else does, but I don't recommend doing it with a big backpack, you'll draw attention to yourself."

Fright and empathy showed in his eyes. "Someone stole your laptop from you?"

"Something like that."

He laughed. "You have some unfortunate luck don't you Michael."

"You have no idea." I continued on to tell him about the recent event with the tall Native man.

Patrick and I got our tickets to 2907 and ate dinner before he decided to take my advice and separate his things. Teary-eyed Andre asked me if I'd checked my email yet, I told him I hadn't and he said it was his computer time *right now* and I could check it if I wanted.

When I checked my email I was a bit shocked to find eight emails from Andre, all with different links to online schools and paragraphs of personal messages. Didn't read much of any of them and, before I logged off, I thought about what Tukahoot stated about human connection. I got off the computer and walked back to Andre.

"What do you think?" He asked.

"Umm. Well you sent me *eight* emails."

"Oh."

"Yeah." Awkward silence. "If you could not do that anymore I'd really appreciate it."

"No?"

"No, sorry man. Really, I don't even want to become a teacher. I appreciate that you think I *could* be a teacher though."

"*Anyone* can be a teacher."

"Alright. I'm gonna go out for a smoke."

"Okay. We're still friends right?"

"Sure."

"I'll print some forms out for you if you want."

"No, it's really alright Andre."

On the outskirts of the crowd I found a place to stand and noticed that a fat bald guy beside me was reading *1984*. "That's gotta be my most favorite book of all time."

He looked over at me and grinned. "It's not one of my favorites, I just found it on the book shelf here. Usually I like stuff like Tom Clancy writes, more action and faster pace."

We recommended a few books to each other and he told me his name was Dan, then he asked if I was new there.

"Not overly. You?"

"I've been here once before. I just got out of prison."

"Oh yeah?"

"Yeah, but you tell me if this sounds fucked up. My buddy beats his girlfriend then she comes runnin' to me so I go over to his house and smash his lights out."

"Sounds like he had it coming."

"Yeah but it was assault with a weapon so… Anyway! I have a job but I'm waiting to get sent out so I'm stuck here. I'm a driller." *Driller Dan.*

"Nice, when do you think you'll get sent out?"

"Hopefully within the next three months, but she'll be smooth sailin' from there on out. I clear three thousand dollars every two weeks out there."

"Geez, I wouldn't even know what to do with that kind of money."

"I do! Blow!" He laughed. "Drink, women, fuck - you name it you can do it. You can do anything when you got money!" *Until it runs out.*

We finished our smokes and went inside, he went downstairs and I went to the dining room and sat down with Greg to watch the movie of the night. His sheriff moustache was gone and now he looked about ten years younger.

"How's it going kid?"

"Not bad you?"

"Not bad. Workin?"

"Tryin'. You?"

"Naw." Greg leaned back in his chair and relaxed. "Hurt my ankle. I'm trying to get on EI. Been waiting for a while now, you know how the government is. I had to wait for over a year for my dental surgery."

"Dental surgery?"

He smiled showing his rare white teeth, then pulled half of them out. "You thought they were real didn't ya?" *Isn't that the point?* "You probably think I lost em to drugs or something."

"Well not *now*."

"Kicked in the face by a horse."

"Yeah that'll do it. Sorry to hear man, that sounds terrible."

"No it doesn't." Smirking, he relaxed back into his chair. "Got me off work for a whole year. There's a lot you wouldn't guess by looking at me."

"Like what?"

"Like I used to be a heroin addict." He sat back up taking his jacket off. "Used to be skin and bones, now look at me!" Slapping his bicep he flexed as hard as he could. "Give er a feel."

I felt the firm muscle and I was pretty impressed, with his jacket on I would have thought he was just a regular Joe.

"Not bad. How long you been clean now?"

"I've been off heroin for five years."

"Congratulations, Greg, that's a long time."

"Yeah well my whole life's gone now. Got into it when I was in my thirties and now I'm sixty. Broke. Homeless."

"You're *sixty*?" Didn't look it.

"Pretty good lookin' for an old timer eh? I may be a mess but I still take good care of myself." He yawned. "Ah, I'm tired." Pointing at the TV, he rose from his seat. "Let me know what happens tomorrow, I was getting into that."

For his sake I actually stayed up and watched it even though I was about to go to bed too. Once the movie was over I went down to bed 207 and sat in my bed looking at the rows of bunk beds that felt like home to me. *So this is what it's like*, I thought before falling asleep to the sound of snoring.

"He's not waking up." Arwin tried to say not quietly at all. *Well, good news is he's not talking about me. Bad news is he's not talking about me.*

"He was written down for a four thirty wake up but I don't think he's *breathing*." My eyes and ears open, I tried to listen but all I could hear was my heart pumping adrenaline.

"No, he's not breathing," the other Dice confirmed a lot quieter.

"Alright let's go call make the call," Arwin sighed sullenly.

Once I'd heard them go upstairs, I looked around and saw the guy on the top bunk next to me looking down at the Bear God. Peering over the edge of my bed, I looked upon the Bear God who had gone to sleep for the last time.

7

NIGHT AT THE MANSION

*S*crew *this,* I thought standing in line for the bingo cage, *no more.*

I'm done. Barely knew the Bear God and yet his death threw me way out of whack. It could have just been because he died right under me while I was sleeping, but if one thing was for sure, I didn't want to see anything like that again. Drew ball number 86. *Nice.* Still had one smoke left from Donald, so I went out to smoke it. *I'm not getting work today.*

While I smoked, I watched some frazzled guy pace back and forth, repeatedly looking at his phone. Drawing near me, he made it inconspicuous that he saw me watching until he got up close with a quick peer at my boots. "You're not Dave are you?"

"No."

"Do you know a Dave who lives here?"

"I know a few Dave's who live here."

"Well I called the work agency here and they said four guys would be waiting out front but we've been waiting for our forth for ten minutes. Pfff, well thanks anyways." Not far away was his van, full of Hobos and ready to go to work.

"I can go if you want."

"Well, get in the van!" ordered the guy, directing me in the direction of the van.

"Irish," a deep Native voice said as I pushed my backpack into the back seat of the van, and I looked up to see Dorian beside me.

"What's up Dorian?"

"Oh. You're not Irish. I thought you were Irish. The Irish guy. But you're uh, who are you again?"

"Michael. Or Mike."

He nodded. "Irish."

"I'm Tucker." A young Native informed me while he reached back to shake my hand, then turned back to the driver. "Hey - are you paying us at the *end* of the day?"

"Yeah", answered the irritated driver.

"I haven't eaten yet, I need money *now*."

"I'd have to stop somewhere if I was going to give you money now."

"Well you'll have to stop somewhere so I can get something to eat, so that works out, hey?"

We stopped at a gas station on the way to wherever it was we were going and the driver gave us each ten dollars. Tucker and the kid with the red hair who was riding shotgun bought chips and sandwiches, Dorian bought a few bags of candy and I bought smokes, I had some sandwiches from the DI for lunch; bologna and margarine.

We got back into the van and went all the way to where a garage had either caught fire or exploded; quite possibly both. Ashes and charcoal everywhere, the steel frame of a quad, melted cans and propane tanks. Scattered all over the scene were a few nudie magazines which we learned, thanks to Tucker within minutes of being there, still had some pages intact. Our job was to clean it all up. The guys who hired us told us to call them Pop and Junior, for obvious reasons.

For an hour or two, we moved all the heavy stuff into a moving truck and Pop took the red headed kid, whose name I'd learned was Jack, to go unload it all. Junior gave the three of us garbage bags and shovels to clean up all the debris before going to sleep in the van for a little while. Right after Junior was out of sight, Tucker hopped up onto the cement frame of the garage and started flipping through his new porn while I shovelled debris into a garbage bag that Dorian held open for me.

"You drink last night Tuck?" Dorian asked the ground.

"Yeah."

"Drinkin' tonight?"

"I don't think so. I don't feel so good."

"Damn. I was going to say we should get some burs when we're done. You drinking tonight Irish?"

"I don't drink man."

He gave me a curious look. "Oh."

"I'll probably drink with you tonight actually, just give me a little while." Tucker revised while getting up and walking to his backpack to eat some chips. He pulled out his sandwich and took one bite and then gagged. "Oh man." And then he gagged a second time.

"Don't puke on the guys lawn Tuck! Puke in the ally." Dorian looked over at me and shook his head. "Kids can't handle their liquor anymore."

Tucker ran into the back ally and dry heaved while hunched over for fifteen minutes before getting a little puke out, then stood up straight and fell down from the head rush and slid himself against the fence on the other side of the ally.

"You alright man?" I called over to him. Tucker shook his head no. "Do you want your food?" He shook his head no again.

"Do I have any water in my backpack?" He called over.

Checking his backpack I only found empty beer cans and his chips, then grabbed his sandwich from the ground and put it in his backpack. There was a bottle of water in my backpack so I grabbed it and took it over to him. As he drank I decided it was probably best not to tell him I'd found the bottle on the ground outside the gas station and filled it with tap water when we got here, though I doubted he would have cared much. Dorian walked over.

"Judging by the position of the Sun, it's time to take a break." Tucker held the water out to me.

"Drink the rest, I know what it's like to be dehydrated from a hangover, you'll need it," I said while lighting a smoke.

"I'll throw up if I drink anymore of it. Hey can I have one of those?"

"Keep it for later. And no, sorry man."

"I'll give you my sandwich for one."

"You'll need that too."

"I'm dyin' here!"

"I'll give you *one*." I gave in.

Dorian didn't ask, but stared at me until I gave him one too.

We took a break for a good half hour before getting back to work, Tucker seemed a *little* better. It was only ten minutes before Junior got back and ten more minutes after that when Pop came back with Jack. Pop told us all to take a break, then shovelled debris into bags Junior was holding while we watched Pop yell about being triple our age and twice the worker. Once we all got back to work, Pop and Junior took off somewhere in the van leaving us to our own devices again.

Instead of two of us shovelling and two of us holding bags, Dorian and Jack held bags for me to shovel, while Tucker sat off to the side flipping through the porn. Jack must have been more annoyed than me because he dropped his bag and walked into the ally to light a joint. Dorian gave up after that and went to look at porn with Tucker and I went into the ally and offered Jack a smoke or two for some of his joint.

"I don't smoke, you can just have some," he said.

Jack was my age or younger and I thought maybe he'd just come to the DI to work, I doubted he lived there. Eventually we loaded all the bagged debris into the moving truck and Pop took Jack again to unload it all, the rest of us were done for the day. We'd worked from 8:30 am to 4:00 pm and got paid $50.00 cash each.

"Where's the rest?" Tucker confronted Junior. *You earned less than fifty bucks.*

"It woulda been more if I didn't have to give you guys money this morning!" Junior started towards the van and we followed. Tucker tried to open the passenger side door as Junior unlocked the drivers.

"Whoa what are you doing?"

"Getting in."

"*I'm* not giving you a ride back. The Drop In said I only needed to take you one way."

"How are we supposed to get back!?"

"You have money!" Junior said as he got into the van and drove off.

"What a fucking asshole! I'm drinking tonight *for sure* now," Tucker confirmed Dorian's earlier question. Now that work was done I noticed he seemed a lot more functional.

"There's a bus stop this way," Dorian said as he followed the direction he was pointing.

We followed him for nine or ten blocks before finding a gas station to buy bus tickets and ask for directions. As we waited at the bus stop Tucker was writing on everything with a marker.

"Tuck eighty-seven. Your last name and year of birth?" I investigated.

"Yeah that's my tag." It was just written plainly in small letters. "Don't want it to be anything impressive, I'm not an artist. I just want one little signature to let people know I was here, *everywhere*." Now that the sign was tagged he decided to hit the bench. "Tuck eighty-seven." He said in confidence.

"You got em' all over the place?"

"All over Calgary, I got em' all over in Edmonton too, and some in my cell in remand."

"You did time?"

"Yeah."

"For what?"

"Theft mostly. When I did time I got caught stealing a bottle from the liquor store and the guy locked the door on me so I cracked the most expensive bottle I could find and just started chuggin'." Tucker let out a laugh of no remorse.

"That was the only time I got caught, but they were looking for me for other stuff. I usually got away with it. One time I grabbed a bottle from the shelf and held it up to the guy and said 'Thanks.' And then ran out!" He laughed again.

When the bus finally came and we sat down, I regretted sitting with them because Tucker started speaking freely about how he was giving some homeless girl anal behind a dumpster, and no one on the bus was impressed.

Why behind a dumpster?" I interrupted. "That's dirty."

"Where else was I gonna go?"

"Fair enough."

Tucker continued, "We were just walking and she said we should do it! I wasn't gonna say no, but I didn't have any condoms so-"

Dorian pointed out a young woman at the front of the bus that I doubted they knew, but she came over and did some prayers for Dorian and Tucker and asked how they've been. When she got off, Dorian told me she was a church girl that sometimes came and prayed for people during the Sunday barbecue.

"I hate people like that. They go around trying to help 'cure people from their addictions' when *they're* addicted to *God*! They're just as bad as we are, but they're worse 'cause they're so high on themselves that they can't see it, so they go around judging people."

***

Got an early night that night. If I really was done with the condition then I had to be careful with my money. $50.00 wasn't much but it was a start, and I still had over half a pack of smokes. Today I'd help Donald move and if he insisted on paying me I'd probably have around a hundred dollars by the end of the day. I got down to laundry early and wasn't surprised to be greeted by Donald, Ester and Wade, but to my surprise, David beat me down there as well. It was a pretty quiet morning in laundry and I realized it could have been very sentimental for the laundry folk to lose Donald.

David made a little small talk as usual and usually directed it towards Wade, who seemed to be the only one who felt like talking for a change. We ate lunch on Fifth and that was where Donald said his goodbyes to everyone.

"You're not actually *leaving* until *tomorrow*, I should certainly *hope* you *do* come by and see us before you depart." Ester said to him as they hugged.

"I probably *will*," Donald replied with a smile before looking to Wade. "Wade." He said in a strong tone, giving him a stern nod.

Wade smiled and held a hand in the air. "See ya Donald."

"It was nice to meet ya Donald." David included himself, standing to shake his hand.

"Yeah! Likewise," Donald grunted before turning to the elevator.

Al followed to let us down, they had a brief goodbye and Donald decided we should stay so he could say bye to Homer too. Two hours and a goodbye later we were on our way to his storage unit.

"You're really going to miss it there eh?"

"Not the DI. Some of the people though, yes."

"How long were you there?"

"Too long." *Everyone's favorite answer.*

"How long's too long for *you*?"

"About a year. Same time as Ester, since the flood." Referring to a disastrous flood that hit Calgary in 2013, minor compared to ones from other countries that don't even make the news, but devastating none the less.

"That's terrible. You had your own place before that?"

"A room, yes. *Ester* had her own place though."

"I'm sorry to hear."

"It's not *your* fault, you're not in charge of this God forsaken world." After he killed the conversation I realized he probably didn't want to think about that, so I waited for him to take the reigns.

"You like ice cream?"

"Who doesn't?"

"I'll take you to my favorite ice cream place on the way, it's the best in the world. They have *coconut* ice cream." We began walking up some steps into a different area of the city.

"Old Mon Don!!" A construction worker called down to him as he climbed down a ladder.

Donald turned to me. "Used to work here."

The man got down and walked over, they shook hands and the man patted Donald on the shoulder.

"How ya doin' kid?" Donald asked the six and a half foot tall man.

"Good man, good, how've you been? Staying out of trouble?"

Donald shrugged. "No." They both laughed. "I'm leaving tomorrow!"

"Where to?"

"Work!"

"Aw you're gonna kill yourself Don! I'm tellin' ya!"

"I still got a few years left in these old bones."

The guy looked over at me. "Do you think he should be working at his age?" They both stared at me, I was put on the spot. All I could do was grin.

"*He's* thinking about ice cream! We're going for ice cream."

"Well I don't want to keep you! Good luck Don, really." They shook hands and the man went back up the ladder.

"I was working there when he started." He said with half a smile. Walking not a block away to the ice cream shop, I wondered if he chose to go to this way with the intention of seeing friends from his old job.

We got our ice cream and ate while we walked and he was right, it was damn good ice cream. "You like it?"

"It's delicious."

"When I was a kid, much younger than you even, there was an ice cream place my father always took me to. *They* had coconut ice cream." Perspiration in his eyes.

"Is that why you like it there so much?"

"Obviously," he mumbled.

We finally made it to the storage place. When we got in we threw our empty ice cream cups in the garbage and Donald made friendly conversation with the guy at the front before we were buzzed into the room with all the storage units. In his unit there were a few boxes and bags, more than I expected to be honest. We started by separating all his clothes from his tools; he had a lot of tools.

After we packed all the tools into tool boxes and a duffle bag, we boxed up all his clothes and other odds and ends. Donald tightened his tool belt around his skinny waist, it was too big for him but he took it off and packed it into the duffle bag anyway.

"You like this?" He asked, holding up a brand new normal sized black and red back pack. "I don't need it. Zipper's broken anyway."

"If you don't want it I could take it off your hands."

He tossed it over to me and I packed it into mine. Once we finished packing I took all the boxes to the loading gate while he called a taxi. We smoked while we waited. When the cab got there the driver helped me pack everything into the trunk and I sat in the back seat with the duffle bag full of tools. After a speedy and probably illegal drive through the busy streets of Calgary, the three of us took everything into the Greyhound station for delivery and it cost him $187.00 to send it all.

We got back into the same cab and got dropped off at a gas station and that cost him another $110.00 but I'm pretty sure Donald gave him a ten dollar tip too. Inside the gas station Donald bought a carton of cigarettes, a phone card and a few lottery tickets.

"Let me take you to dinner," Donald invited.

"Are you sure? Everything is costing you a lot of money."

He smiled. "Don't worry about it."

Across the street was a very nice restaurant and when we sat down at the bar a pretty young bartender turned around to give us menus and take Donald's order of a very expensive appetizer.

"You been staying out of trouble?" the bartender asked.

"No," he shrugged. They both laughed and she turned to take another order.

"She's a sweet girl. She's had to cut me off a few times."

"You come here a lot?"

"Ester and I and-" He waved his hand in the air. "The rest of them used to come here once in a while." Pointing at the menu in front of me he said "Order anything you want. Let me buy you a beer," knowing I was a recovering alcoholic.

"Don't drink. I don't mind if you do though."

"Come on, I'm leaving tomorrow! Have a beer with me."

"No thanks."

The bartender came back and Donald ordered an aged bottle of wine and I ordered some water. I ended up ordering the burger Donald got once he recommended it to me. While we ate the delicious appetizer he finished the first bottle and drunkenly told me of his days as a university teacher. When he got into his days in the Navy he was asked to quiet down because he started saying some racist stuff.

He got started on his second bottle of wine before our meals came, though this one was less expensive.

I ate while he drank and worked on his fries a little.

"I really appreciate you coming here with me and helping me out today."

"No problem, it was a good day."

"No, no, no, but I mean you could have been out working or hanging out with *younger* people or been doing more exciting things but you came with me and helped me out today and I really appreciate it." It didn't look like he could see me and his face was bright red. Could have been anyone sitting with him.

"It's really no problem Donald."

When I was finished eating Donald got his burger packed up so he could take it up to a friend on the fifth floor. Before we got up to leave he held out $60.00 to me.

"I can't take that."

"You have to take it, you earned it."

"No way, let's just say I did you a favor."

He flipped open the breast pocket of my leather jacket and slid the money in with the note I got from Kelsey.

"I'll be insulted if you give it back."

We left the restaurant and got on the train back to the DI and I told him I was going to get off a few stops early.

"You have to come back with me!" He slurred. "They'll know I'm drunk if you're not with me."

"There's some stuff I have to do but if you really think it'll make a difference…"

I'd planned to print off one of my short stories for Lee, who again last night had reminded me I was supposed to let him read one of my stories. '*I thought you were a writer*' is how he challenged me and I was now determined to prove myself to him.

"It's fine. If they don't let me up to Fifth I'll just get a motel somewhere."

"Are you sure?"

"Positive." I shook his hand then got off the train and walked straight to the liquor store, buying a mickey and a bottle of pop before finding a stall on the third floor of the TD mall on 3rd street.

Sadness overwhelmed me as I reflected on the day's events and Donald's uncertain future. Donald was a classy man who enjoyed the *finer* things in life; he always had the money for it, that's what he was used to. Now these expensive meals and rich liquor served as a reminder of his better days. It all provided temporary comfort, but now he was out of money and whatever he was able to earn was spent carelessly on relief. But who was I to judge? I just found it interesting.

It wasn't until drinking on a public toilet with my pants around my ankles that I realized all the money Donald had just spent probably came from the same batch of Welfare Wednesday cheques that Brad was going to use to pay Dave the Dealer. I pondered how Donald must feel leaving his friends at the DI, especially Ester who he quite obviously admired. My mickey was finished by the first round of mops and I staggered out of the mall and to the library while chain smoking cigarettes. Upon finding out the library was closed I made my way back to the DI.

"You're too drunk to go to the Warehouse Michael." One of the Dice in the doorway affirmed.

"I'm not too drunk to go to the Warehouse, I haven't even been drinking." I replied while the ground tilted in all directions.

"Okay. Well we might be able to get you onto Second but there's a wait list. You might have to sleep in the lobby tonight."

"Fuck eh?" Walking straight into the lobby I let out an obnoxious laugh.

"Michael!" Patrick called over and shook my hand. "Were you working late too?"

"Yeah."

"Yeh you smell like you've been working."

"A friend paid me to help him move some stuff."

"My boss made me work a twelve hour shift today! I didn't even have a lunch or anything and now I'm hoping to get onto second floor. Can you believe that? *Hoping* to get onto Second? Ugh."

Ray walked over to me with a smile. "Michael uh, you stuck down on First tonight?"

"I'm going to the Warehouse." I slurred back.

"Oh, uh, cause uh, we have an extra bed in Intox. Came out here to see if anyone wanted to take it. *You're* chill. Intox is better than Second, in my opinion at least."

I patted Patrick on the back. "Patrick needs a bed!" And Patrick followed Ray to Intox with a look of concern draped across his face.

Gave it about twenty minutes before trying to act sober while asking another Dice about my bed at 2907, but unfortunately for me I was still just as intoxicated. I went outside to smoke and saw a very tall middle aged man who reminded me of a tower. Hunched over I think he was a full foot taller than me. He was wearing a blue and yellow jacket, standing by himself looking around for someone; when I lit a smoke he approached.

"Can I use your lighter?" I handed it to him and he lit a half smoke and put my lighter in his pocket then held his smoke out in front of me. "Oh man I've been saving this in my pocket all day. I hate picking up butts but too many people do temp labor, I never get any work. Do you do temp labor?"

"Lighter."

"Sorry." He handed it back.

"Yeah temp labor blows. I'd like it more if you got paid cash per day, but not the way the DI does it."

"The place I go to pays cash per day."

"How much for an eight hour shift?"

"Eighty, a hundred. Depends on if you get an advance and if it's skilled labor or not."

"That's not bad."

"I can show you if you want. Are you staying on Second?" The burning coal of his half-butt hit the filter and when he noticed he flicked it away.

Hopefully. Fuck man, I can just give you a smoke, why the fuck not, you're chill." With a touch of pity I whipped a smoke out for him.

"Thanks man. I'm Steve." We shook hands.

"Can I call you Steve Tower?"

"Okay, why?"

"Because you're massive and that's an epic name."

"Are you drunk?"

"Kind of."

"Do you have any money?" *Yes.*

"No."

"Oh, cause I was gonna say if I'm taking you to the temp agency we should say fuck the DI and drink somewhere. I'll pay you back."

"No money sorry man."

"Alright. Well if we both get on Second I'll take you to the place anyway."

Both of us signed up for second floor and instead of letting people up according to the list, the Dice just started letting people up. *First come, first served, I guess.* When we got up on Second we tracked down a couple of empty floor mats, and I spent the night giggling beside Steve Tower while trading some of the horror stories of the DI.

He pointed out some old guy trying to start a fight with Twitch for walking around asking for smokes but because of Twitch's condition it settled down pretty quick. We used our backpacks as pillows and when we were woken up at 4:30am, we still had all our things. After grabbing some sandwiches we were on our way to the Steve Tower temp agency, crusty eyed and groggy.

"Morning Geo."

"Stan right?"

"Steve. This is-" Unsure, he turned to me and I introduced myself to both of them.

Geo told me since it was my first day he'd make sure I got sent out, and Steve Tower said he better get sent out for bringing me. We got sent out on the same job with about ten other people. Our objective was to toss big steel bars from warehouse shelves that were brought to us endlessly by an army of forklifts and throw them into a giant dumpster. Steve Tower and I worked together like a well-oiled machine. We were a two man team, a regular Mario and Luigi, some might say. When the shift was done, our boss for the day signed off that we were skilled labor even though we weren't so we'd get paid more and asked us to come back next week, it was a Friday.

We cashed our cheques at a booth right inside the temp agency and Steve Tower was right, I had eighty-five bucks. Steve Tower didn't need to know how much I really had so I put the money in my decoy wallet. Thinking about what Trent said about being able to keep an eye on me through the DI's system, I wasn't sure if I wanted to go back tonight and face Kelsey about being too drunk to go to the Warehouse the night previous.

"You wanna drink?"

"Naw man I don't drink."

"You were drunk last night!" *Dammit.*

"Yeah I guess I was." *Where's an excuse?* "I need to go home anyways, there's someone I gotta talk to."

Steve Tower laughed hysterically. "Did you just call the DI *home*?"

"Uhhh…" *Holy shit.*

"I'm gonna start calling the DI 'Mike's place'."

Steve Tower and I went to drink some beer inside an open garage in a sketchy ally while he told me an inspiring life story. Out of respect to Steve and the goals he's pursuing, I can't share any of it with you; but I *will* tell you he's the only person I will ever respectfully call The Muffin Man.

Buying another case of beer each, we stashed them in our pockets and backpacks then continued walking aimlessly.

"Went up to two hundred bucks playing blackjack last night and lost all of it!."

"You any good at poker?"

"Just blackjack."

"Is there a casino around here?"

"Kind of close."

"We should go, you play blackjack and I'll play poker."

"Can't gamble tonight man I need to save my money, and it has to last me all weekend."

"If you're feelin' lucky I can spot you forty bucks, but you gotta pay me back as soon as you win."

"I'm down."

Inside the casino we turned our bags into the check-in desk then made our way to the washrooms. We each took a stall and cracked a beer.

"We're not going to get caught?"

"No, I do this all the time."

"I do too, but never in a bathroom *this* nice."

Someone came in and we drank our beer in silence. Right after the man stepped out of the bathroom Steve Tower cracked another beer and we both laughed.

"You're already on your second one?"

"Yeah man."

"I'm only finished half of my first."

"Slam it!" I did and then cracked another one.

"How much you got left?"

"Like half."

"Alright when you're done wait a minute and we'll shotgun our thirds," Steve Tower laughed.

"Alright."

We finished our second beers then grabbed our third and punctured holes in our cans, Steve's sprayed all over the place.

Counting down together we slammed our beers before making our way to the sink where Steve washed the beer off his face and jacket. When I handed him $40 he asked "You playing blackjack?"

"Never win at blackjack, poker's my game."

"Well how will we find each other after?"

"If I win or lose I'll come find you at the blackjack table, if you win or lose you find me in the poker room." We started walking out of the washroom.

"Alright man. Don't ditch me okay? People always ditch me." He looked genuinely worried.

"I'm not gonna ditch you man, you're my brotha."

Immediately after we separated a security guard intercepted me, requesting my ID.

"You're too drunk Michael."

"To play poker? Isn't that a *good* thing for you guys?"

"It's not a good thing for *you*, I'm not going to let you play."

"Fuck off, are you serious?" He nodded. "Fuck you man that's bullshit. Let me tell my friend."

"No, no, you need to go *now*." He grabbed my arm and started taking me in another direction.

"I don't want to ditch my friend man, let me go tell him, he's at the blackjack tables."

"You'll see your friend again."

"Let me grab my backpack at least." I showed him my item ticket and we got my backpack from checkout.

The security guard followed me outside and I propped my backpack up against the wall and sat down on the steps for a cigarette. The security guard stood beside me while I smoked. "Are you seriously just going to stand here while I smoke?"

"Yes."

"Why?"

"I have to make sure you leave the premises, but I'll let you have your smoke."

"What's the big deal if I want to drink and play poker?"

"You'll lose your money."

"So? What's the minimum buy-in here?"

"Forty dollars sir."

"So what if I lose forty dollars? What's it to you?"

"Forty dollars is a lot of money."

"No it's not."

"For some people it is. Have you seen some of the homeless people in Calgary? For some people forty dollars is too *much*." Fighting to swing my backpack over my shoulders, I stood up and began backing down the steps.

"*I'm* homeless man." He took on a look of concern.

"Really?"

"Don't you see my fucking backpack?" Tears stung my eyes as I accepted the sad reality of my situation.

"Let me see your ID again, maybe I can let you back in."

"No it's alright, I'll go somewhere else." I turned my back on him and walked in the same direction for an hour before I sobered up enough to ask for directions to the other casino.

Around midnight I finally found the place. Much bigger, much nicer and much more expensive. Buy-in for the poker room was $100 and after the beer I bought and the money I gave to Steve Tower I was left with less than twenty dollars, five of which I used to buy a beer during the poker game.

The room was spinning and I don't remember how the game went. I was probably up, I was probably down; you know how gambling is. I do remember thinking the guy beside me looked remarkably like an older version of myself and during the game I daydreamed about what it would be like to meet yourself at a poker table. *That'd make a good story. Would you be fooled by your own mask, or would you see right through it? I supposed it would be different for everyone, but underneath the mask are we really all the same?* I'd met a lot of masks, inside and out of the DI. *Are all of society's adversities just consequences of our frivolous masks?*

It wasn't my choice to get up and leave the table, I was out of money. I lost; multiple times.

Walking out of the casino, squinting at the Sun as the cold cut any fiber of my skin that it touched, I counted out twelve dollars. *I hope they're open Saturdays* I thought as I directed myself towards the Steve Tower temp agency. *Now I know how Tucker must have felt.*

8

ANGELS & ANGEL DUST

Besides Sunday, I had work for the last week and a half. Though Steve Tower was signed on to work with me the following week, he never showed. I hadn't seen him at all actually. During the entire week I imagined what may have happened to him. *Maybe he got arrested. Maybe he did extraordinarily well at blackjack and is now filthy stinkin' rich.*

Today I was one of the guys who was too drunk or hung over to get sent out. The look in Geo's eyes when he told me to sit down told me I shouldn't even have come in at all, I just walked right out the door. No money, but at least I had smokes. Guess you could have considered it a full-blown relapse; I didn't. Still told everyone I didn't drink, meanwhile getting wasted in bathroom stalls and movie theatres. Even openly on the computers at the library with some hard liquor mixed into a big gulp if it was early enough.

If I'd learned one thing from Donald it was to not be afraid to treat myself. It was good shelter for your mental health while living in such a stressful uncontrolled environment; an escape. How did I spend all my money? Beats me, I blackout almost every time I drink.

It's a miracle I'm not dead, I thought with a smile on my way to the library.

I sat in a nearby Tim Horton's with an empty cup of the same brand that I found on the ground outside to avoid harassment of my loitering; it was a trick that I was both proud and ashamed that I taught myself. Once the library was open I went up to the third floor and went straight onto YouTube. Lately I'd been watching videos where pranksters team up with the homeless to conduct social experiments to see how they were treated in public settings. I'd dug that rabbit hole empty and sat wondering what to watch next and somehow I remembered the name of the documentary Patrick had recommended to me, Streets of Plenty.

It was about an hour long and exactly what I anticipated from Patrick's explanation, only I felt it was fairly pretentious. It featured a guy who faced the streets alongside his brother for twenty-five days, a majority spent in shelter. Still, in the heat of the documentary he did cover *most* of the bases, it was both informative and entertaining, and it had a very human ending with a strong message. I walked out of the library, unsatisfied with the film I'd just watched, - the man beat me to it and it was better than what I had hoped to achieve. Though I'd past his month mark, I felt I had learned very little; he finished filming in less time. He and his brother clearly did a fair bit of planning and research before setting out on their journey whereas I pissed directly into the wind in hopes of spelling my name. I suppose I was envious of the fact that he had a place to go when the process was done whereas I was actually sinking into the condition. I hated him, but what was I mad about? I'd already given up.

If one thing was for sure, I needed money. I was on my way to see Mac, the accountant Malcolm introduced me to. It'd been about a month, surely the revenue agency had received enough of my T4's to get enough cash back to get a bottle of liquor and another pack of smokes.

Basic math told me I was expecting nine T4's, and all nine were accounted for. For at least two hours I sat while the slow well-dressed old man forced his fingers to crunch numbers on his keyboard while staring blindly into the screen - but this still seemed easier to him than breathing. *Old man Willy should've taken up accounting.*

"Fourteen hundred seventy six fifty eight." My eyes probably bulged out of my head. "But you owe the government money. Three hundred sixty two seventy six." *Right down to the penny eh?*

"Eleven-hundred thirteen dollars and eighty two cents is what I can give you. Cheque or direct deposit?" He cut me a cheque and sent me to the bank he does his business with to get it cashed. The entire way there I weighed out what to do with the money. *Go back to Red Deer? Get a place in Calgary? Save it and get a job?* A new laptop is what I elected; I wasn't done yet, I just felt naked without my voice.

The only pawn shop I knew of was closed by the time I got there. *That will give me some time to rethink my decision* I thought. Down the street a block or two I came upon one of my favorite restaurants from my past life. Dropping my backpack beside a stool at the bar, I sat down to make some more mistakes. Highballs were on sale and I took a double whiskey and coke while I browsed the menu. *I'll have one nice meal and play it safe from here on out.*

By the time I was finished eating I had also finished seven highballs and was feeling mighty fine. Paid my tab and left the woman a sixty dollar tip before stumbling out of the restaurant. I'd forgotten how cold it was outside and my jackets were open and draped clumsily around my shoulders.

I dropped my backpack and lit up a smoke while I buttoned my zippers and zipped up my buttons.

When I was finished my cigarette I was feeling pretty thirsty again and fancied a drink.

Back in the restaurant I sat in the same spot right up at the bar. The bartender was friendlier this time around and remembered my order of double whiskey and coke as she put one in front of me before I'd taken my jackets off again. She smiled at me. "So, what do you do for work?"

"Oh, ya know." I mumbled as I took a swig. "I'm a writer."

"Are you published?"

"Not yet." I took another drink and looked down at the cup half full. "But I will be." *Then how do you make your money?* Is what she probably wanted to ask me.

Drunkenly I mumbled about different projects I'd worked on and who knows what else while I drank forty more dollars-worth of highballs until I decided it was time to leave, but not before I gave her another forty dollar tip. After living in the condition for a month, spending money senselessly never made me feel so visible. Couldn't even remember the last time I tipped a server.

***

In the empty theatre of I don't know what movie, I was woken up by a scared teenager who worked there while his friends, who also worked there, stood back and watched as he approached the unconscious Hobo laying on the ground in the front row.

"Hey man!" Shouted an unfamiliar voice. "Are you okay?"

I pushed myself off of the ground out of what was *probably* my popcorn and tried to focus on the kid that was standing all over the place. Taking an apprehensive hop back, he threw a glance at his snickering friends.

"Shit sorry man."

"Show's over!"

"What time is it?"

"It's almost six!"

"Thanks." Before I threw my backpack on I attempted to organize myself, make sure I had everything.

"You need to get out of here!"

"I'm going." Me heading towards the exit made him anxious because it was also in his direction.

"I'm calling security!"

"I'm fucking leaving kid, what's your problem!?" I stopped and looked at the scared kids working minimum wage at a job that *should* be fun, a job I had once. They followed me all the way out of the theatre.

Walking towards the library with a pounding head ache I attempted to reassemble my mind. Only had a couple hours until the library closed and about an hour after that to get back to the DI for the last 2907 shuttle. Reassembly wasn't the only reason I wanted to go to the library, I also had a hunch that I'd be able to find some weed there. I felt like death and cigarettes obviously weren't the answer; and I was afraid if I drank again I'd hork my liver up. There was still half a mickey of whiskey in my pocket I didn't remember buying anyways.

Bowser and most of his crew were posted up at the chairs in the sitting area, there were at least ten of them. Nearby I watched and waited until one of them broke from the group. A girl, one of the only young ones living at the DI walked over to the elevator and I walked up beside her, tapping her on the shoulder. "Do you know where I can find some shit?" I asked as she took her earphones out. She looked me up and down and shook her head.

"No, sorry."

"No I don't think you understand. I need some shit." We looked down at my open wallet full of fifty dollar bills

"Oh. One second okay?" She walked back over to Bowser and they spoke for a minute or two while I realized I may as well of just flashed ten sketchy people a thousand dollars or however much I had left. When she waved me over I sloppily lugged my backpack over. Bowser and I gave each other a nod of the chin and I eyed all his piercings and tattoos.

"What do you want?" He asked me.

"Just weed man."

"How much?"

"A twenty bag?" All the eyes laughed while Bowser looked around, he looked at the girl then back at me.

"You gotta get more than that. *I* don't got it. I gotta call someone for you."

"Is a quarter cool?"

"I guess." Bowser called up his dealer and said it'd be seventy dollars for a quarter but it was really prime shit.

I told him I needed to get change and four of them plus Bowser came with me to the Tim Horton's across the street. Leaving my backpack with them outside while they smoked was my inebriated strategy to see if I could trust them. There really wasn't much in there and it was all worth less than what was in my wallet. I'd planned to go in alone and count my money but one of them, a seventeen year old kid that told me he didn't live at the DI, came in with me saying he was planning to buy a coffee.

On the way to the front of the line I slid a fifty dollar bill into my decoy wallet and then pulled out another one to make change at the till. We met Bowser outside and went to the courtyard of the abandoned government building Tukahoot showed me. Only Bowser, the kid and another guy came, the rest stayed behind watching with the eyes of vultures. On the plus side, my backpack was safe and sound.

We waited for about twenty minutes for the dealer, I'd smoked three cigarettes and had to give another three out each time I lit one. Finally he showed up, from what I remember he was like a short Denzel Washington. We shook hands and Denzel pulled out a handful of small bags of weed and I held out seventy bucks.

"I said eighty right?"

"No you said seventy."

"Did I?" He looked over at Bowser.

"Yeah you said seventy," Bowser replied, looking in another direction.

"Well I need eighty, this is primo shit dude, I promise."

Choked, I pulled out another ten and held eighty dollars out to him in exchange for seven little bags of weed.

"Thanks." With the intention of walking away I gave a nod to Bowser.

"Hold up hold up, don't you want to blaze?" Denzel asked.

"Sure." My compulsive sense of indisposition got me again even though I was very uncertain of my newfound friends.

"You roll this one I'll roll the next one, sound good?"

"I guess. I don't have any papers."

"I got papers!" The kid called out, then took one of my small bags to roll a joint. He rolled it pretty quickly and handed it to Denzel who sparked it as soon as it touched his fingers.

"Don't you want my phone number in case you need weed again?" Denzel asked me.

"You got an email?" They all laughed.

"What? You're gonna email me for weed?"

"I don't have a phone."

"You got a pen?" Didn't have one.

"No. If it's simple just say it and I'll remember, I got a photographic memory."

"Alright it's-" And I have no idea what it was.

"Got it."

"Say it back to me."

"I can't remember, say it one more time."

"It's-" Still didn't catch it. "What is it?"

"Uhh.."

"That's not a photographic memory."

"Sorry man I'm a little off right now."

"Are you drunk?"

"No I don't drink." I slurred. "I used to drink. I used to be an *alcoholic*, but not anymore! Now I'm sober." The only one that didn't laugh was the kid, he seemed to think it was sad.

"Yeah you look sober buddy. You a cop?"

"No."

"You seem like a cop."

"How do I seem like a cop? I'm clearly wasted." I was. I was a God damn mess. Directing my attention to the kid who seemed like my only ally at the moment I asked "Do I seem like a cop?" All he could do was shrug.

"Yeah you do." Denzel cut back in. "Show me your wallet and prove you're not a cop."

"If I was a cop I'd have to tell you I was a cop when you asked. Isn't that the code?"

"I don't know. I'm not the one with a photographic memory." He grinned. "Let's see your wallet." Bowser walked up beside him and looked at me.

"Don't show him your wallet." He looked over at Denzel. "He doesn't have to show you his wallet."

"If he's got nothin' to hide then he can show me his wallet!" I pulled my decoy wallet out and handed it over to him.

"Don't even have ID man." After he poked through the card holders he passed the wallet back with twenty dollars still in it.

"Don't worry I'm not gonna take your twenty dollars man." He hit the joint and passed it over to me.

Something persisted to bother him as the joint went around the circle until it got back to him. "I heard you had a wallet full of fifty dollar bills."

Bowser wasn't looking anywhere in my direction when I looked over at him.

"No man, I had a *couple* fifties but you have most of em' now."

"Empty your pockets." The kid shook hands with Bowser and took off saying he had to get back home. Bowser and his other friend talked nearby, not paying much attention to me after seeing my empty wallet. *The only one that saw it was the girl, she's not here.* I touched the pocket containing my wallet and weed.

"This is the pocket with all the weed." Pulling out a handful of bags seemed to satisfy him as far as *that* pocket went. None of my pocket contents seemed valuable to him, then I patted my backpack.

"There's nothing in here, just work stuff and a blanket."

"I know." He tapped the breast pocket on my leather jacket. "What's in there?" Foolishly I pulled everything out and held my hand open for him to see. His eyes lit up when he saw the memory card and I held up the note I'd got from Kelsey to try and throw him off.

"This just a note I got from a girl."

"No, no, let me see." Gently he opened my hand and looked at the memory card. "You don't need that do you?"

"Yeah."

"Come on man we're being really nice to you. Here, I'll give you something for it." Denzel reached in his pocket and pulled out what I thought could have been a box for a bracelet or necklace.

"I'm good man I don't need anything." *All my writing's on there…*

"It's MDMA, really good shit man. Come on it's a good deal, I just want to get rid of this."

"Alright." I pretended to hand it over and dropped it in the snow, then stepped on it and slid my foot around trying to make it seem like an accident but it all probably looked pretty stupid. "Shit sorry man." When I bent over to pick it up for him, the mickey fell out of my inside pocket. He picked it up and looked at it while I grabbed the memory card from the snow.

"You don't need *this* do you?"

"No, you can have that." The mickey went in his pocket and I held the memory card out to him.

"It probably doesn't work anymore." My memory card lost its importance to him.

"Give me the twenty dollars and you can have this." He held the box out to me again.

"I really don't want that man."

Twenty dollars appeared in his hand pretty quick once he started pacing and once we made the exchange he said he had to head out. Bowser re-lit the joint we were smoking after Denzel left and passed it to me.

"You want to walk back with us?" He asked pointing a thumb at his friend.

I walked with them for half a block before heading off in a separate direction, specifically to the liquor store. *It could have been worse.*

***

In a familiar bathroom stall on the third floor of the TD mall on 3rd street I started drinking, and came to hours later in a nice unfamiliar bathroom rolling a joint. After the joint was rolled I looked at myself in the mirror and tried to gain recognition before walking out into God knows where.

It was the restaurant Donald had taken me to and I barely remembered showing up. There was a spot at the corner of the bar that I assumed I was sitting at where there were two appetizers and a meal all partially rummaged through, and a half empty double whiskey and coke beside it all. *I'm so stupid* I thought. As soon as I sat down I miserably looked at the bartender in hopes that she would tell me I was in some person's seat, but she just smiled. "Can I get you anything else hun?"

"I'm going to go out for a smoke, I should probably pay for all this."

"It's on your tab. You've already went out three times, I trust you." She started filling a pitcher of ice with water. "I have your backpack anyway, it's not like you're going anywhere." *I didn't even notice I didn't have it.*

"Alright." She put the pitcher and a cup in front of me.

"Maybe I should cut you off."

I poured half a glass and drank it in one fluent motion, maybe.

"I'm fine, I just need a smoke."

Stumbling off out the door and around the corner I went to smoke the scraggly joint I rolled in a state I considered acceptable at the moment. It hardly lit and I was too drunk to smoke it anyway so I lit a cigarette instead and walked down the sidewalk a bit in hopes of seeing Orion's Belt in the sky. I don't know if I saw it or not to tell you the truth, but I do remember feeling free and without a sense of time or responsibility. I was also very cold.

When I got back in I sat down and made an attempt to eat the burger I'd ordered hopefully not too long ago but I felt absolutely disgusting. Looking down the bar I noticed a Pleb my age that hadn't been there as far as I could recall, he was brooding over a beer. "Here, you want these?" I asked, holding out a plate of dry ribs. With hungry eyes he ogled them, then looked at me.

"I'm good." He took a drink of his beer and looked away.

"You sure? I've only eaten two of them. I don't know why I ordered them, I got all this other shit."

With a shrug he decided to take a chance. "Sure thanks man."

Right when I finished my double whiskey and coke I ordered another one, and asked to pay my tab. The bartender came back with a tab of one hundred and twenty seven dollars and my drink and I gave her the cash with a small tip. *Do I even want to know how much money I have left?*

"Cheers man." The guy said as I looked over to see him holding his beer in the air with one hand and a dry rib to his mouth with the other.

"Cheers." We each took a drink of our drinks and went to drinking in silence for a few minutes.

"You here by yourself?"

"Yeah."

"Me too man, friends ditched me. Well not really, they went to the club-" Glancing over his shoulder he made sure the bartender couldn't hear him. "I don't have ID."

"Shitty dude." *That's what you're pouting about? There're bigger problems in the world asshole. I guess I'm not any better.*

"What about you?"

"Tried to roll this joint but I'm too wasted to roll a joint." He laughed when I held up the quarter smoked scraggly.

"Yeah that's pretty bad." From his coat pocket he pulled out a bag of marijuana that was so big it was hard to imagine it would even fit in a backpack. "I got a bunch of weed man." Smoothly he tucked it away and looked around.

"I got some weed too."

"That's alright, I'll roll one up once I'm done my beer."

"Alright." He moved to the stool beside me and told me all he had was enough for one beer and that he was a dealer and he had ton of cocaine back at his place and if I bought him a pitcher or two he'd hook me up fat. Told him I'd think about it and when we finished our drinks I paid for a second beer for him. He went to the washroom to roll a joint and I put my head down, I almost threw up when he shook me awake and I ran to the bathroom and did just that.

***

"Is someone in there?" *I recognize that voice, this room.* "Hello?"

"Yeah! Sorry."

"We're already closed you need to get out of there right now."

"Sorry! Sorry!" Standing up to find I was dizzier than ever, I waddled to the door. The look on the bartenders face when I opened the door said I didn't look so good. I looked over at the bald fancy suit manager and got a piercing glare of pure repulsion in return.

"We have your bag upstairs, I thought you forgot it." The bartender said.

"I'll get it," the manager said before he stormed off.

"I'm sorry."

"No, I'm sorry, I should have cut you off a long time ago."

"No one ever cuts me off, it's fucked up."

"Well maybe you need to learn self-control."

"I went to rehab."

"Well maybe you should go back." *Sound advice.* "You're not really a traveler are you?"

"I told you I was a traveler? I've never left Alberta."

The manager struggled to carry in a backpack that could easily have been the same weight as him and dropped it in front of me, then wiped his hand off on his pant leg like the bag could have been contaminated with something; I suppose it could have been. When I flung the backpack over my shoulder and adjusted it onto my back it felt a hundred times heavier than before.

I staggered out the doors and up a few blocks until I found a hotel. The check-in clerk wanted nothing to do with me. He tried to send me the other way and I insisted I had the money, in fact, I showed him. Then the security guard showed me the way out.

Continuing on, I staggered until I found a row of taxi cabs lined up the street. First taxi, the guy told me to get lost; I told him I was cool but when I opened the door he said he was going to call the police. The woman in the second cab just shook her head and pointed to the next one. Then I leaned into the window of the third cab.

"Hey ma-"

"What the fuck!?" He jumped and it made me jump and we stared at each other. "Jesus Christ!"

"Do you know of a hotel or a motel that will take me in right now?"

"It's three thirty in the morning! You got a credit card?"

"No."

Sighing, he looked out the other window. "God dammit! Get in! Put your backpack in the trunk."

After plunking my backpack in the trunk I hopped into the passenger seat and made myself comfortable.

"Look out the window." The sound of his voice woke me up.

***

I was still in the cab, he must have taken the scenic route; we had to have been outside of the city. The high rises lit up the scenery, and all the lights from the city shooting up into the black sky and white winter mist were quite stunning.

"Do you really want to be on the streets of a city that beautiful?"

"Not really." A tear may have come to my eye, but it's hard to say. Told him I was a writer and on the way to the somewhere motel, this nameless taxi driver became the first person to hear me admit I was homeless as I came to the realization for the second time. *A Hobo. Struggling in the condition.*

We pulled up and the cab fare was around fifty dollars. I pulled out three twenty's and handed them over, then he gave me my change. He took a deep breath while studying me, then handed me back one of the twenty's.

"Thanks a lot man I really appreciate it."

"I hope you do."

We got out and there was an old East Indian woman standing outside the motel office already watching us.

She took one look at me. "No, no, no!" She began waving her arms in the air.

"Come on! Where's he supposed to go!?"

"No! No rooms! No service!"

The driver turned to me. "You got money right?"

I nodded and he looked back at her. "He's got money."

"Check-out's eleven in the morning!"

The driver looked back at me. "You got seven hours with the room, you want it?"

I nodded again and he looked over at the woman. "He's got the money for it. He wants the room, just let him stay."

Glaring at me, then back at him, she nodded with a look of doubt in her eyes.

***

"Check-out in one hour!" A deep voice commanded in combination with what was possibly the loudest knock on a door I've ever heard.

I awoke on the floor of a ratty motel room with a furious itch all over my body and a hangover that made the unrelenting body itch feel as miniscule as the dirt under my fingernails. The aftermath of hurricane me, it'd never been this bad. Everything was everywhere and then some, plus I was missing a sock. Actually missing a sock, I couldn't find it anywhere, but I did find an empty mickey I didn't remember bringing in with me; and my money was scattered all over the place. *As far as I remember I came in and went to sleep.*

The room had two beds and neither had been touched. A rolled joint was sitting on the night stand and I walked to the bathroom to smoke it while scratching the Hell out of myself - not literally, I'm afraid.

I turned the shower on to the hottest temperature and put a towel against the base of the door, *a nice warm steamy hotbox.* Halfway through the joint I turned the water off, collapsing to the floor. I felt *high*, not just from the weed; unless it was laced. It was a high I'd never experienced before. My heart was on fire and pumping ridiculously fast, I laid shivering in cold sweat fighting back the urge to vomit for around ten minutes until I stripped my clothes off and managed to stand myself up.

When I looked in the mirror I was revolted. My pupils covered their iris, the bags under my eyes were vicious and I was whiter than the walls of the motel were supposed to be. Smiling in the mirror to check my teeth, I could see that they had turned a nice shade of yellow in only a short amount of time. I didn't look twenty-one, I looked a generous thirty. I wiped my nose and there was something brown on the top of my hand, then the mirror I could see that I had this brown stuff in both of my nostrils. *What the fuck?* Knowing my pockets were empty I walked out of the bathroom in the stark to find the box I got from Denzel.

Naked, I searched the room high and low until I finally found the box. Inside there was a small bag ripped open that could have contained a fair bit of the brown powder that was spilled inside the box. *That's not MDMA.* I was sick to my stomach. *What the hell is it?* It could have been dirt. *It could be angel dust for all I know.* Whatever it was, I didn't remember taking it and it looked like I took quite a bit; almost all of it. After I threw the box and the mystery substance in the trash I went straight to the shower.

My itch didn't come from bug bites, it looked like a rash but it was hard to tell because I'd been scratching so much. *It could just be from the drugs.* Bearing in mind I didn't have much time left with the room, I tried to clean myself as thoroughly as possible because it had been a while. Coming out of the shower the itch didn't seem so bad, however when I put my clothes back on the itch flared up again. *Maybe it is bugs.* I decided it was probably best to get the room for another night even though I suspected there might be fleas.

Even moving around as little as I did, I felt like I could collapse at any minute. I wasn't in good shape. Somehow I got all my stuff organized and cleaned the room in the little time I had. When it was all over I smoked a cigarette while I built up the courage to count my cash. *Three hundred and eighty,* plus change. *Sweet mother of God. How?* Once I finished my cigarette I went out to the motel office to find the East Indian woman who was working late the night before.

"I know its check-out but I'd like to get the room for another night."

"We have to move you to a single room."

"That's alright."

"It's cheaper."

"How much?"

"One hundred seven."

"How much did I pay for the double?"

"One *twenty* seven. And a one twenty seven deposit."

"Alright." My ears were ringing and the room was shaking.

"You'll get that back when you check-out."

"Okay!" I held all my money out to her and she took it with a look of question.

"I don't need this much sir."

"Take what you need!" At the end of my tunnel vision was a chair I dropped into.

The woman counted out the one hundred and seven dollars and put the change and the rest of my cash on the counter with the new keycard.

"Sir! Your things."

"Yeah, one second okay please?" I said with my head in my hand, leaning on the arm of the chair. She waited patiently and eventually I got up and thanked her and moved all my stuff to my new room. I lay down on the bed (naked if you must know, because the itch was less severe) until the roof stopped spinning.

It was four in the afternoon when I finally got dressed and left in search of a pawn shop. It was dumb luck that I actually found one after walking up the same street for about an hour. Didn't have much for laptops, everything was ridiculously over-priced. Only two of them were affordable with what little money I had left, and one looked like it probably didn't work to begin with.

"Can I help you?" an employee asked. Lucky for him I was easy prey.

"I want that one." I said, pointing at the half decent one for $220.

The guy threw in a free laptop bag, more than likely because the laptop wasn't worth $220, then I left the way I came, without much on my mind besides laying back down. Still tortured by the itch, no part of my body was worse than my feet. The quarter-sized blisters on the bottom of them from waddling in the size fourteens made the situation even worse.

On the way back I got a cheap T-shirt, jeans and socks from the someplace mall on the way back to the somewhere motel. *Guess I'll have to go commando.*

Ten dollars is all I had left and I bought some fast food before leaving the mall. When I got back, I put everything on the desk in the room and laid down in the bed naked again, this time under the blankets. *I hope these sheets are clean.*

It was the middle of the night when I finally woke up. Bulging blisters on my feet stopped me from standing to get out of the bed so I ripped all of them open and painfully oozed them onto the floor.

Gross.

While I showered I regretted not buying a toothbrush and a good brand of toothpaste instead of the cheap clothes, but the regret subsided a little once I put them on and the itch was bearable enough to not scratch at.

I hooked up my new computer and got it online with the motel's Wi-Fi. *Just one YouTube video* I thought. Unfortunately, this laptop was so old it could barely run YouTube videos. *Maybe that's for the best.* I grabbed the memory card and searched for a place on the laptop to plug it in and see if it still worked. Of course there was no memory card slot on my new-old computer. *Idiot! What am I going to do now?*

After a while I repeated my online hunt for my writing while downloading a comedy film. Some was much needed humor - I needed to forget about the horror that was my prevailing addiction and failing mental health. By the time I gathered all my writing the movie was only half way done downloading. Again I tried to start writing the book and wrote nothing. Instead, I ate my cold fast food and read some of my old writing until the ten o'clock check-out guy came by.

The movie was ten minutes from downloading and I took my last hour to have another long shower. *I've failed,* I thought. *I came into this completely unprepared. I'm just a hopeless egotistical homeless uneducated high school graduate.* I'd played my cards left alright, pretty God damn left.

***

I searched the streets for the city train with no luck and eventually stopped at a bus stop where I got the stink eye from people when I got on with my big backpack. Standing was my only option because the bus was so packed and I could tell people thought I was taking up more room than I had to, but I wasn't exactly being inconsiderate.

Today was Saturday and I only had a hundred twenty dollars left and no work for the next two days at the very least. *No choice but to go back to the DI.* It had been two weeks since I saw Kelsey and I avoided coming back during the hours she was working. Now, it was time to face her. I got off the bus at the train station and got on the train to Hobo central.

On the way back home I actually remembered to print one of my short stories off for Lee. It only cost me sixty cents, ten cents a page. *Could have printed it off a million times by now.*

When I got inside the DI I saw a few familiar faces among the Dice at the front door. It felt as though it had been a long time since I'd seen them because I'd shown up drunk most nights lately. Some of them gave me a nod and the guy doing bag checks said I was cool with a smile and waved me through. *I'm one of the good ones?*

Upstairs I saw Kelsey talking to an old man at the end of the invisible gated walkway down the middle. As I walked up to her the old man walked away and she smiled.

"Hey!" I smiled

"Hey! Where've you been?"

"I've been… just really stupid lately. I relapsed." I admitted it.

Tilting her head she still maintained her smile. "That's okay, relapses happen. Don't be too hard on yourself, that won't help."

"You're right."

"I was thinking about you, I thought you left. I thought you went back to - well you're not from here right?"

"No I'm from Red Deer."

The way she nodded told me she knew that already. Of course she knew; she had access to my file. *I don't know why she'd pretend not to know already, unless she didn't think I'd know she knew, but even if I didn't know she knew, why wouldn't she want me to know?* Maybe I was overthinking.

Brad walked in with a smile showing teeth I felt less arrogant about now.

"Red Deer! What's up buddy!?"

He walked up uncomfortably close to Kelsey and she stepped away.

"Brad we're talking," she said to him.

"Alright, but I just need to tell him something really quick." He faced me. "I did morphine the other day for the first time! It was nuts I pushed the whole thing right into my vein and apparently you're not supposed to do that and I started tripping balls." I looked over at Kelsey then back at Brad.

"Can you give us a few minutes man? You're being intrusive."

"Fuck I didn't know we were allowed to date staff, maybe I should go look around for a cutie."

"No. you need to go for a walk."

"Aw. really?"

"Yeah, until dinner. I'm serious."

"I'm gonna go out on the smoke deck," He said and walked off to the smoke deck.

"Sure. Just go." She said to him, smiling at me.

"The dynamic between the three of us is hilarious I think."

"Why?"

"Because we're all the same age." There was a quick silence. "Well, I don't know how old *you* are, but I know he's a year younger than me."

"You're six months older than me." Kelsey shot back quickly, another quick silence. "I hope you don't think it's weird that I know that, I saw it on your file."

"I don't think that's weird." We smiled at each other.

"Did you go to school in Red Deer?"

"Yeah. Well, I was in Sylvan Lake for part of elementary."

Her eyes lit up. "What grades?"

"Kindergarten to grade three."

"I went to elementary school there until grade three too! Do you remember your teachers?" *Small world.*

"Ms. Batting for kindergarten. I can't remember my grade one teacher's name. Mrs. Winter for grade two and Mr. Davidson for grade three."

Her smile widened. "*I* had Mr. Davidson." We looked into each other's eyes for a moment.

"Were we in the same class?"

"I *think* so!" God, I was shaking. Thought it could have been from the heart I could feel beating in my chest.

"That's the craziest thing I've ever heard." We talked about people we both knew from elementary school and a little about how we spent our middle school and high school days until it was time for me to catch the 2907 bus.

"Oh yeah, you're still staying at the Warehouse. I forgot to ask, have you checked the office for any messages?"

"No why?"

"I hope you don't mind but I told my shift leader about you and they said they were going to get you a bed on the fifth floor. That was a while ago now."

"Thank you, I appreciate it, I'll definitely check it out. Have a good rest of your shift."

"Thanks, have a good night. I'm working tomorrow two to ten, you should come see me. If you're here."

"Definitely." Waving and smiling as I backed away, I made my way downstairs to get my ticket for the bus.

After that I got my message from the security station at the front. All it said was 'Janet' with a phone number underneath. I saw Lee waiting outside for the bus and gave him the short story I'd printed off for him. Lee actually looked excited to have it in his hands, he read the first few sentences right there.

"I'm not going to read it now. Too cold. I'm not going to read it at dinner, too messy. I read at night. It's what I do before I go to bed. Read then go to bed. Yes. Maybe that's what I'll do tonight."

"Thanks for reading it."

"*I'll* decide who needs to thank who once I read it. Tonight! Before bed." We got separated in the usual disarray of Hobos getting on the bus and by the time I was lining up for dinner he was already sitting down eating.

"Irish!" Dorian was standing beside me with a big grin on his face.

"Hey man."

"Last time I seen you you'd been drinkin'. But you don't drink."

"The last time I *remember* seeing you was... Working at that burnt down garage."

"I've seen you twice since then."

"Really?" *I need to stop drinking.*

"Maybe, I don't know. I been drinkin'."

Dorian and I ate in silence while we watched the news, featuring a story about a young man that got hit by the city train. Patrick came in on the second 2907 bus by the time we finished eating and I walked up to him and shook his hand.

"Patrick! I thought you'd be gone by now."

"Not yet, boss owes me a thousand bucks!" He pointed to the doors to the smoke pit and we made our way outside.

"For like the three weeks you've been working for him?"

"Well he's given me five hundred alrea'y, but he was supposed to pay me the rest yesterday."

"Brutal."

"I'nt it?" We lit our smokes.

"Yeah man. Fifteen hundred isn't that bad for three weeks though."

"For the long hours he's been pullin' on me? And now he's got me working Saturday's. What about you? You been working?"

"Yeah, actually, but I've been spending my money like an idiot."

"Don't we all?"

"You too?"

"Nah, I still have most of the five hundred to be honest wiv you." He said with a smug grin.

"Right on, are you going to get a place out here?"

"To be honest wiv you Michael, once I get that thousand bucks I'm getting straaaaaaaaaight out of here." A serious tone while his eyes rolled.

"You don't like it in Calgary?"

"Ugh, with all the disgusting things I've seen here and the stories I've heard… Even nice guys like *you* get beat up here. And did you hear about the kid from the DI that got hit by the train?"

"Just saw it on the news, didn't know he was from the DI though."

"Is it on the *news* already? Yeh, I heard people talking about it while I was standing in line for my ticket, apparently it only happened an hour ago. Heard the train driver saw the kid on the tracks and didn't even slow down."

"Well, if you're going that fast it might be better not to."

With a shrug he stared off with eyes that were attached to a brain that was taking his mind to a place where a kid was getting hit by a train; the same place mine was.

"I suppose."

We smoked in silence for a minute before I sparked conversation about Streets of Plenty. The conversation didn't last very long though because I went straight downstairs after our smoke, exhausted from nothing yet again. Under bed 207 in the Bear God's spot was an old man laying straight up, stiff as a board. Didn't even want to give him a nickname. *I hope he's not dead.*

Lying down in the bed, more or less sober for the first time in a while, I was vexed and itchy. It was quiet for once and I acknowledged the new stability of the bunk bed. Very tranquil, but it was an aggravating tranquillity that only exposed the absence of the Bear God. *Why couldn't I have been a painter?*

9

BED BUGS

Arwin tried to wake me up at 5:30 am like I asked, but I was too tired to get out of bed.

Until the first wakeup call, I just laid there itching and scratching.

"GOOD MORNING EVERYONE!! IT'S GOING TO BE MINUS FORTY OUT TODAY SO MAKE SURE YOU WEAR A LOT OF LAYERS AND A WARM PAIR OF BOOTS. I HAVE SCARVES AND GLOVES IN THE OFFICE."

"Yo, is dis a bed bug?" Some guy asked.

Hopping out of my bed, I landed in my size fourteens and followed Arwin to where the voice came from. There was a tall African guy holding his clothes bin up beside him, looking at a small red dot on it. Arwin put his face right up to the red dot.

"Yep! That's a bed bug alright!" He looked over at me. "Get a good look at it before I kill it!"

Didn't put my face quite as near, but sure, there it was. Bigger than I'd expected, I found it hard to believe they could warrant a successful infestation but I didn't doubt it. After all, different species can manage all sorts of bizarre abilities. A ferret can squish its body to slide under a door frame, damn rodents. Up till now I had been considering staying at 2907 for a while longer instead of occupying a bed on the fifth floor but with this newfound development at hand, fuck it.

Upstairs I saw the Dave's, and when I walked up I could tell I was the same sort of annoyance to them as Brad would be to say, Kelsey and I.

"I owe you a smoke," I said to Dave.

Dave III looked over at black-eye Dave and snickered. Never actually met Dave III, but he was pretty tall and had really long hair. If he ever spoke it was so quiet I don't think whichever Dave he said it to even heard because they barely acknowledged his presence.

"Thanks man." Dave said as he took the smoke.

I stood waiting awkwardly for some sort of acceptance but it was apparent they didn't want my company. I went to the office and received my first scarf ever from Arwin then went into the dining room trying to figure out how to wear it. A random Hobo came by and showed me a couple different ways to tie a scarf before all of us got on the bus to the DI.

***

Ralph was limping around on Second like a chicken with his head cut off. He was holding a staff card, so I approached him and asked if they needed a hand in the basement. I followed him to the elevator.

"Boy, am I glad you showed up, I was just up hya looking for someone. Wade said he's not workin' today and Esteh says she's going to an early movie latah! And you know *Al - he* won't be in the basement fah long." We got in and started riding down. "I tell ya, I can't wait until weya done and I can smoke a big old bowl."

"You smoke weed?"

"Of course I smoke weed, ah you kidding me!? Do you know wheh I live?"

The elevator opened and we joined David and Ester to fold bundles. After a half hour or so Al came down with a tall guy wearing an aviator cap, a polo T-shirt too small for him, sweats and sandals. Over time, I became bothered by something he did that no one else seemed to mind, or did a damn good job hiding that they did. The guy would constantly wash his feet in the sink with the dish soap. This was a sink where dirty dishes waiting to be cleaned were sitting. *I'm never drinking another cup of coffee in here again.*

The nickname I bestowed upon him was Footsink, not aloud, of course. Footsink didn't talk, today nobody really did; with the exception of Ralph.

"I'm getting so sick of folding these bundles, a man like me shouldn't have tah do this fah no pay. Ray had the right idea!"

"*That's* not why Ray isn't here," Ester began to correct him. "Gus *accused* him of *drinking* down here and now he's been *suspended.*"

"Oh, that's bologna, he told me he got that all swoted out. I could undastand him not comin' down when Gus is workin', but not comin' down at all and leavin' us to do all the work is uncouth!" *Uncouth?*

"Speaking of not *being* here, I have a *movie* to get to. I hope Wade is still waiting for me!"

Footsink threw his leg over the side of the sink and turned it on, scrubbing his red, already scrubbed feet with some paper towel and dish soap.

"Yowah going to the movie with Wade?"

"I certainly am." Ester got her book and crossword and pen packed into her purse while Footsink washed his other foot. When she left, Ralph followed her to let her out. He limped back after a couple minutes. David just remained chill as always in the corner, pumping his foot to the rock on the radio.

"See what I mean!?" Ralph exclaimed. "Everyone just leaves *me* to do all the work around hya. *I'd* like to go to a movie for a change."

Leaning on the counter beside me, deciding to take Ester's spot and a break from folding, he continued his rant, knowing I was the only one paying attention to him. Footsink finished washing his feet and was now sitting on the counter drying them.

"And if you take a look around, guess who ya don't see!?"

Al rolled a cart of dirty laundry into the room behind Ralph.

"Al!" Ralph continued.

Al glanced over and went on to the washing machines.

"Whenevah I don't work I nevah see him upstahs, but whenevah I'm volunteering *my* time I nevah see him *down hya*!" He turned to the counter to start folding bundles. "Anyone who thinks that's a coincidence is brainless, let *me* tell *you*."

Al opened the washing machine and startled Ralph who peered over to see Al in his hazmat suit.

"Oh, hiya, Al!"

"Hi Ralph," Al replied while continuing what he was doing.

Ralph leaned in to me with a guilty grin. He didn't hya me did he?" *Sure did.*

"You're good."

There was a brief moment of silence and I thought back to a time when Donald was still here and Ralph was on one of his rants. When he walked away Donald pointed at me like he did with the woman he said had FAS and said like a mad man; 'diagnosis!?'

My guess was posttraumatic stress because of the way he fidgeted and the nervous way he spoke in addition to a few other things. Donald said that his guess was that Ralph too had FAS and based on some of the things Donald ended up telling me about FAS, the shoe fit.

"So anyway like I was saying," Ralph continued, "I can't wait to get back to my old job!"

"What's you're old job?" Humoring him was the least I could do, maybe he'd get back to folding.

"I'm a roofa! How do ya think I broke my leg!? Well *hip* actually, *and* femur."

"Did you hurt it roofing?" I asked in confidence.

"A six story fall, yes. Half my hip is a steel plate."

"Jesus."

"Isn't that somethin'?"

"That's somethin'. I wouldn't go back to roofing if I fell six stories. I'm afraid of heights, I probably wouldn't roof in the first place!"

"*I'm* not scared of heights! I'm not scared of anything!" He folded a bundle. "I've been roofin' for thirty five yeah's, if you can believe *that*! I don't have anothah job to go back to."

"Thirty five years eh? That's a long time. How old are you?"

"Sixty five! And wouldn't you know it right before I turned sixty five they changed the age of senior to seventy! I sweah theya tryin' to kill me!"

"What'd you do before roofing?"

"I was in the Vietnam war."

"Really?"

"Those were crazy days, let me tell *you*! You're lucky kiddo, when I was yowah age I was in the jungle shakin' in my boots!"

"My generation's spoiled, I know."

"Don't even get me stahted!"

"Don't even get *me* started. How'd you get into the army?"

"I came ovah to America as a refugee and when the Waw stawted they let me enlist in exchange for my citizenship! That was *one* good thing that came from it."

"Where you from?"

"Czechoslovakia. That was even worse than the Waw! When I was nine or ten yeah's old I'd walk around the streets in my bah feet and pick up bullets and old weapons from the debris left from bombings and I'd sell them so me and my motha and my little brotha could eat."

"That's intense."

"Intense isn't the right woid fah it! Unimaginable!" He folded another bundle. "No one should have to see the things *I've* seen, believe you *me*!"

"Did you see action when you were in the war?"

"Mmmmmmm*eeehhhhh,* I saw *some* things, not necessarily *action* because I was a medic, but I saw a lot of severe injuries and people die, but it was nothin' I'd nevah befoah seen. The only times I'd evah see action was when we'd have to leave the helicoptah to get the guys."

Shuddering in a retrospective moment, he went on. "Runnin' in those fields, every time you'd heah a little whistle you'd know that a bullet was inches away from takin' yowah life!"

Footsink was washing his feet again. *I could have been right about the posttraumatic stress,* I thought.

We went upstairs to fifth floor to eat lunch and I took a look around, wondering which of these beds would be mine. There were probably twenty or so rooms on the side we were on, which was the male side. None of the rooms had a door but there was only two bunk beds per room. Other than the rooms there wasn't much to the fifth floor besides the sitting area with the T.V and the smoke deck, plus the office, I guess. When we were done eating we went out for a smoke. When we got onto the smoke deck, Al held a smoke out to me.

"I have smokes, thank you." I put one in my mouth. "I think I owe you a few." My hand was on the first row of cigarettes ready for the draw but Al shook his head.

"No that's okay, you keep them for yourself. Your a nice kid. *I* have a son you're age."

"I'll take a smoke, if ya don't mind," David said nervously, with his hands in his pockets.

We smoked for a minute and Ralph asked me for a smoke. After the stories he'd been telling me I couldn't possibly refuse. Al and David finished their smokes and went inside and, when they did, Ralph said he wanted to smoke a bowl with me in exchange for a few smokes. I was reluctant because I had left what was left of my weed at the somewhere motel with the intention of getting sober again, but I wanted to hear more of Ralph's stories. He said we should at least wait until Homer gets back.

About an hour after lunch, Ester and Wade came back with a big bag of theatre popcorn.

"How was the movie?" Al asked.

"Good!" Ester answered. Wade just looked at her.

"Good!" Al replied.

"It was terrible!" Grumpy old Wade put in. "It was supposed to be an action movie about battle and lore but they turned it into a *love* story! Rated 'R', my ass." He took a handful of popcorn. "The only good thing was the popcorn. Anyone want some popcorn?"

"I'll take some popcorn." Homer said walking into the room. "Movie theatre popcorn's good eh."

"Homer! How's your new place!?" Ester shouted excitedly.

"Good, good." Homer, his hands in his overall pockets, nodded his head. "It's nice to sleep in the peace and quiet eh." He laughed to himself. "Still don't have a bed yet, I just sleep on a big pile of blankets. The DI's supposed to be giving me a bed one of these days, I just need to go to the storage warehouse to pick it up,"

"Congratulations, Homer, I didn't know you were getting out so soon!"

"Yeah well it was time eh, I've been living here long enough and now that I'm working here and making money I really have no excuse not to get my own place. Life's good eh."

"You're here early." Al said putting dirty laundry into the machine.

"I was just feeling really restless at home eh, had to get out of the house. Went to the library to find a DVD, but I found one right away, usually it takes me a while eh, I like to check the backs of all the movies and read about who's in it and what's on the special features. The run time, rating, why it's rated the way it is, what languages it's in, look at the *pictures*." He threw his staff vest over his overalls.

"Pictures are neat eh, I really like them."

Well since all of you ah hya now, me and this fine young gentlemen," Ralph announced, putting his hands on my shoulders. "need to be gettin' out of hya. We deserve a break too!"

"Yeah you guys go take some time for yourselves, you need to do that once in a while eh. Don't go outside though it's freezing cold." He looked at me. "Are you coming back today?"

"Probably not, there's someone I need to meet on Second."

"Alright, you're a good kid eh, stay out of trouble."

"Don't worry it's just staff that I'm meeting."

Homer followed Ralph and I to let us out. "Come down anytime eh, bud."

Ten minutes later Ralph and I were outside walking to a spot he knew. It wasn't far from the DI and I was surprised I'd never been there before. We sat on a bench beside a big wall of vibrant graffiti. "Theh's a camera right theh." Ralph pointed a camera out to me. "The cops know about me but they don't do anything, you know why?"

"Why?"

"Cause *I* know how to talk to cops." We smoked two bowls out of a sticky metal pipe while he told me about a few experiences he's had with the cops, all the crazy things he's done and how the only thing on his record is a jay-walking ticket. By the time we were walking back to the DI I was pretty stoned, and when we got to the second floor I'm *pretty* sure Ralph ditched me. I took a drink from the water fountain and when I was just about to go downstairs I saw Patrick looking around at everyone with a look of distress, but he smiled once he saw me.

"Michael, am I glad to see you!"

"Yeah? Why what's up."

"I just saw someone get stabbed in front of the DI!"

"Geez."

"Oh, it was horrible. There's something about this place that just seems to drive people mad."

"Yeah, it's sad."

He nodded. "I was thinkin' about how you watched Streets of plenty and I thought about another documentary that may interest you. Have you ever heard of 'strategic relocation'?"

"No."

"It's, well-" He looked around. "I've got it on my computer if you'd like to watch it, I just hope no one takes it."

"I think it'll be alright. Let's just find a place and watch the people around us before you pull it out. Not everyone's bad. Most people here have their own computers anyway, it's not worth it to get barred from the place."

"True enough."

We walked through the crowed and, for the first time, I sat down at a table on Second. For a few minutes we sat there observing while he told me what the film was about and mentioned a little about the government. There was a very brawny man sitting close by, listening to every word we said. When I made eye contact with him he took it as an invitation to join in and slid closer, extending a boxing glove of a hand to me.

"I'm Davin." I shook his hand and he put it in front of Patrick.

"Michael."

"Patrick."

"Okay. Okay." Davin said suspiciously as he leaned back in his chair. "You know what I hate? The government man."

Patrick and I looked at each other then back at Davin.

"They're everywhere, the staff here work for em', the banks work for em', the police work for em'." He scrutinized us again. "You guys could even work for em'."

Again, Patrick and I looked at each other then back at him. "We don't work for the government man, we're homeless."

"Yeah. Well that's what you'd want me to think if you were spying on me though right." Davin laughed nervously. "No, nah, I can't trust ya. That doesn't mean I'm suspecting you of anything, I'm bigger than they are." Inhaling a large breath through his nose his eyes darted around the crowd. "There was one time I was walking back here to the DI and there was a guy somewhere over there-" He pointed in three directions, "following me. I knew he worked for the government, man, I fucking knew it. He followed me for like a block man and he was on the phone with the army." Patrick and I looked at each other again.

"What'd you do?" I asked.

"I knocked him the fuck out! He was snorin'!"

In my peripherals I could see Patrick looking at me but I was still looking at Davin. "You *are* making sure you're 'knocking out' the right people though, are you?" Patrick asked with a shuddering voice.

"Yeah."

We didn't say anything as his head nodded, he didn't stop. As Davin's paranoia evolved Patrick and I grabbed our shit and got out of there without a word to each other.

"See what I mean? This place is dreadful." Patrick said.

I saw Kelsey watching everyone as Patrick asked, "Would you like to go to the library with me?"

"Might be able to meet you there; I need to talk to someone right now."

Patrick seemed to be under the impression that I just didn't want to hang out with him but he smiled and shook my hand before leaving anyway. Kelsey smiled with a look of excitement and a sparkle in her eye as I approached.

"Hey! I have something for you." She reached in her pocket and handed me a folded piece of paper. *Another note?* I unfolded it and it was a class picture of Mr. Davidson's grade 3 class. Blood was inflating my heart.

"Which one's you?"

"That one." She pointed at a girl in the front row with a big smile. My eyes made their way to a fat kid in the back.

"Do you know which one's me?"

"That one." she said, indicating the fat kid. "I remember you."

"Seriously?"

"Yeah." We held each other's gaze for a moment. "You were the class jackass." She broke the tension and I blushed, looking back at the picture. *She really does remember me!*

"That's too cool."

When I tried to hand it back she shook her head. "Keep it."

After folding it, it went in the breast pocket of my leather jacket; the pocket of memoirs. We talked a little longer about people we knew from grade 3 and a few other things like how much the town Sylvan Lake has changed since we were kids and so on. Then Brad walked up with a look I'd never seen on his face before and, because he didn't say anything *inappropriate*, Kelsey wasn't immediately annoyed.

"You okay?" She asked him.

With a frown, he pointed at me. "No I just wanted to talk to Red Deer." He looked me in the eye. "Sorry, I call you Red Deer because you're from Red Deer."

"Yeah man, I know."

"What's your name again?"

"Michael. Sorry man we're just talking right now, can I talk to you later or something?"

"My best friend got hit by a train last night and I wanted to see if you'd come for a coffee with me, but forget it." He walked away with his hands in his pockets while Kelsey and I comprehended the truth. I looked at her.

"I'm sorry, I'm actually going to go with him, I'm good with this kind of thing. My good friend Ben died a couple months after graduation."

She smiled. "Okay, good luck."

Brad and I made our way to Tim Horton's once I caught up with him, me wrapped in my scarf. "He was too young, man, too young."

"How old?"

"Seventeen."

"I had a friend that died at seventeen."

"Life's so cruel!" He shouted with a smile on his face.

"Yeah, I'm sorry to hear about your friend man."

"You knew him too!"

"I did? It wasn't Lyle was it?"

"No, fuck that kid. It was Andy, man! You remember Andy, don't ya!?"

"No, sorry man, I don't." There was a silence. "How long did you know him for?"

"A couple months." He grinned. *And he was your best friend? Yeah right.*

When we got into the Tim Horton's he started talking about how he still wanted to have sex with his 'girlfriend' and went on to make orgasm noises, trying to impersonate the sounds of the hypothetical scene. Then, he spoke about what a miserable bitch she was for not having sex with him. I stood with him at the till but said I didn't want anything. He ordered then told me he didn't have any money. Once I paid for his stuff he went to the washroom and I ditched back to the DI.

"That was fast." Kelsey said.

"Yeah, he didn't care about the kid who died - he just wanted attention. I hate that shit, I was pretty empathetic towards him because of my friend Ben, but it turned out he didn't even care." I shook my head angrily.

"That's not right."

"People like that piss me off. I hate the way society responds to death. It should be a celebration of life not a group pity and mourning session."

"Everyone deals with death differently. Hmm, maybe you should write about that! It might help."

"I always write about stuff like that. Death, loss. Tragedy in general. I always thought it helped me cope with things but I'm starting to learn all I'm doing is making it a part of me."

"Can you do something for me?"

"Three positives?" I asked grinning.

"No. From what you just told me, and based on what you've told me about your work, it sounds like you only write depressing, negative things. Maybe you should write something positive for a change."

"No way, that's not my style."

"Please? For me?" She asked smiling and swaying.

"For you? Does that mean you're going to read it?" She held her smile, gave me a nod then looked around guiltily. *Is that allowed?*

"If you want me to!"

"I'll give it a shot, but I can't promise no one's going to die."

"Trying is all I can ask for."

We spoke until one of the Dice, probably a supervisor, came and told Kelsey she had to go work on third floor. After our goodbyes she left. Even though it was just about time to catch the 2907 bus something compelled me to go buy a bottle of liquor and find a bathroom stall to drink it in. Because it was Sunday, there weren't a lot of places open late, I had nowhere to drink. Ended up going to a McDonald's washroom and drank it within minutes because there was a line up for my stall. *That's fast food for ya.*

It was around eight when I was on my way back to the DI. Under the bridge I saw the middle aged woman that was always there.

"Hey honey, lookin' for anything?" She offered in a chipmunk voice. *Gross.* With barely any acknowledgement I kept walking towards her because the DI was on the other side. "I give really good head."

Half blacked out, I had some sort of moment of compassion for this woman, though she worked in an industry I had absolutely no respect for.

"How much would it take for you to not have to suck dick for a whole day?"

"A million dollars," she laughed.

"How do you live with yourself?" *Christ.*

"Wait!" She called after me as I started walking, I turned to see extremely hopeful eyes. "I make around two hundred in a day..." I pulled out the cash I had left in my wallet, I think it was around ninety bucks.

"Have a nice night." Feeling like a hero I was about to walk away, until I saw her smile; it disheartened me. *I forgot you were a human being.*

"Oh, my God! Why!?"

"Everyone deserves to smile *sometimes*," came off the top of my head, but I couldn't even smile back. She hugged me for a long time before letting me go.

They were still setting up for Second by the time I got back but the building was packed full because of the cold weather.

Everything's a little blurry but in the end I was laying on a blanket in the lobby using my backpack as a pillow.

"This is fucking bullshit!" I heard a man yell, and looked up to see Harold the web designer red faced, smashed and in a mood. "I come to this place for shelter and they put me in a room with a bunch of lunatics!?" He caught a lot of other people's attention and I pulled a toque over my eyes so he wouldn't notice me. Kept my face hidden until he was escorted out while having his temper tantrum.

Then I saw Driller Dan, *also* wasted, talking to one of the Dice. They were close enough that I could hear.

"Here's the difference about *me* and these *other* fucking bums, okay!? I have a fucking job, these guys? None of them are goin' anywhere man, they *live* here. *I'll* get a couple checks and *I'll* be gone because I'm not a bottom feeder. Fuck these peasants."

"Oh really!?" A younger man in a ponytail was getting riled up, he was friends with the Dave's.

"Well now that you said that you can leave," the Dice said.

"Fuck you, man, I'm better than these people!"

Tukahoot sauntered in and spotted me and we gave each other a nod of the chin and he sat down across from me.

"It's for your own safety man." I heard the Dice say as he escorted Driller Dan out.

"How are you?" red-eyed Tukahoot asked with a smile.

"Not bad man, you?"

"Not bad." He pulled a bag of chips out of his backpack and started munching away.

"You want some chips?"

"I'm good man."

"Aright." He laid down on his backpack and mowed his chips while staring at the roof like he was looking at a sky full of stars. "I'm so hungry man I got mad munchies right now," he laughed. "Can't wait until tomorrow."

"What's tomorrow?"

"Hopefully getting out of here. I just have to sell *one* more picture and I have enough to go to Vancouver, *with* a bit of cash."

"Awesome man, I hope you get out of here!"

"I hope *you* get out of here." He said. "I heard Casey has it out for you."

"You know Casey?" Raising an eyebrow I sat up concerned.

"Yeah, bro. I have half a mind to give you my ticket to Van!" *Fantastic.*

"I'll be fine, man, you gotta take care of yourself. I appreciate it though. And thanks for the heads up!"

"What are hommies for?" he asked before shoveling some more chips into his mouth. Tukahoot fell asleep soon after he finished two bags of chips, but I couldn't sleep. What was more pestering than the uncomfortable floor, or the coughing, or the smell, was the Dice in the lobby making jokes and laughing like there wasn't anyone trying to sleep.

When morning came I convinced a woman working in the front office to let me into Daysleep - it wasn't hard, due to the fact I look terrible with no sleep. Who doesn't? I asked them to wake me up early though, because I had plans for the day. At one O clock they woke me up and I went to Second to call the Janet number I got the other day. Janet answered saying she would send someone down to talk to me. Seraj, an East Indian Dice came down to see me.

"Michael is it?"

"Yes."

"I'm Seraj." We shook hands. "I understand you've been saying some suicidal things to Kelsey," is the way he put it.

"I *did* say some suicidal things, yes."

"We'd like to give you a room on the fifth floor but we can't have any concern of you killing yourself up there, it would disturb some of the occupants." *Is he being facetious?* "Do I have your word that if we move you up to the fifth floor that you won't do such a thing?"

"Sure."

He nodded and I followed him up to the fifth floor office. In there he went through a screening process with me and when he was done, he gave me a choice between forth or fifth floor, which he said was rare.

"I'm only giving you this opportunity because you mentioned you don't associate with the youth here. Forth floor is generally our youth and fifth floor is generally seniors. Also there are no women on the Forth."

"Fifth floor for sure."

I had to wait until the regular 2907 time to get all my stuff and when I did I got a ride back from one of the Dice. That was it, 2907 was behind me. After I got all my stuff organized in my new locker, I took a shower in a shower that, in all honesty, was really no better than anywhere else the DI could offer, besides the fact it wasn't contained in a public washroom.

When I got out I went out to the smoke deck and looked at the Calgary Tower shining in the night. There was an old man standing beside me and he was also staring at the tower.

"When I first went homeless I didn't expect to get a free room with a view." I said to him with a grin; he didn't seem to think it was very funny.

When I went back inside I met one of the three new roommates I had in my doorless room. His name was Sergei, a small middle aged man with a Russian accent, the way he spoke reminded me of a con man. He informed me that the man I'd be sharing my bunk with had some form of Tourette's syndrome and constantly repeated 'piece of shit' through the night. *Great.* The good news was the guy worked night shift somewhere as a janitor so he wasn't always there, and tonight would be one of those nights.

Sergei also filled me in on a few of the other old folks on the floor and explained that most everyone on that floor has a job. He said they wouldn't suspend you for drinking or anything as long as you didn't try to come up intoxicated, you'd just have to stay on Second for that night. Already it was very obvious that my situation had improved tenfold, *maybe the DI isn't so bad after all.*

It was around two in the morning and I was out of smokes. On the freezing cold smoke deck I was checking through a big barrel full of cigarette butts I saw some other guys poking through earlier, ready to roll some butt-tobacco. Just then a young woman came out onto the deck.

"Here," she said before I saw her.

When I turned around she was holding a smoke out to me. "I hate seeing people dig in that disgusting thing."

"Thank you, I appreciate it."

"No problem." We didn't really talk but her presence stopped me from focusing on my thoughts. *Just for a moment, I'd like to be by myself outside of a bathroom.* I finished half the smoke before she left and when she did I put out the half smoke and started looking through the barrel again. A middle aged man wearing a leather vest over his jean jacket, a ball cap and glasses came out. He smoked while I found my butts and right before I rolled a smoke he tapped me on the shoulder.

"Here, you want some of this?" He was holding half a lit smoke out to me.

"Sure! Thank you."

He shrugged. "It's just a cigarette. What's your name?"

"Michael. You?"

"Lester."

"You work?"

"No, but I'm in a job training program."

"EST?" His eyes widened.

"You already know about EST!?"

"Heard of it, at least."

"It's a good program. Really good. Once I get my tickets, I'm going to get a job and then I can start making money from the job I get." *Brilliant.*

"Sounds like a good plan. How'd you end up homeless, if you don't mind me asking?"

Lester told me about how his parents and siblings left him to take care of his poor old grandmother on her farm, and how he'd stuck around until she died. His mom inherited the farm and sold it leaving Lester with nothing. He thanked me for listening to him and suggested we get matching haircuts, said it'd be cool; we'd look like brothers. *I guess my hair is getting a little long.*

Once Lester went inside I sat down in a chair and rolled a smoke from the cigarette butts I'd gathered. After it was rolled I sparked it and looked down at the bright lights coming from the city bellow, contemplating my new homework assignment. *Write something positive huh?* This was going to be harder than a book on the homeless condition. *Now what am I going to do?*

LINCOLN'S ON FIRE

By: Michael Jesmer

(Unedited)

She said I should try to write something positive. Was she kidding? I couldn't do that. After all, I was still getting used to using my left hand; my writing looked like chicken scratch. I was right handed before I lit myself on fire; the stubs that remained were just a bitter reminder.

The doctors and nurses avoided telling me what happened, saying things like "You just made a mistake" or "You hurt yourself" because they wanted to avoid severe posttraumatic stress. I had experienced so much shock during and after the incident that I didn't quite remember how everything went down; at first.

I did however remember everything I had felt and known from before the incident and I knew damn well it was no accident. Red, the bassist from my old band had actually been the one to fill me in on what happened. He was one of the only people that came to see me in the hospital after the allograph surgeries. In fact, he was one of my cadaver skin donors; what was left of my skin was not nearly enough.

I was somewhat vain when we were in our band. Because I was lead guitar, singer and song writer, I had wanted to call the band *Lincoln's on Fire*. Higgins really didn't care what we called the band, he just played for the music. Red, like me, wanted the fame and fortune. He wanted the name of our band to be something universal and inspiring.

We played a few shows here and there and developed what I guess you would call a "cult following" in our city. We even put out an album with eight tracks. We called ourselves *Within You.* We played metal - not my style. I wanted to play blues, so I went solo under the name *Abraham.* Higgins never forgave me.

After I had played four shows I realized most of the people coming to see me were old fans from *Within You,* and they weren't diggin' the blues. Every show I played, the audience seemed to get smaller and smaller, maybe because they were pissed that I broke up the band, or maybe, more realistically, my tunes just weren't good. For my fifth show I advertised that I would be playing metal again, and it was the biggest show I got. I alm sold nearly two hundred tickets and that wasn't even counting the tickets that were sold at the door.

Red told me that during my first song I was shredding metal on stage, no lyrics, and at the end of the song I let out a growl that made the crowd cheer. He told me I then took off my shirt and asked the crowd; "You wanna see me go up in flames?" The crowd cheered louder as I pulled out a milk jug full of gasoline and undid my belt. Subconsciously, I guess I knew I was gonna live - why else would I have stripped my clothes off? The crowd loved it but Red said the minute I was naked on stage security started tripping out. I poured the gasoline all over myself and as security began running up to the stage I lit a match; and poof.

After I heard the story, I remembered everything. I remember the sound of the audience going wild until they realized it wasn't an act, and the sound transforming into united panic. I remember my body being engulfed in flames within seconds, feeling my eye lashes burn down to the skin, hearing all the hair (and there was a lot of it) on my head sizzle and singe, disappearing within seconds. I remember feeling the skin all over my body rise as it blistered and boiled. I remember feeling my testicles melt. I remember hearing myself scream like nothing I'd ever heard before. And after what seemed to be eternity, I remember the fire being put out .

I was inable to see the crowd around me with my open eyes. My skin was hot and raw, the air felt cold and it hurt like hell. I took one step and felt mycontracted skin pull at itself. After that, I blacked out; only vaguely remembering sirens and the EMT's making jokes about trying to kill myself in such a way. But Red told me I didn't pass out, he said I grabbed the microphone and said 'I hope you all burn in hell!' then stood in that spot grasping the mic until the ambulance showed up.

I don't remember the first weeks or maybe a month of my treatment. I just remember the guilt and hate that I felt towards myself and the world. I was deaf in my left ear and could barely understand what the nurses would say to me while they were cleaning my burns and changing the dressing (bandages); this was called *debridement*, and it would happen multiple times a day. I really didn't care what they had to say to me and I was thankful I didn't have to look at them due to the dressing covering my face. My mind was clear by the time I came out of my second allograph; coherent enough to meet with the head doctor on the floor. To my knowledge, this was thefirst time we'd met.

"Ben, by now you must have comprehended what is going on."

I couldn't see Dr. Frost, but I could hear the coldness in his voice. He either looked down on suicide, was desensitized like most doctors, or both. I tried to grip the arms of the chair with my right hand and was reminded that I couldn't by a searing pain that seemed to travel up my entire arm. My left hand, the one I used to douse myself, was able to complete the task but I released the arm immediately when the pain hit me.

"Yeah." I could barely recognize my damaged voice.

"Ben you're suffering from a severe full thickness burn, meaning your epidermis and dermis, first and second layers of skin, have been completely, and irreversibly damaged. Meaning they no longer exist." Cold as ice. "You have many surgeries ahead of you Ben, your body contains no undamaged skin and you are unable to provide yourself with a proper skin graph."

The room fell silent and I realized he wanted me to give him some kind of indication that I heard him.

"What does that mean?"

"That means you need cadaver skin, skin from another person. Your father and your friend Earl-"

"Call him Red," I interrupted. Earl always sounded weird.

"Red, have generously offered to take part in your allograph."

"That's all fine and dandy doc, but I'm still gonna kill myself."

"I'll be blunt with you Ben." Like he wasn't already.

"Call me Link," I interrupted again. Ben always sounded weird.

"You won't be able to do anything of the sort in your current condition." I hated his accent, it was a mix of British and asshole.

"But you're fixing me up, right doc?" If I could have smiled I would have; I thought it was clever. I could hear some pages rustle and I wondered if he was just moving things around to add tension.

"If that's the case, it is too early to move you into the psychiatric ward. I'll see to it you're on constant watch." Great. "I'll call a nurse to come and get you, but Ben,"

"Link."

"You've already put your friends and family through enough. Don't waste their good spirits."

He called in a nurse who then wheeled me out of the room..

It was a few months until I was able to walk again and, even then, I needed the wheelchair more often than not. When I'd walk, I would have to take baby steps and use the pole attached to my IV and catheter as a support. I still never spoke to any of the nurses unless I absolutely had to, and if I did I kept it to a bare minimum. Most of them didn't want to talk to me anyway. They must have seen me as selfish and miserable and not worth their time. By then I had finished my fifth allograph and most of my skin had been restored; if you can call it that, and I was able to see again, though I was partially blind in my right eye.

I'll never forget looking in the mirror for what felt to be the first time in my life. I was *hideous*. My hair, my nose, my ears, my lips, my *face*; it was all gone. What skin wasn't covered up by bandages looked patchy like grid paper, stretched out and discolored. Whatever stood looking back at me in the mirror was not me. It was a monster. I raised my previously talented hands in the air, my left was somewhat recognizable as it only suffered second degree burns. My right hand was an ugly stub. Tears started running down my face, but I could barely feel them. It was like feeling a butterfly crawl across your skin without looking at it while you are distracted by something else. That was the moment I realized how much I had going for me before I scarred myself for life. Before I took my looks, before I took my body, before I took my future.

I had been putting off seeing visitors. Whenever they'd shown up I would tell the nurses to send them away, eventually people stopped showing up all together. They asked me to call when I was ready but it must have been a couple months by this point. I was ready, I asked one of the nurses to call my dad.

When he walked into the visiting room, I could tell he had been expecting the worst. I was expecting him to react as if it had been even *worse* than he had thought.

"Oh my God, Ben," he said,picking up his pace as he cme toward me. He started going in for a hug but stopped when his arms touched my shoulder and looked me in the eyes. "Can I hug you, will it hurt?"

I looked at his arms and saw the bandages and scars from his donation to me.

"Go ahead." I was bitter but I hugged him back with my left arm. It hurt a little but it was the only real human contact I'd had in months. I could see that the nurse was monitoring our visit, but I didn't care. It felt nice to get a hug from my dad and, for a moment, I felt comfort.

"How are you doing bud?" He asked and then cupped his mouth while tears welled in his eyes.

He was fighting back a raging storm of tears.

It reminded me of me when I was little and he'd hit me, saying he'd give me something to cry about. I must have got it from him. My comfort turned to anger in an instant and I looked away, fighting back tears of my own. I think we had a moment of understanding; we had to regain our bearings.

He hugged me again. "I'm sorry Ben. You could have talked to me."

"Don't tell me that." I said, and he let go and looked at me. "Don't fucking tell me that."

My dad had always treated me like a friend rather than a son. He gave me my first beer, my first cigarette, my first joint and even my first line of coke all before I was sixteen. When I asked the nurse to call him, I didn't know what I was thinking. I guess I wanted my *dad*. Nevertheless like father like son, he had a short fuse too.

"You can't put this on *me* Ben, you didn't even reach out to me." I had nothing to say. "Have you seen yourself Ben? I don't even recognize you."

I tried to jump up in a fit of rage but was reminded by my contracted, seemingly plastic skin that I couldn't do things like that anymore. Didn't stop me from yelling though.

"Of course you don't recognize me, you pathetic mother fucker! I haven't been myself since I was twelve years old! And I have *you* to thank for that! You're right, maybe I should have come to you, I could have used some beer and drugs!" I could feel my heart training to fight Mike Tyson, I wanted to kill my dad.

The nurse rushed to his side.

"Mr. Lincoln you have to leave right now, you're bothering his heart rate."

She led him out of the door then turned to ask if I was alright. I blacked out after that, I don't even remember the rest of the day. The day after I met with Red; but only for about five minutes to hear about what had actually happened at my show and then I sent him away.

In two months I had another allograph and probably a hundred more debridement's. During that time I had been diagnosed with PSD, *posttraumatic stress disorder*. It hadn't hit me until I was able to see and smell. I was often reminded of the incident by the smallest things, such as water being poured from a pitcher, hearing people cheer or smelling something burnt. I couldn't even handle eating hotfood. Anytime something triggered a memory, I'd black out and begin running amuck; cracking my still healing skin badly on several occasions.

Luckily, my skin infections were never too bad and I continued making a positive recovery. I became more open to physiotherapy and began working with the nurses more, but was still completely withdrawn. Interacting with people had lost all worth and meaning. I was ashamed of myself. Who I was then, who I am now. What I'ddone. Everything. Just *everything*.

Then came that fateful day. I was walking around the unit and was starting to get the hang of it. Dr. Frost relieved my watchdog nurse from duty the day before and it was a nice change of pace to be on my own. I was still suicidal, but Frost had made the decision based on the fact that my attitude and commitment to life were moving slowly in a positive direction, not to mention the nurse and I didn't like each other.

His exact words were "Ben, (of course I told him to call me Link) I'm going to let you be by yourself for a while, I don't think I will be needing to put you on the psych unit as long as we keep that *nasty* nurse away from you." He said it sarcastically with a smile, and I wondered if he was beginning to like me a little, or understand me at the very least.

In the lobby I looked around and saw other recovering patients; some were amputees, some were people who were recovering from things like car accidents or surgery, but I still felt withdrawn and alone. I couldn't talk to these people, why would I? They all tried not to look at me, but I could tell I was subject matter in the unit. I was the worst one there.

I looked around the main lobby and saw people sitting in uncomfortable chocolate brown pleather chairs gathered around a T.V, the carpet blue with stained ugly pink diamonds in the design here and there. I walked over to the window and the sun hit my face; I rarely looked out the window because, when I did, it was way too bright for me. But this time was different, this time I saw the world, the beautiful world, and I realized I hadn't been outside for five months. Then I was distraught, I couldn't go *outside*; what would people think? I was being judged and pitied by people missing limbs, what would *normal* people think? What was *normal*? The beautiful world turned black again, I cursed it and retreated to my room.

When my dad had come to visit he brought my old song books and my pen, though I hadn't even thought about looking at them. I pulled one out and began flipping through the pages. Not only had I not been outside in five months, but I hadn't written in five months. I hadn't played guitar in five months, I hadn't sang in five months, shit, I hadn't done *anything* in five months. I turned to a blank page and picked up my pen, then thought for a few minutes. I wasn't sure if I would be able to write, I had written my left arm off as void years ago but now it was all I really had. In physio the nurses had urged me to learn how to write with it but I was bitter and wanted nothing to do with it. Knowing me, they never pushed me too hard out of fear of what I may become. What had I become? Then it came to me:

"Drain my bleeding heart

Make me whole again

Remind me what it's like to be callous

Take me back to the nothing where I dwelled before this

I was strong, I was weak

I broke my mask, I saw my face

I remembered

What it's like to bleed

Can I have it back? My mask?

It's broken, it's salvaged, and it's yours.

What are you?

Reflection? Illusion? Memory?

I keep misery company, now that I can bleed

Make it stop

My fruitless sacrifice

I wish not to bleed in vain

Drain my bleeding heart

Make me whole again"

I had read it over half a dozen times when she walked in.

"Hey I'm just coming to check up on you!" She smiled while she spoke to me, people didn't do this much and I was surprised that I had to fight back a smile.

I looked up at her.

"Ok." My response didn't seem to satisfy her, her eyebrows showed a bit of distress and she tilted her head a little.

"Is everything alright?" Yeah, right.

"Everything's fine." She still didn't seem satisfied, but for some reason I found it hard to look away from her captivating eyes. She looked down at my song book.

"Oh you're writing!? That's awesome good for you!" She smiled again, and again I found it hard to fight off my own smile to the point that it hurt.

"Thank you." It was quiet for a few seconds. I detested how drawn to her I was, I wanted her to leave.

"Would you mind if I take a look?" A part of me was expecting her to ask, but when she did, I got butterflies for the first time in God knows how long.

"*If* you can read it. I think it looks like trash." It did, it looked like a three year old's coloring job with a few legible letters here and there. Regardless, I handed it to her. I didn't expect her to be able to read it but she read it out loud. I had to correct her on a few words but I was impressed, people could barely read my writing beforehand, no pun intended. When she was done reading, it looked like she gave it a quick skim over before she looked back at me.

"Is this about you?" She spoke soon and I took it as a sign that she either didn't like it or was about to take my song book away so I reached my hand out to take it back.

"Kind of."

She held it out to me and I took it, and then looked away.

"It's a wonderful poem, but it was pretty negative."

"It was supposed to be song lyrics but it didn't-" I looked it over for a few seconds. "I guess it *is* a poem."

"You're a song writer?" At this point I almost forgot I was a burn victim; if you could call me a victim. I was just a normal guy talking to a beautiful woman.

"Actually, I'm a musician!" I said with confidence, then realized the truth and lifted my right arm as if she didn't already know my situation. "Well, used to be." I'm not sure if my face was capable of looking sad, but after I said that she looked concerned and comforting.

"Aww, well I'm sure you can still be a musician! You obviously have a-"

"I can't be a fucking musician, look at me." Her genuine concern turned to a sad uncomfortable look.

"I'm sorry. If you need anything I'll be around, we're all here to support you." She waited for a little bit but I didn't say anything, then she turned to leave and began walking.

My rotten attitude had lost me a lot; right then and there, in one second, millions of lost opportunities flashed through my mind - friends, relationships, jobs, family.

"Wait,"

She stopped and turned around slowly as if she wasn't sure if I had actually said anything. I stood up out of the bed and walked towards her.

"I'm sorry," *I'm sorry*? When was the last time I said that? "It's just, I used to play the guitar, and I used to sing. Now…" I held up my right arm again like she didn't see it the first time. "Now I don't have a proper right hand and I'm deaf in one ear. Plus I've been hooked up to respirators on and off since I got here; my voice is getting worse and worse." I looked down in self-pity.

"Well…" it seemed she was uncertain if she should say what she wanted to say, but she was the kind of person that spoke her mind, the type of person that could be herself no matter who she was speaking to; she was *real*. "Maybe you should exercise it more."

Then she smiled again and I couldn't help but smile back. Her smile was contagious and perfect. I didn't even know I could still smile; it had been at *least* five months. I didn't know if she was insinuating that I should practice my singing or talk to her more, but I wanted to do both. I felt warm inside, like nothing I'd ever truly felt before.

"No one is going to believe me when I say you smiled! I'm so excited for you!" I smiled even bigger and she did too. I could feel my heart pounding harder than Ron Jeremy on a Saturday night.

"I'm Link." No I wasn't. "I mean, I'm Ben Lincoln." I quickly corrected myself. Then I realized that there was *no way* she didn't already know that, but she played along anyways.

"Nice to meet you Ben, I'm Mary Dawn." She held her right hand out to shake mine then quickly changed to her left. For just a second I was a bit offended, but I started laughing and so did she.

After that day I felt human again, I felt hope for the future. She made me feel like a normal person and I held onto that. I started writing again and singing in the showers. I began talking to nurse Dawn whenever I could, which was easy because after that she became my debridement nurse. I told her all about *Within You* and *Abraham*, my old family and friends; even in such a short period of time she was the most valuable support I had in my entire life.

Every time I'd hear her laugh or see her smile, it made it hard to believe that all the mistakes I made in my life were the wrong choices; without them, I never would have met her. It hadn't even been a month and I was convinced I was falling in love. She was stunningly beautiful, empathetic and honest with a gifted mind, warm heart and the most amazing smile. Absolutely, undeniably perfect. After a few weeks of trading stories she had convinced me to reach out to outside sources again. I still wasn't ready to see my father again, but I had still not yet thanked Red for his cadaver skin during my allographs. I asked nurse Dawn to call Red for me, and I asked if he could bring my guitar.

When he showed up, I was expecting him to be like me, different. But in walked Red, long red haired, leather jacket, tight plaid pants, combat boots Red. He sat down with a smile, however there was a look in his eye I couldn't put my finger on.

"Link! Good to see ya, man." He slapped my shoulder like a prick. "Well, not really! I mean it's good to see you but-" Red always had a way with words; that's why I was the writer.

"I know what you mean."

"So how ya been, man?" He looked around. "Got this place all to yourself?"

The room was covered in ugly, assorted flower wallpaper, there was one couch and two love seats, all the same uncomfortable pleather as the chairs in the lobby; no pillows and no bed. Red was smart too.

"This is just the visitor's room," I looked around. "Did you bring my guitar?" Red's face looked puzzled for a minute.

"Yeah, yeah I did! It's out in the car, you wanna go for a smoke?" He realized it was a stupid question before he finished dribbling it.

"Don't smoke anymore." Then he made a stupid face while he raised his right index finger attached to his thumb to his mouth while he sucked in some air to allude that he meant smoke a joint. I just looked at him.

"Oh, uh, alright. I'm gonna have one then I'll be back with your guitar, alright?"

"Sounds good. Thanks Red." He walked out.

While he was gone I began to wonder why I was so bitter towards everyone; everyone except nurse Dawn. When it boiled right down to it, there was no excuse. Sure, *now* I was dealing with PSD and recovering from full thickness burns, but I'd always been like that. Red had been a friend who stuck by me and even gave an unknown amount of skin to save my life, and I was treating him like shit.

From now on I'd be a better friend to him.

Nurse Dawn let him back in, and he came in with a brand new guitar; black with red designs that almost looked like flames. It looked expensive, more expensive than my old one.

"Ta dah!"

At first I wasn't impressed with it but I knew I'd adapt. After all, that's what humans do.

"The old one's toast eh?"

"Yeah man, but me, Link senior and a couple others pitched in on this for ya once we heard you wanted your guitar."

He handed it to me and I held it in position, playing with the frets with my left and trying to figure out what to do with my right. I was right, the guitar was much higher quality and much heavier than my Gibson

"Frankly, we were a little surprised you asked."

"It's great, thank you Earl!" There was an awkward silence; I'd never called him Earl before.

Earl always sounded weird.

"No problem. Hey check this out!" He jumped over beside me and pulled out his phone to show me a video.

The video started off with roaring flames, and I could feel my skin start to blister and boil. I started sweating, I was in tons of pain and the anxiety was incredibly overwhelming, this was the worst PSD attack I'd had so far. I felt like I was going to explode but I tried as hard as I could to hold on to myself.

"We kept the name *Within You*, hope that's cool!"

The video continued and the crowd, along with my nerves began to calm down, then one of our old songs began playing, except it wasn't me on stage. It wasn't my guitar, it wasn't my voice, but those were my lyrics. Higgins wasn't even there. The blistering and boiling of my skin hadn't left yet but now my blood was boiling. I was furious with feelings of jealousy and betrayal. This piece of shit just stole not only the lyrics to this song, but most likely every song I wrote for the band. Fuck it. Fuck him.

"Fuck you!" Without hesitation, without thinking, I hit him as hard as I could- with my stub.

"Ow! What the fuck man?"

"You plagiarizing mother fucker!" I hit him again, then again then again until he stood up and took a couple steps away.

"You're bat shit crazy, you know that Link!? Shit I was hoping after all this bullshit you might be half a decent human being, but you're not. You're hopeless." He spit on the ground in front of me "Enjoy your guitar bitch."

I could see tears in his eyes before he turned around to head for the door. He opened it and went to leave but right before it closed he turned around and opened it.

"I'd tell you to burn in hell but you already did. You got what you deserve, bitch." He stood there, hands shaking for a moment, then he turned and the door slammed.

The second time he called me a bitch was unnecessary, but now I didn't know what to think. I had a right to be mad but at the same time I knew he was right. I was at a loss for thoughts. I sat in the room for a half hour pondering until nurse Dawn came in.

"I didn't realize he left." I was crying.

What happened?" She sat down beside me and I told her everything.

"It sounds really shitty, but you need to look at the bright side!" She smiled *that* smile. "Now you have the opportunity to write all *new* songs! Your work before seemed to be so negative, you should try writing something positive!"

I'd never written anything positive before in my life.

"I don't think I'm capable of that. Everything I've done has been dark."

"Well maybe that's why you have such a rotten attitude!" I must have looked insulted because she continued-

"Your words not mine!" She smiled again.

The only quality that outweighed her beauty and kindness was her wisdom. She was right. I needed to write something positive for a change. I'd always thought that expressing your anger and pain and sadness was a way of getting it out of you, but it is just a way to keep it a part of you. I took this as a real test of my artistic ability. It took me a week to even figure out where to start. Then, for some odd reason I began writing a blues song about a man that finds love while living on the street.

Only it wasn't blues, it was something completely different. It had soul, it was unique.

I began singing what I had written so far religiously and I could feel my voice getting stronger, getting better. I had thought about changing the song out of fear of what nurse Dawn may have thought, but I had to keep it the way it was; it came from the heart. After a few weeks I had finished writing the lyrics and had them memorized. I even had the tune and riffs in my head; I was blessed with the gift to write music down in my head before I put it down on paper.

Nurse Dawn asked me every day that she worked how the song was coming but I was a bit elusive, I didn't want to show it to her until it was perfect, like her. I had hit the seven month mark by the time I felt it was at the level I was ready to show her. Then she was away for the long weekend so I worked on it like there was no tomorrow to impress her when she got back.

I walked into the main lobby to see her kissing *some guy* at the front desk, and like when I was with Red I was jealous and overcome with a ton of emotions. I couldn't expect her to fall for someone like me, especially in my current condition; but it still hurt. She smiled her smile to him and he left, she was blushing. My heart was training for a rematch with Tyson and, before she noticed me, I hid my newest song. She walked over smiling but I didn't have it in me to smile back.

"How's the song coming?"

"Good I guess." I looked away to avoid getting lost in those eyes.

You *guess*?"

"Yeah," I held onto the papers in my pocket while I spoke. "It's not quite finished yet."

"Well, that's alright! How is everything else going?"

"Everything's fine."

I knew she knew something was up, the way her eye brows crunched. I guess I made it kind of obvious. She looked towards the door where her boyfriend had walked out; her intuition was keen as always. "

I didn't get much sleep last night," I hadn't, I'd been working out the kinks in the song. "I'm gonna go lay down."

She looked a little confused, but mostly disappointed. She knew exactly what was going on. "Oh, alright Ben. If you need anything let me know."

"I will." And with that, I left for my room.

When I got there I began looking over my song again, I wanted to change it. I had, however, become regrettably attached to it. But at the same time, I didn't want to feel the soul that it seemed to have before.

I was feeling like an unwanted burn victim again after seeing Nurse Dawn kiss that other guy. I felt withdrawn, anxious and embarrassed. She didn't care about *me*, she was just being nice. No, not even; she was just doing her *job*. I despised her. For a minute I felt myself turn back into the hideous monster, mentally and physically. As I looked around the room with tears in my eyes, grief in my heart and suicide on my mind my eyes fell on the guitar Red had given me.

A new light came over me. I had manifested my recovery, my new found ambition, my sanity and my music into Nurse Dawn and that wasn't what I was supposed to do. She was a catalyst for the possibilities in my new life and I couldn't let jealousy get in the way of that. Nurse Dawn - Mary was my best friend, even if I wasn't hers. I smiled and again felt like myself, more now than ever. For the first time since I'd been in the hospital I felt strength coming from myself rather than her.

I picked up the guitar for the first time since I got it and pulled out the notes I had written down. "Now how the hell is this going to work?" I thought as I moved my stub around the strings. Even my left hand on the frets seemed awkward and out of place; not only had I not played the guitar in seven months and went through extreme mental trauma, but the skin pulled when I tried to spread my fingers across the neck. I started picking with my stub, it actually seemed to work, but fuck was it painful. I realized I'd have to rebuild callus and reteach myself how to play guitar if I ever wanted to play again.

While I was smiling and messing around with the guitar, Mary knocked on the door and I looked up.

Hey how are you doing?"

"Good. Hey I'm sorry about that I just-"

She was already smiling that smile. "It's ok, you're playing guitar again!"

"Well, trying to." I grinned. "Picking it up again is going to be a stretch." Pun intended. "I'm so happy for you!" She was smiling the biggest I'd seen her smile, it made me happy that I had the ability to make her do that; even if there was no romantic interest.

"Well, it's all thanks to you!" Her smile faded a little but it didn't let up. I thought she might bring up her boyfriend and try to make me feel better about it but I was already past it. "I mean, I know I am the one that is making the effort to get going again, but you opened my eyes Mary. Thank you so much."

She looked relieved. "Aw well thank you! I'm very proud of you!"

"Thank you!"

"Is that your new song?" She made a head motion to the music and lyric sheets. Busted. "Yeah. I lied to you earlier, it's not finished, but I want to play it for you." That was a new thought that had rolled off of my tongue, but I knew I was now bound to it.

"Well I'm looking forward to it! When do you think you'll be ready?"

"Give me a week or two and I'll figure it out." I grinned because I realized I was still myself. Call it confident, call it cocky, but it was a part of me. But that didn't mean I had to be the cynical, pompous douche I had been my whole life. It looked like tears might have been building in her eyes, but I could tell she was just proud.

"That sounds great, Ben. Do you want me to leave you to it?" Any time before this I probably would have said no.

"Maybe, just for a bit."

She smiled and nodded with the same teary proud look and walked out. The feeling I felt was unreal, I felt as though I could take on the world. I practiced guitar on and off that entire first week to the point my stub was raw and bleeding. Although I was extremely committed I felt as though I was making minimal progress, but progress none the less. It was time to take a break.

I stood looking out of the window as I often did since the fateful day. I looked over to see Mary and we smiled at each other. We had barely spoken that week, unless she was changing my dressing which now only happened once a day, if that. I think she was letting me get used to walking on my own two feet and knew I'd approach her to perform my song when I was ready.

I returned my gaze to the streets below; the streets that had somewhat inspired my song. I was ready to go outside again. Not only that, but I was ready to leave - even though Frost and some of the reciprocating staff had mentioned on several occasions that I could stay as long as I needed. I was almost finished with my physiotherapy and was able to complete necessary tasks such as getting dressed and taking a shower with no problem. As much as I would like to stay institutionalized and see Mary as often as possible, I felt as though it was finally time to move on.

My stub took another week to heal and, right on the two week mark, I asked Mary if she wanted to hear the song. She did, of course. I sat on my bed with my guitar and asked her to close the curtains. I looked around at the curtain walls that were our privacy to be reminded of my decision to leave. After she closed them she sat down in the chair, excited to hear the song. I could tell she would be supportive even if she didn't like it, but I knew it was good.

My voice was stronger than before because I had to put much more effort into it, and the damage to my throat gave me kind of a raspy tone that I thought sounded wicked. I was also very impressed with the lyrics, more than anything else I'd written.

I placed my fingers on the frets and began playing but I kept fucking up. I had to keep restarting and I was getting agitated which made me mess up earlier into the song every time.

"I'm sorry."

"Don't be." She smiled at me and I smiled back, I felt as though I could do it this time. I began playing and got further into the song but the second I began singing I screwed up again.

"Dammit!" I rested the guitar and looked over at Mary sitting patiently. "I can't do it. I'm sorry."

She smiled.

"Just sing it, it's ok, you'll get it. Most people in your situation wouldn't even try."

I took a minute to catch my breath, I was nervous about singing without hiding behind the notes of my guitar. I began singing and I believe it was the best I had sung in my life; if I couldn't play the song perfectly I wanted to at least nail the vocals. I could tell as the words came out of my mouth that they were touching her heart. I was surprised to find that even though she knew the song was about her, she was looking at it objectively as a piece of art. As I held the last note and looked over at her I saw a tear slide down her cheek.

"That was - incredible."

I don't think she was expecting it. I felt like her reaction may have been a little exaggerated but it was still mostly sincere.

"I wish I could have performed it with the music." I could tell something was on her mind.

"What's up?"

She looked at me with the look that said she wasn't sure if she should say anything. "You might not be open to this, but have you thought about showing this to Dr. Frost?" Dr. Frost?? Was she joking?

"No, why would I?" I asked with a confused *Are you high?* grin.

"You probably didn't know, but he's a musician as well." I was amazed; that crafty bugger! "He might be able to help you out."

"How?"

"Well maybe he could find someone to play the guitar for you until you feel a hundred percent! You have a fantastic voice." I wasn't interested.

"Nah, if I'm going to get up on stage again, *I* need to be playing. It'd be too weird singing in front of people without a guitar."

"Well think about it! I'm sure he could get you a performance at the Stadium at the very least, but you'd probably have to prove to him that you're ready to go up."

That caught my attention. *The Stadium.* I couldn't even imagine the number of people that would be there - my biggest show had only been around two hundred people; the Stadium could fill nearly twenty thousand. The thought of the cheering crowd brought on an intense PSD attack. My entire body hurt, my skin began to rise and at the same time my mind began fighting me. How would I ever be able to get in front of a crowd again? She sat beside me and rubbed my back and every time I felt her hand move it felt like blisters and boils were being popped and irritated.

I opened my eyes, my head hurt. "You fainted." I heard Mary say, but my vision was still blurry.

I couldn't see if she was smiling or not.

"What time is it?"

"It's only been an hour."

I tried to think, and then recalled performing my song for her. I sat up.

"How're you feeling?"

"I've been better." I smiled and shrugged. "I've been a lot worse."

I imagined her smiling but I was shielding my eyes from the light. We sat in silence for a couple minutes while my eyes adjusted to the light while I gulped down a cup of water she gave to me. "Thank you."

"You're welcome."

"I decided I'm ready to go home." I looked at her and she looked surprised. I assumed she was going to try to convince me to stay a bit longer but I should have known better.

"That's great! You know you can always come back if you need to though, right?"

"Of course." We smiled at each other and I hoped that my time with her wouldn't end after I didn't need to be in the hospital anymore.

Two days later I had a meeting with Dr. Frost and a few of the other medical staff. They seemed reluctant to release me and ensured that if there were any complications to come back with no hesitation, and stressed the importance of at least coming in to get my dressing changed every few days. I didn't get a chance to talk to Frost about music because there were others in the room, I wasn't even sure if I wanted to. I wanted to do everything all on my own, I was still stubborn. That afternoon after all the paperwork was signed, my dad came to pick me up and that was the first time I'd seen him since our fight. It seemed like we had a mutual understanding and were just thankful to have each other back in our lives, although we didn't talk much during the walk out of the hospital.

Being outside again was bizarre, foreign, downright sideways. There seemed to be so many people, so many cars and *so* much noise. Even though I could only hear out of my right ear every sound seemed to be enhanced. The smell of fresh air was something I felt I had never experienced in my life. It had been eight months since I had been outside and I felt alien to my surroundings, especially to the people who, unlike the folks in the hospital, would stare as they walked by. I didn't care though because I was in awe. I didn't move for almost five minutes as my dad stood waiting, letting me take it all in. After I began to notice all the people staring at me, apprehension began to take me away. I already wanted to go back to my safe little room in the hospital where nothing and no one could hurt me. I was scared.

"Come on buddy, let's go home," my dad said in a comforting tone. He put his arm around me and as we began walking to the car. I felt like I had my dad back.

On the way home we stopped at a gas station so he could grab a pack of smokes. In the store I saw a fedora on the shelf and bought it; I suppose it was a way of reinventing myself. A new mask, which isn't always a bad thing as long as you aren't hiding behind it.

We picked up dinner at a drive through because I wasn't up for sitting in a restaurant and a grabbed a movie that was an old favorite of ours when I was a kid, *Ace Ventura Pet Detective: When nature calls*. I even remembered to thank him for his donation to me. That night was the best night I'd ever had with my old man, it's as heartbreaking as it is inspiring how such tragedy can bring people together and make them appreciate life.

I had practiced guitar nearly every day over the next two months and saw Mary at least three times a week; I'd only go in to get my dressing changed when I knew she was working. I was still getting the hang of going out in public. Though it was still awkward when people would stare at me, I would just smile or wave or both. Eventually it became second nature and I felt I was spreading positivity wherever I went. I developed a bit of a reputation around the city; a local paper even interviewed me and did an article on me, although they cut out the interview. I was still too anxious to provide a solid interview.

After the article was released, I got a call from Higgins; that was the first time he and I spoke since I broke our band up. I wasn't sure if I should answer it at first. One of the reasons the band broke up was because Higgins' mom had committed suicide when he was a kid. We were best friends so I saw firsthand what it did to him, the rest of his family and even me; When I went through my suicidal *phase* he began despising me more and more. When I went solo, I can see why he didn't want anything to do with me, I let him down on every level. Still, he was, and always would be, one of my best friends. "Hello?"

"Hey is Link there?"

"No but Ben is," I grinned.

"Oh good. Can I talk to him please?"

"Hey Jon." It was quiet for a minute, I knew he didn't hang up but I thought the line might have been cut off.

"Shit man you sound like an old geezer!" I didn't know what to say.

"How the hell are ya? I saw your article in the paper, it seems like you're doing really good!" I had to think about it; I guess I was.

"Oddly enough, I am doing better than I was a year ago."

"Shit man, that's fucking awesome to hear."

"Yeah man. It's good to talk to you!"

"Yeah." It was quiet again for a few seconds. That feeling you get when you're talking to an old friend and you remember why you were friends in the first place. "Look uh, I know we've had our differences, but if you ever want to talk or hang out or-"

"Yeah man, that'd be great."

"Cool! Um, we could, like, smoke a joint, or like, not. Whatever you wanna do man!"

"What are you doing today?"

"Hanging out with you! Wanna come over?"

"Let's go for coffee or something." Even over the phone I could tell that surprised him.

"Sure!"

Two hours later we met up at a coffee shop. It was busier than I would have liked but it wasn't so bad. We hung out for like three hours reminiscing over old times, telling each other about new things going on in our lives and sharing our new music. He showed me some of his recordings from his new band, *Discard Death,* and they rocked! They were miles better than *Within you.*

I let him read some of my new songs - I had fournow. I could tell they weren't really his style, but he appreciated the new tone and said he was a fan of the lyrics.

"Can you still sing?"

"Yeah my voice sounds a lot different but in my opinion it sounds better." When I said that I think we shared the same thought; 'is it actually better or am I just trying to be optimistic?'

"That's awesome man congratulations."

It seemed without even thinking, he extended his left hand out to shake mine. Like when Mary would talk to me, I felt he was just talking to any other person. To him I wasn't some monster or misfortunate being to be pitied, I was just a friend. I was Ben Lincoln, his buddy from grade three.

"You can't still play can you? I mean-" He motioned his head to my right hand.

"I'm getting there."

"Seriously? Shit man, you're an inspiration." I was filled with pride.

"I should get going though," he continued."I need to jam early tomorrow. But, fuck dude, it was good chillin' with you again! We'll have to get together more often!" We both started getting our jackets on.

"For sure!"

I saw Higgins digging around in his pockets.

"Yo, please don't get mad, but Red wanted me to give you this." He held out a capo for my guitar. "He says he's really sorry."

Red was a friend of Higgins, I had never really been too fond of him. He always seemed to put in a solid effort to be my friend though, I think he admired me. It might have been time to meet up with Red again, but I wasn't ready for that. Even though I still had my newfound positive attitude I also still had my short fuse - and Red *always* found a way to light it.

"Thanks. Tell him I'm sorry too and I'll give him a shout in the near future." He nodded and we left.

During the next month I got to where I felt I was good enough to play my guitar at the Stadium; maybe. My last dressing change and final appointment with Frost was coming up and I had decided it was time to speak to him about my dreams. Before I met with him I met with Mary one more time, it seemed now that we were much closer friends than we were patient and nurse although I had never spoken to her outside of the hospital. I asked her for her phone number and, to my surprise, she said yes; pressure was taken off of me with this confirmation that she wouldn't be out of my life forever when I walked out those doors. After that, I met with Frost.

"Alright, Link," he grinned like an asshole and looked at me waiting for a response.

I smiled embarrassed.

"It's Ben." I sort of laughed to myself.

"Yes, I heard you were going by your name now. I was wondering if you wanted to remain an outpatient or if you want to be completely on your own?"

That question made me anxious and Frost knew it.

"You don't need to answer now. At any rate, we will have to set up an aftercare plan for you.

Now, this may be a silly question, but do you plan on working?"

That was my opportunity. I told him I wanted to get a job and went on to tell him all about my plans to continue as a musician and it appeared to me that he had already been informed. He set me up for medical employment insurance and let me know that if I had decided to get a job to let them know promptly.

After all the paperwork for aftercare and medical E.I were signed he let me know of a venue where I would be able to audition for him and Cal, his connection at the Stadium. That night I called Mary and told her about it and asked if she would come. She said she would, of course.

Later in the week, I went to the venue Frost had told me about. I was glad to find there were no pitchers and no crowd. They told me I was to perform two songs and then they would make a decision on whether or not I would be able to play at the Stadium. Mary wasn't there when it was time to perform my first song. Even though I was nervous and a bit disappointed, I didn't let it bring me down. I rocked it and I could tell Cal was delightfully caught off guard, but Frost retained his stone cold expression. At the end of the song I realized Mary was sitting off to the side with her boyfriend. I waved to them and they waved back.

"This one's called 'Street Light From an Angel.'" I was looking right at Mary when I said it and she blushed; she knew it was the song I'd written for her. When I was finished my performance, Frost and Cal immediately began talking.

"Please give us a few minutes, Ben." Frost said professionally.

Mary came up to the stage while I was putting my guitar on the stand and hugged me, kissing me on the cheek; my heart was hammering on my chest cavity like it was building a house in Kenya.

"Wow, Ben, wow. I'm so proud of you." She hugged me and looked down at my stub that was now my organic guitar pick. "You've come so far! I-"

"Ben," Cal came up to the stage. "I like your music, and you are unquestionably talented, but from what Gary tells me about your condition, I am not willing to put you on my stage." He may as well have stabbed me in the heart with an icicle; I thought *Frost* was cold.

Mary looked over at me with sad eyes, unsure of what my reaction would be. Frost was standing beside him.

"But Gary would like to have a word with you - it's his judgment call to make."

I could tell by the look in Mary's eyes that she had faith that Frost would let me go up, she knew him better than I did.

"I'm going to be candid with you, Ben, you have potential-" He thought for a minute and as he was judging my music with his half British half asshole accent, he reminded me of Simon Cowell. "But you need more. There's something lacking." I knew what he was getting at.

"You need a band Ben, you aren't a solo artist, I'm sorry."

I was trying to put something together in my head fast but Frost gave me an opening.

"Do you think you'll be able to find some musicians to play with you?" I was hoping he'd smile but he didn't, this was business.

"I *know* I can find musicians."

"In three weeks?"

"Yes." I was still unsure, but my instinct said act now, figure shit out later.

Frost stood thinking for a moment.

"I can't let you play your own show at the Stadium."

I could feel my lungs getting smaller. I looked over at Mary who still contained hopeful eyes and then back at Frost.

"But I can let you open for mine."

I couldn't believe my ear. Mary registered the information before I did and began hopping happily and celebrating while I stood in shock. Without thinking, I held out my stub to shake Frost's hand and he shook it.

"I know you won't let me down." He said with a wink. That crafty, crafty old bugger. He seemed like he could be a character straight out of a story or something.

After Frost left, I had coffee with Mary and her boyfriend Todd. They informed me about Frost's band and explained the reputation they had. Apparently Frost's band had gone on a few cross country tours and had four albums out. They were bigger before Frost got his doctorate, but played at least once a year and always had a huge turnout. They were a Christian rock band called *Peace of Heaven*. I'd heard of them but never listened to their music before that night, and they were actually pretty good.

The next day I called a meeting with Higgins and Red. It started off a little awkward because Red and I had still not patched things up in person, but I had to act fast. We sat in Higgins' basement where we used to jam; it looked completely different not hazed by smoke. You could actually see the posters of *The Doors* and *Pink Floyd* and *Iron Maiden* clearly. I appreciated that they had probably let it air out and weren't smoking in there for my sake.

"Guys, I gotta cut right to the chase."

Few words were spoken before this. They both looked at me intently.

"Have you ever heard of *Peace of Heaven*?"

Red scoffed but Higgins wanted to see where I was going with it.

"They're that bible pushing band right?"

"I've heard of them."

"They want me to open for them at the Stadium." Higgins instantly got up and went in for a hand shake.

"Fuckin' eh! Way to go man!"

"Are you serious?" I could tell Red was jealous but also disgusted that I'd be collaborating with Christians, even though he knew I believed in God.

"But I've got one problem." They both knew what I was going to say. "I need a band." Higgins withdrew his hand but now Red seemed a bit more interested.

"Shit man, I'm already so busy with *Discard Death*."

I had expected them both to mention their bands, but I thought Higgins would be eager to help.

After Higgins put that out there Red's interest diminished.

"Me too, with *Inside You,* I mean." I forgot to mention Red was original too.

"You renamed the band, huh?"

"Yeah man, I didn't want any tension between us."

I'd put down money on him continuing to use my lyrics. I couldn't let that bother me, not now.

"I'll write all the music, all you guys need to do is practice with me. It's in three weeks, so we'd have to jam more often than not, but I promise it will be worth it. You can even wear your band T-shirts during the show. Please?"

"Fuck it, I'm in." Higgins looked over to Red expectantly.

He stood looking at us like we were trying to shoot apples off of his head with exploding arrows.

"Shit Link, you know I'd go to Hell and back for you, but *Heaven*?"

The apple stare continued until finally he pulled out a coin. He flipped it then caught it, putting it in his pocket without looking at the result.

"I'm in."

I felt like my whole life was riding on that moment, and I got the ideal result. We'd reformed our long lost brotherhood.

In a weeks-time we had everything memorized and sounded great. Everything else after that was just practice. Come show time, we knew we'd be ready. We agreed to keep the name *Within You*, Red said his band wouldn't mind, but I doubted he asked permission, it didn't seem to be his style.

Everything was coming together like that *Beatles* song.

"Wake up man. Fuck, wake up! What do we do man, shit, do we call an ambulance?"

I started waking up. I was a mess, I was a fucking mess. Backstage of the show, hearing an enormous crowd talking and laughing made my skin rise, bubble and simmer. I could hear and feel all of my hair singeing and shriveling back to my face. I was covered in pounds of cold sweat and I felt like throwing up; and man did I ever throw up. I couldn't go on stage; I hadn't been on stage in a year to date.

"Come on Link we practiced too hard, our future is on the other side of the curtain! We were supposed to be on two minutes ago."

"Shut up Red, you don't know what he's going through." I could finally see properly and I sat up.

"I need water."

Higgins ran somewhere to fetch me a bottle.

"Just remember that somewhere in the front row is that nurse you have a crush on." I thought about it; I couldn't let her down. I couldn't let myself down.

"How many people are here?"

"Last I heard, ten thousand thirty five." Jesus Christ.

"Here's your water! Throw er back man, if we're gonna get out there we gotta do it now!" I slammed the water back and held my left arm out.

"Fair enough. Help me up."

They both supported me as I got to my feet and we made our way onto the stage and as we did, ten thousand people began cheering. I felt like a used stick of dynamite. I tried to stay in the moment but couldn't. I could see the milk jug of gasoline beside the amp, the pitchers, the crowd, the blisters, the boils, the fire, the pain, the - I was going to be sick again.

Then I saw Mary smiling in the front row, and the sound drowned out. All I could feel was Mary hugging me and kissing me on the cheek, all I could hear was her saying "I'm proud of you, you've come so far."

Higgins sat up at his drums and waved the audience to calm down and slowly but surely they did. I grabbed the microphone and looked out at the ocean of invisible faces attached to bodies of shadow, then back at Mary. Then, it was quiet. Ten *thousand* people were waiting to hear me speak.

"Hey everyone, this song's -"

The microphone screeched. My stage presence and charisma had disappeared with my hair and face. What were all these people thinking? Were they silent because they wanted to hear me speak or because I was hideous?

"I call it -"

I couldn't think about that. I looked back down at Mary.

"I call it 'Street Light From an Angel!'"

The crowd must have sensed I was nervous; if there were crickets they'd be beating the shit out of my ear drum. Even Mary looked worried. I forgot to give Higgins and Red my cue.

Higgins screamed into his mic.

"Ladie's and gentlemen! WE-ARE-*LINCOLN'S ON FIRE*!" Higgins screamed into his mic The crowd went wild, and this time it didn't bother me. I was too overwhelmed by power and, as I waslooking into Mary's mesmerizing eyes, Higgins tapped his thimble, giving Red and I the cue.

That night, we set the stage a blaze. We rocked the Stadium, the crowd absolutely loved us. I wasn't even thinking while I was playing but I could feel those butterflies crawling down my cheeks. I wasn't playing for fame and fortune, I wasn't playing for the audience, I wasn't playing for the love of music, I wasn't playing for Mary, I wasn't even playing for myself -I was just living my life.

10

CASEY

Four days is what it took me to write 'Lincoln's on Fire', and on the fifth day I gave it to Kelsey.

Midterms were coming up so she asked me to give her some time to read it; it had since been a week. During that time, I managed to find my way back to the public washroom on the third floor of the mall on 3rd street every day after work, anticipating my next meeting with her. Today was that day.

The Fifth floor staff didn't know I was drunk when I'd come back, or didn't care. Often times I would come back around midnight when most of the floor was asleep so I wasn't 'triggering' anyone, and I'd show them my hour sheet explaining I worked the evening; lies.

Through the first week I only made one friend on fifth floor besides my roommate Sergei, his name was Vince; a very, very old self-proclaimed doctor from Vienna. His accent was thicker than the Earth itself, so I had to pay close attention when he spoke. I'd play chess with him once in a while, one game here, two games there.

We'd probably played about a dozen games and he beat me every time. Over the course of the last two weeks, Patrick and Tukahoot were nowhere to be seen, I presumed they made it to Vancouver.

Today, almost like déjà vu, Geo said with a certain look in his eye "Sit down and we might be able to get you some work, *later*."

I was out of money again and was determined to work today so I'd have some cash for the weekend for *cigarettes*. The office was packed today and I was unable to find a place in Geo's line of site, so instead I took a seat near the back. There was a woman sitting across from me who I recognized from the DI, she was relatively new. Due to her incredibly fine posture, constantly darting eyes and consistent look of paranoia, I gave her the nickname 'Knife Lady'.

Her purse was always sitting on her lap and most of the time she had one hand inside of it. My assumption was that she didn't have friends because she was always with different groups of people and, if she ever did sit by herself, her back would be pressed against the wall. Gauged her to be in her mid-thirties, not many wrinkles, but crow's feet from lack of sleep; I didn't take her for a substance user. Her hair was greasy and black, pulled back in a ponytail, and she wore a long army green jacket.

A small old man sitting next to us could see her slaughtering him out of the corner of her eye.

"Do they know you're here?" He asked her in a friendly voice, referring to that rule of thumb of making your presence known.

"Do I look fucking stupid!?" Knife Lady shouted as he cowered. "I was one of the first ones here this morning!" There was a stress of abuse and injustice to her voice.

I could tell he wanted to explain to her what he meant, but she hurt his feelings. She was offended that *he* thought she was stupid because she's a *woman*, and also that she's not going to get work because she's a woman. The old man was right though, if she'd made her presence known she'd most likely get work, she was in better condition than almost everyone else in there; myself included.

I can't sit here anymore, I thought after about an hour, *there must be dry cigarette butts somewhere.*

I walked for an hour or so, unable to find anything but snow soaked butts. Walking up and down Hobo central more than once, I built up the nerve to ask someone for a cigarette. Yes, I've asked for smokes before, but not while homeless. I was always too embarrassed, expecting immediate rejection.

Near the library, I spotted a chubby man wearing a suit and noticed he was smoking a cigarette.

Casually, I moved towards him.

"Hey man, I'm really sorry to ask, but do you think you could give me a smoke?" After a quick inspection he promptly pulled out his pack.

"Oh, sure," he said with a pinch of pity. It looked like he was going to give me more than one, but he just pulled one out with a smile.

"Thanks a lot, man!"

"You're more than welcome."

As I walked to the DI, I reviewed my past interaction with Plebs, and realized I'd had very little. Besides the French woman and the guy that just gave me the smoke, I'd only encountered passerby's staring. I wasn't about to force any interaction with Plebs, but I came to the conclusion that perhaps I shouldn't be so closed off towards them either. *They're people too.*

As soon as I got back to the DI, I went down to volunteer in laundry. Right now, Ester was the only one down there, but it was still early. Once Al pulled a fresh batch of laundry out of the dryer Ester and I went to folding and Al went upstairs to find some more volunteers.

"So *where* have *you* been this week?"

"Working."

"Ah! Did you talk to that young lady about the story you wrote for her?"

"Tonight!" I replied with a giddy smile. For some reason I'd told Ester about Kelsey, but I left out her name and the fact she was a DI employee.

"I'm *very* excited for you! I would like to read the story if I may."

"Sure, I just need to get it printed off. I told her she could keep the copy I gave her."

"There's no rush."

Al came in with a shrivelled old man I'd never seen before. He was wearing a baseball hat and glasses.

"Jim! It's been *too* long since you've come down to volunteer!"

Jim shrugged as he walked over to the bread table to make some toast.

"Weyall, I wouldn't say *that*. Hyah hyah hyah hyah hyah!"

"You haven't seen Ralph anywhere this morning have you?" Al asked Ester.

"*Nooo* I *haven't*! I *did* see *Wade*. *He's* not doing very well; I don't think he'll be down here anytime *soon*."

"I talked to Wade." Al gave a confirmation nod as he turned toward the elevator.

"What's wrong with Wade?" I asked her.

"Wade suffers from *depression*; I won't speak *much* on it without him here. He's just been feeling a little *down* lately. If you're a writer you should talk to *Wade*. Now *there's* a story!"

"Oh yeah?"

"Oh *yes*. *Oh*, all the death; all the loss. Such a sad, *sad* story. I have *very* much respect for Wade."

"I'll have to talk to him."

Jim rinsed his plate off in the sink before walking over to join us.

"I don't know if it will help with your book on the *homeless,* but it certainly *is* a story!"

"A book on the homeless!? Who's writing a book on the homeless!?"

Ester made a motion towards me with the sheets she was holding and Jim looked at me.

"*You* are!?"

With a grin I gave him a nod.

"Well keep *me* out of it! Hyah hyah hyah hyah hyah!"

"No promises!"

"If I ever see my name written anywhere, boy, let me tell ya." He tilted his head towards me and gave me a serious look.

"Maybe I don't want you in my book *anyway*!" I said playfully, he came off to have a good sense of humor.

"Oh, trust me, *I'm* the guy you want in your book."

"Why's that?"

"I've lived at the DI for over twenty five years."

"*You're* the guy!"

"Hyah hyah hyah! I'm the guy, that's me, hyah hyah hyah!"

"I thought you were a legend."

"Who says I'm not?" We all laughed. "So a book on the homeless eh? What are you going to write about?"

"Well, I think there's definitely discrimination towards the homeless, but I think the homeless are just as bad for it."

"You try to get a job here yet?"

"Just temp labor."

"Put the DI's address on your resume, go hand a few out then come back and tell me that."

"I might give it a shot actually, that might be interesting."

"If you're living at the DI and you're looking for a job you're better off using a friend's address or getting a PO box."

"Hmm."

"What else?"

"Addiction is unquestionably one of the bigger issues."

"Uh-huh. And what else?"

Maintaining a grin of fascination for the guy, I once again remembered *I don't really know what I'm doing.*

"You're missing half the issues here, kid! Mental health, addiction, abandonment. Ugh, the sex trade."

"Well that's the thing though, people just throw it all into a pot and call it a problem but there's a lot more going on under the surface. It's a mess."

"A *big* fuckin' mess."

"I was surprised to learn the government has nothing to do with the shelters, despicable really. I think it's pretty cool that we run on donations; restored my faith in humanity a little bit."

"Yeah, well don't let it."

"What do you mean?"

"All the donations come from big corporations that haven't spent all their money from their budget yet so they throw it all into the DI or some other charity and call it a tax write-off."

"Seriously? There's gotta be other people that donate."

"Weyall, maybe a hundred dollars here, a thousand dollars there. But the big donations, the one's we are able to run off of, are all tax write-offs."

"Huh."

"Do you know how much it costs per person at the DI per *day*?"

"How much?"

He smiled because he didn't know.

"A *lot*."

We continued folding for a few minutes while I think he was hashing out good information for me and I was writing out a list of questions for him.

"Why does everyone go to Vancouver?"

"Why *does* or why *did* everyone go to Vancouver?"

"Both I guess. A lot of people I've met here who got out left for Vancouver."

"Weyall, that's where ya go if ya wanna live on the street! Hyah hyah hyah hyah!"

"Why *did* everyone go to Vancouver?"

"You ever heard of Expo eighty six?"

"No."

"In nineteen eighty six they evicted a whole section of Vancouver for *tourists* during the world fair and, long story short, we have modern day east Hastings."

"I've seen a few documentaries on Hastings, but why would people go to Vancouver because of that? That's a reason *not* to go if you ask me."

"A lot of the people they evicted were on welfare or disability, so they offered two thousand dollar cheques to everyone who was evicted. Weyall you know how people are, soon as they heard that they came runnin'."

"You can't get that *now* though, can you?."

"No, now it's just because Hastings is what it *is,* and Vancouver's one of the richest cities in the world. People who panhandle in Vancouver could make a fortune if they didn't spend all their money on drugs! Hyah hyah hyah hyah hyah!"

"You ever do drugs?"

"You a cop? Hyah hyah hyah! No not particularly. Experimented, but what kid doesn't."

"*I* never did drugs," Ester joined in.

"Oh pff, you're high right now."

"No I'm not! I haven't even went outside today!"

I thought eventually David would show up, but the only other volunteer who came down was a young girl who was there to work off a speeding ticket or something, and since she was an outsider we put our conversation on hold.

We were eating our lunch on Fifth when Jim asked "Have you met Joel yet?"

"I don't think I have."

"Oh, I bet you have," he said, "I bet you know who he is." Jim saw my confusion and added, "Twitch."

"Yeah I've seen him around. I didn't know his name was Joel."

"Not many people do. But they all know *Twitch*. You want this?" He held his plate out to me and I grabbed the piece of pizza that didn't have a bite out of it. "Tastes like cardboard. I'll stick to my soup. But *Joel*, yeah. Interesting character, Joel."

"Why?"

"Weyall, he got abandoned here by his brother."

"Wow, really?"

"Hard to say. All I know is he came here two years ago with his brother and his brother's girlfriend when he was seventeen, they're not here *now* but *he* is."

"That's pretty sad."

"No, that's not sad," he said, "that's *life*. People are fucking horrible. Hyah hyah hyah hyah hyah!"

After lunch, Al decided to fold bundles to help us catch up and Ester left not too long after that. Homer showed up early again and, for the first time to my knowledge, there were *two* Dice *working* in the laundry room; and the God's were cheering. Folding of epic proportions took place.

"Michael, how ya doin' bud, is everything goin' good?"

"Yeah I'm good, how are you doin' Homer?"

"Oh I'm doin' good bud. Keepin' sober?"

"Trying. I've been slipping up a lot lately."

"Oh well, it happens eh, come down here any time. You're a good kid eh, we don't want anything bad happening to you. It's not all that exciting down here but at least it'll keep you out of trouble."

"Yeah I might come down more often. Planning to get work tomorrow though, I have no money. I've been dying for smokes."

"Oh you don't have smokes? Would you like to go for one?" He asked holding one out to me already.

"Sure."

"Homer, do you mind if I take off when you get back down?" Al asked. "It's my son's birthday today."

"Oh shit, he's not gonna be my age anymore!"

"No, no, my other son." He reassured me. "I still have a son your age." When we got outside I noticed Homer seemed angry about something for once.

"What's up?"

"Oh, the stupid DI. Well, not the DI here, the storage warehouse."

"What happened?"

"Oh, I went to go pick up my bed and some other stuff, eh. Went with a ticket sheet I got from one of the counselors and they told me they didn't have any beds and that's not true, eh. I used to work at the storage warehouse." He shook his head. "I think he was being rude to me because I was wearing my staff vest, but I lived here for three years I deserve a bed, eh."

"Yeah you definitely do. You should talk to someone, I'm sure there's someone who can help you out."

"No, I hate people, eh, people suck; I'm not good talking to em."

"I've considered you pretty good with people in the time I've known you."

"Thanks, eh, that means a lot to me."

"I never would have thought you hated people."

"Not all people, eh, just the bad ones - but there are a lot of bad ones. People just exclude people, eh. The world's just a lonely place for some people. I don't take rejection very well, eh, that's why it took me so long to even go there for a bed. I've had the ticket for two or three weeks now."

"I don't take rejection well either. Actually, I just asked a random person for a smoke the *first* time today since I've been homeless."

He puffed on his smoke while nodding his head with a smile.

"I was like that too. Before I heard about the DI, I was homeless for months. Never asked anyone for help, eh, not even smokes or food. Sold my car just so I could go get somethin' to eat."

"How did you hear about the DI?"

"Kind of a funny story, actually. It was a few days after I'd spent all the money I got from my car and I hadn't eaten anything, eh, so of course anything looks good. I saw half a sandwich on the sidewalk and picked it up off the ground and started eating it." He smiled to himself. "This one couple was grossed right out but it was actually a homeless man who came over to me and said 'You know where there's a place you can get some free food, eh?' Been here ever since, well, until I moved out."

When we got back down Jim was holding up a really nice tool belt. "Lookin' for work!? Hyah hyah hyah hyah! Ask and you shall receive!" He tossed it over to me.

"This is a carpenters belt. That's actually what I did before I started my company." It fit nicely.

"Must be a sign, eh. You can take it if you want, hopefully no one comes looking for it! Oh uh, you need a hammer?"

"Sure!" Homer rummaged through the lost and found and pulled out a brand new hammer with the price tag still on it. *Stolen?*

I looked through after and grabbed a tape measure but there wasn't much else of use. As I got ready to leave I crammed it all into my backpack. "Thanks a lot guys, that's awesome."

"You're gonna be out of here in no time bud, I know it."

"Thanks Homer." I checked the time and it was around three thirty. "I need to meet someone, can you let me upstairs?"

"You bet!" Homer said as we walked to the elevator. Walking backwards, I thanked Jim for the stories and said I hoped to see him around. Homer gave me three smokes before sending me up to Second. I saw Kelsey when I got upstairs but I snuck out onto the deck to have a smoke and un-spike my nerves before talking to her.

"Hey," I said sneaking up beside Kelsey.

"Hey!" Sparkling eyes.

"Did you read it?"

Her face already told me the answer. "Yes, it was amazing. I can't believe you wrote that in four days. Did you already know all that stuff about burns or…?"

"I did a bit of research on the first day."

"You're so talented. I really think Lincoln's on Fire could be novelized."

"Maybe. Honestly I just wrote it for you. Besides Scarves and Spaceboots, I doubt I'll attempt to write another book. I'll continue writing short stories but the dream is to direct my screenplays. Scarves is just something special."

Swaying a little, she went through a list of questions in her head similar, I thought, to the way I did with Jim.

"I was wondering, why was the doctor the one who came through for him in the end?"

"I'm really not sure actually, it just kind of happened. Guess I wanted to put out a positive image of doctors in there, since I'm not the biggest fan of them. Tried to keep it positive."

"Who's he based on?"

"A doctor I had in a psych ward. That guy was a good doctor."

One by one, she asked who the rest of the characters were based on and, when there was only one left, nurse Mary Dawn, she stopped and blushed. I didn't want to tell her; I thought she knew.

Suddenly there was a loud crash and we both looked over to see a man nearby convulsing. Kelsey stepped in front of me trying to block my view, but I could see the whole scene right beside her head. She tried to distract me with conversation and I humored her because I simply wanted to talk to her, but most of my attention was on the convulsing man.

Eventually the crowd around him got bigger and I couldn't see him anymore. Paramedics got there about ten minutes later and took the man out on a stretcher. All the people that were originally around him were crying and holding each other tightly. *Did he die?*

A few minutes after that, the live band started, giving me the indication I had to catch the bus to 2907. I told her I was going to go but I'd talk to her tomorrow and she stared back at me, smiling "What?" Getting lost in her eyes seemed appropriate.

"Do you remember your promise?"

"Don't kill myself for two weeks?"

"Yeah, that was how long ago? A month?"

"Around that, a few weeks at least."

"You seem a lot happier. Writing really is your passion, hey?"

"That's part of it."

"Keep writing! You write very well and it makes you happy, that's a great tool to have."

***

Standing in line, I remembered I had a bed on Fifth; *I don't need a ticket to 2907.*

"Read your story." Lee said before I got out of the line.

"Oh yeah? What'd you think?"

"Hrm, it was good! Just like a book! Gimme another one!"

"I'll try to get one to you, but it might be hard, I'm on Fifth now."

"The fifth floor!? Movin' on up! Yes."

We shook hands and I tried to go back upstairs to talk more with Kelsey but was blocked by a Dice that said something like 'We're serving dinner right away, go stand in line and wait for a meal ticket.'

In an attempt to sneak up anyway, I told him I had a room on Fifth, but he said I had to take the elevator up, then escorted me to the elevator doors. *Next conversation with Kelsey will have to wait.* I ate dinner watching TV with the old guys, but sat by myself. After I had a smoke, I saw Vince on the way to my room and stopped.

"Hey Vince."

"We play chess?"

"Not now, maybe later."

"Later, we play chess later." Vince, although very old and possibly senile, had a sharp look in his eye. I actually believed he was a doctor, but there was no way to prove it.

Piece posted up in front of our room on a chair. He was heavy-set and usually wore his trucker hat so that it covered his eyes, not that they hid much. There was a particular emptiness to them that gave me the willies. At first, I thought he looked friendly, but the first time I looked into his eyes, I saw an innuendo in them that told me: *this guys gotta be homicidal.*

"Pieeeece of shit!" He shouted as I got in the room.

Since the first time I met him I had to set my laptop up a specific way so he wouldn't get mad at me and his preference seemed to change daily. Piece shared the bunk with me; we'd had a couple run-ins but nothing major. There would just be really minor things, like me having my bin sticking out from under the bed or my laptop cord hanging over a sliver of the space between our beds and he'd yell at me. Sergei filled me in right away to take him with a grain of salt; that he's not *all there.*

When a Dice walked around the corner followed by a husky middle-aged African guy, I sat up to greet him.

"Alright Mando, this is going to be your locker here," he said unlocking it. Then he pointed at the bunk under Sergei's. "That's your bed there."

Mando came in with the demeanour of a sad puppy dog, so I slid to the edge of the bed and, when he turned in my direction, I stuck my hand out.

"Hey man, I'm Michael."

He smiled a big white smile, his eyes lit up and he shook my hand. "Michael! I'm Mando, pleased to meet you!"

"Let me know if you need anything Mando, I'll be in the office." The Dice said.

Mando waved him off and turned back to me.

"Yo so yaoung Maike! What are you doing here?"

"I ran a company into the ground." There are only so many ways to say it.

Mando blinked his eyes a few times like he was impressed.

"Will you try again?"

"Maybe."

"You *have* to Maike! You see, failure is part of de process. Without failya, you cannot achieve *success*!"

"That's what they say."

"I'm telling you! Maike, listen to me. I've been trying to run my own business since I came to *Canada*, and I'm *still* struggling! Look! I'm *here*! With *you*!" He put his bags down and took his jacket off.

"Where you from?"

"Central Africa, but I lived in Montreal for ten years."

"What do you do?"

"I'm a web designah."

"Oh yeah?"

He talked my ear off about this *thing* he had going on and how he could teach anyone to do it, to the point that I thought he was leading into an attempt to recruit me into a pyramid scheme, but he didn't directly ask me to jump on-board.

After literally three hours or so of listening to him he stopped and sat down on his new bed. I went out for a smoke and when I came back he was sitting in the same place with a big smile and looked over at me like he had something else to tell me.

"Maike!"

"Yeah?"

"I think God brought us togetha!" *Um.*

"What makes you say that?"

"Because!" He stood up and walked towards me passing an invisible ball in between his hands. "I've been hoping I would find a good *pearson* in the DI. I've been so scared since I got to the DI, I've been *praying* to find someone good."

There are good people all over the DI, I'll introduce you to some." Blinking his eyes a few times again, he continued to smile.

"See! You attracted good people because you're a good pearson, Maike! If you think about good things, good things will come, if you think about *bad* things, *bad* things will come."

"Are you talking about the Law of Attraction, Mando?" He did his blinking thing again.

"You know the Law of Attraction?"

"Yes sir, since I was seventeen." Mando smacked his forehead.

"Maike. That's why we here."

"To discuss the Law of Attraction?"

"No! So I can mentor you."

"I'm really not looking for a mentor, Mando."

"God works in strange ways Maike. I *know* he wanted me to meet you."

"It's possible."

Jumping back up to my bed I figured it was late enough that I could get away with calling it a night.

Piece came in and saw my laptop bag on the ground near the bed and he kicked it across the room.

"Hey don't kick my shit around man!" He didn't say anything.

"You're fucking lucky my laptop wasn't in there." He walked right up to where I was sitting up on the top bunk and was tall enough to get in my face.

"Who the fuck you think you're talking to, bud?"

Piece was easily twice my age but I didn't notice how tall he was until now, he was sitting most of the time. Like I said, looking in his eyes you could tell he wasn't all there; he told me the first time I met him to be patient with him because he had brain surgery twice. I'd tried to be understanding with him so far, but he didn't have a right to damage my property. He retreated from the room and I hopped off the bunk bed and followed him into the common area where everyone was watching TV.

"Hey don't walk away from me, man, we need to talk about this." Piece turned around and got in my face again.

"I don't want to talk to you!" he shouted.

"You don't need to talk to me, but if you ever break any of my shit, it's coming straight out of your pocket, bud."

Piece took off, but now everyone was staring at me so I got out of there too. An older man, who I wouldn't have guessed lived at the DI if I saw him on the street, caught me on the way to my room.

"What happened?"

"He kicked my laptop bag across the room. It wasn't a big deal, but if my laptop was in there it would have been toast!"

"Yeah don't let him push you around, a lot of people have had problems with him. He should be in a mental institution, that guy. My name's Garrett."

"Michael."

"Let me know if you need anything, alright?"

"Alright."

Garrett went back to watching TV and I went back to my room, Mando was standing there with a smile, blinking repeatedly.

"Maike! Why did you lose your patience so quickly?"

"Had problems with him before. I'm a writer and all of my writing is on my laptop, I'd be really choked if I lost it all."

"Let me tell you something Maike. I used to be like you, filled with a great deal of anger."

"I'm not an angry person." I shot back. He put his hands in the air.

"Okay!" He smiled. "*I was* an angry pearson. I would get so mad at things people would do, but one day I heard something and do you know what I heard?" Annoyed, I sat back up in my bed.

"What did you hear Mando?"

"That God stands before me in every human being. Now, no matteh how much a pearson annoys me, no matteh what a pearson *does* to me, I will *not* stop loving *them*." *Deep.* "Do you know why?"

"Why?"

"Because God is within them and God would nevah disturb my spiritual temple." Convinced, I gave him a nod of approval. *What a commendable way of life.*

"I really respect that Mando, but I'm different than you and shit like what that guy just did disturbs the fuck out of my spiritual temple. I need to work in the morning so I need to go to bed, but it was good to meet you."

"Wehking? Tomorrow?"

"Yeah."

"Wheh?"

"Just this temp labor place."

"What time? I'll come with you."

"Four thirty is when I'm waking up, they open at five thirty but I try to be there early."

"Fouwa thehty? I need more sleep than that tonight Maike." *Good.*

"Well if you're not working tomorrow you should get some volunteer hours in."

"Yes! Volunteeya houwas! I was thinking maybe the kitchen."

I shook my head "Check the laundry room, it's really good down there for hours. They could use the help right now too." We shook hands again.

"Thank you! I will go to the laundry room tomorrow! How do I get to the laundry room?"

"Just ask one of the staff on second floor in the morning and they'll get you down there." I laid down. "I'm going to bed, night Man."

As I rolled over I heard him sit down, but he didn't move again. *Hopefully he's not just staring at me, he's probably just thinking.* Took me a while to get to sleep, but I laid there as still as possible to avoid more conversation with Mando. *Why does Mando annoy me so much?* There was something about his presence that just pissed me right off, I couldn't figure out if it was some psychological reaction to other people's happiness as a result of living in the condition, or if it was just a juvenile response to people who try to mentor me.

Geo put me on a job the next day, it was even skilled labor. Said I'd need my fall protection ticket which oddly enough was the only one I had. A tall Native and I were squished in the backseat of a tiny car, the driver had his bitch riding shotgun; a purebred German Shepard. The Native guys' legs were so long that one of them was squished right up against mine even though I was pushing my legs into the door. When we got to the job we met two more Native guys who the one I was with seemed to know, one covered in tattoos, the other was young with a ponytail.

Our boss for the day came out with four safety harnesses and dropped them on the ground in front of us. We all started equipping the harnesses, but I couldn't figure mine out. The tall Native I road in with came over and started helping me put it on.

"You've never put on a harness before?" He asked in confidence and irritation.

"It's been a while."

"This guy's a hard ass." He said with a head jerk to the trailer door. "He'd send you home if he seen this."

"Thanks man I appreciate it a lot."

The boss came out looking at a sheet.

"Which one of you is Casey, and which one of you is Mike?"

I looked over at the tall Native and realized not only was he Casey, but he was also the guy that told me Casey didn't want to talk to me. When he looked over with a smirk, I knew he knew it was me the entire time. *Forgiven?*

"Casey." He said putting his hand up.

"Casey, you go with Nathan to zip-tie the tarps. Drew, Mike's gonna be your helper on the roof today."

"You mean I'm in charge!?"

"You've been with us for three months, I think it's time we give you a little more responsibility."

Drew and I spent the morning on a way-too-God-damn-high roof taking down temporary rails along the edge that were set up for the concrete workers. He told me that he and Nathan had been on this site through the temp agency for almost three months and were about to get hired. Also said that the three of them, Casey included, lived at the DI.

"I knew Casey lives there but I don't think I've seen you or Nathan."

"We've seen *you*." He said.

After lunch, Drew and I finished up on the roof then went down to help Casey and Nathan tie the tarps. I had never done it before and I was having a really hard time with it. Casey minded me and tried to teach me a few tricks but I wasn't picking it up as fast as I've picked up other things and I was getting very frustrated because it was a simple task.

"Don't worry kid you'll get the hang of it," Casey assured me.

We were all spread out across the scaffolding, I was farther than the other three listening to their friendly conversation.

"You don't talk much hey?" Nathan said looking over at me.

"He probably doesn't understand what we're saying. Hey come speak Indian with us!" Drew called out.

We all laughed and I went over and joined them, though I still didn't say much. When our shift was over, we cashed our cheques and walked back towards the DI together. Drew's plan was to go to the casino; Casey and Nathan were going drinking. Both parties invited me, but I declined; I wanted to make it back in time to see Kelsey. If it had been a week day and Kelsey was not working perhaps things would have been different. Unfortunately when I got back to the DI, Kelsey wasn't able to talk because she was working in the second floor office. After a brief conversation we agreed we'd try to talk the next day.

After dinner on Fifth, I smoked a cigarette and when I came in was invited to a game of chess I couldn't refuse; Vince had already set it up. We played two games, and I lost both times. *Vince 14; me 0.* Don't get me wrong, I wasn't bad at chess, Vince was just very good. I did beat him however on our third match; I checkmated him with most of our pieces on the board still. It surprised both of us; it was really more of a fluke than anything. Vince stared at the game for half a minute.

"I won!" I shouted shocked.

"We go back."

"Go back?"

"Yes, yes, we go back." Reaching his hand out to the piece I just played, he grabbed it and rearranged the pieces more or less accurately to where they had been two or three moves back. "There, there."

"Alright."

We continued from there and he counteracted my checkmate and beat me, then lectured me on what I did wrong in the match.

"Well thanks for the game Vince."

Heading back to my room I saw Sergei at the doorway, it looked like he'd been watching from a distance.

"You won, ah?"

"Yeah. Well, kind of."

"What'd he do?"

"Moved us back and beat me."

He nodded with a smile on his face.

"That's what he does. That's why no one plays with him."

"Aw, really? He said he doesn't play with anyone because no one else is a good enough chess player to give him an exciting match."

"Ha! Say's that to everyone, sorry kid."

We talked for a little while and then Mando came back. After they introduced themselves,

Mando told me about his day in laundry, I guess he liked it. Then he went on to repeat almost everything that he said to me the day before; word for word like it was scripted, it was even taking up the same amount of time.

He picked up on my irritation I think because he pried about it and I told him I just didn't like hearing the same things repeated and he apologized, saying he doesn't mean to do it. But then proceeded to do it though, for another two hours, until I called it a mock early night again.

The frustration Mando was causing me made me regret leaving 2907. *I'll get used to him.* I thought. *Mando's a good person, he's just too much for me right now.*

I didn't get much sleep that night because Piece didn't have to work. For hours, while Mando, Sergei and I were trying to sleep, Piece was yelling profanities, mostly 'Pieeeece of shit!', and when he did finally fall asleep, he woke up and told Mando to 'Turn that fucking music off!'.

Out of the curiosity of not hearing anything, I looked over to see if Mando was even listening to music. He was, and instead of holding his ground on his music that was cranked to three, he smiled with a nod and turned his music player off and just sat in the dark in silence for the rest of the night.

Why do I hate him?

11

CORNERSTONE

Jim was right, after close to a full two weeks of job searching I'd come up empty handed. Not only did I have a solid resume, but I actually landed four interviews. Even got a haircut after the second interview because there was a comment made during the first one, I also stopped hauling my travelers backpack around and took up the one Donald gave me. In my opinion all four interviews went extremely well, however, when I mentioned I was living at the DI, as I thought necessary for my *experiment,* they all said the same thing; "We'll call you."

I managed to get a few days of temp labor in over that period of time and, as you may have guessed, I didn't manage to save a cent. Besides that, the only constant remained the anticipation of seeing Kelsey on the weekends.

It was April already, and it was a Saturday. *Most guys my age must be out meeting women, spending their hard earned money. Maybe they're still at work, maybe at a camp up north.*

Me? I was sitting on the 6th floor of the Mansion enjoying some coffee and cookies provided by a Dice whose side-passion is to give lectures on our society's waste of fossil fuels and energy. Only occupants of Forth and Fifth were invited, only ten of us showed up. A few said they were just there for the snack but during the lecture these Hobos showed their true colors; strong compelling opinions and ideas and views, not just that, but a majority who spoke up offered thoughtful solutions. Besides what I learned from the slideshow presentation, I didn't know enough about the subject to contribute to the conversation, but listening to the back and forth between the Hobos and the instructing Dice was remarkable. When he was done the presentation he pulled out a petition and asked us to sign it.

"You know I'm really passionate on the subject." One of the Hobos mentioned while signing.

"But what the fuck am I supposed to do? What are any of us supposed to do? *We* don't have a voice."

"Everyone has a voice," the Dice retorted.

"Easy for *you* to say. If I got up in front of a crowd of people I wouldn't have the respect you do, you can't deny that."

"It doesn't happen overnight. You can't give up when no one listens the first time." The Hobo handed the pen to the next guy and stood to the side.

"Well *you're* our voice in this. Because on this piece of paper we're just our names, they won't know we're homeless. If they knew *that,* they'd crumple it up and throw it in the garbage and you know it."

The Dice ignored the man and he left once his two friends signed off on the petition. I was the last one and I told him I thought it was cool that he got the Hobos involved in what he was doing.

"I love doing this here, I try to do it at least once a month." He said. "The support I get from these guys is amazing every time. When I present to other crowds I don't get the same response."

He gave me a couple boxes of cookies to take down to Fifth and we walked down talking about the presentation.

"If you don't mind, I have a suggestion for your presentation."

Disorder was in his eyes and I could tell he didn't take criticism well, but I continued.

"A lot of Hobos read; the ones who would be interested in this kind of thing anyways. If you don't get the same results from 'regular people' it's probably because of the pace. You have a lot of really good information in there but it's delivered so slow. We live in a time where the next great invention is going to be an alarm clock that turns itself off; the generation you're appealing to has the attention span of a house cat. They spend their free time watching movies and listening to redundant vibrations." *He doesn't get it.*

"You know, 'Bwah bwah bwah bwah bwah bwah'" I tried to mimic dubstep.

"I get it."

"If you spiced up your slide show a little bit, or even made a video, I'm sure people would pay more attention to what you're doing, you just need to make it interesting."

By the time we reached the doors of Fifth he was pretty chaffed, I didn't get the impression that he appreciated my advice, but I thanked him for the cookies and wished him luck. When I got in I put the boxes of cookies on the table in the lobby for everyone and went to my room. Mando was sitting on his bed with his big white smile like he was waiting for me, as he often did.

"Maike!"

"What's up, Mando?"

"You said you wah looking for a construction job, raight!?"

"Yeah."

"Framing?"

"Yeah." He held out a piece of paper for me with a name and phone number on it.

"I just saw the ad on Kijiji!" He pointed at his computer with an open internet browser. "It said to call as soon as possible. Call *now* Maike!" *What the hell?*

"You have internet up here?"

"Yes!" He pulled out a new smartphone. "You see, I can create an internet hotspot right *here* off of my phone!" Smacking his forehead, he did his signature blink a few times. "Is that not incredible!?"

"That's pretty cool."

"Look! I'm even wehking on a website for someone!"

Mando clicked over to another tab and showed me a website that was under his construction.

Blew my mind like Paris Hilton on a Friday.

"Maike! I don't know why anyone in Calgary would evah live outside of the DI!" I hoped he was referring to homeless anyone's.

"How'd you afford all this stuff?"

"Temp labah! You see Maike, if you save yowah money -" signature blink - "you can have *anything*!"

He started playing around on his phone. "My boss says I'm the only one that saves his money. Everyone else is always asking for advances *every day*! Can you believe that!? How can someone spend all that money they make in one night!?"

"Yeah, hah! Suckers. I better go make that phone call." *Jerk.*

On my way to the fifth floor public phone, I noticed that all the cookies I brought down were already gone. I made the call and my new boss didn't mind me living at the DI as long as I knew what I was doing. He said I could start on Monday and I wrote down the address he gave me.

When I got off the phone, I saw Vince walking over with the chess board. I sat down to have one of my now occasional matches with him, although I stopped trying to give him my best, knowing he'd never let me win, even if I beat him fair and square. Unfortunately he took my new lack of skill as an opportunity to tell me what I'm doing wrong and how I'm *not as smart as he thought.*

Tonight I was going to beat the bastard. It was a match even the gods could not compete with, a chess-travaganza. He had three pieces, I had four. I was planning my course of action for this pivotal point in our match. Must have taken two minutes, three at most.

"Hurry up!"

"What?" *Sometimes I wait five to ten minutes for this man to make a move; surely he didn't just say what I think he said.*

"Hurry up! Hurry up! I don't have all night, make a move!" *I didn't even want to play.*

Right then I stood up and started walking away and Vince yelled at me, everyone was watching.

Coming up to my room, I saw Mando talking to two of his friends; Carl and Pierre. Carl was a husky Columbian guy who was still learning English. I'd thought he was younger than me, but everyone said he was thirty five - I didn't know if they were serious or not. Pierre was a very tall, very proud French busker in his fifties - he was also teaching Lester to play guitar a little, but Lester only interacted with people one on one. The three were sitting at a table across from my room with plates full of chicken drumsticks left over from dinner that Pierre scored from volunteering in the kitchen.

"Chickon?" Pierre offered as I walked up.

"Sure."

He lifted a plate of chicken from the top of a stack of plates for me to grab one, then put his back on top. After I loaded up my plate Pierre gave me some hot sauce that I doused it all in.

"Thanks."

"Any time, my boy, any time! Just don't you forget old Pierre when you get out of here!" he said with a wink.

"How could I forget *you* Pierre?" I countered, biting into a piece of chicken that had been long massacred and forgotten. Mando and Pierre didn't pay me or Carl much mind as they went on to speak French during the meal. *So this is how you feel huh?* I thought looking over at Carl.

"Michael.. Boots." Carl said before laughing.

"Boots?"

He nodded and I looked down at my fourteens. "Oh yeah, they're pretty big hey?" I made a hand gesture for *big*.

"No. No. You wear, always."

"Yeah, well I don't have anything else really." He pointed at the sandals he was wearing.

"Two dollar."

"Where?"

"Dollar store. Beside um…" He thought for a few moments then tapped Pierre on the shoulder.

"Um, Michael." He made the same hand gesture I did for big. "Boots." Then he pointed at his sandals and Pierre looked down. "I say Dollar store. Um. He wants where."

Pierre leaned in like he was about to tell us some big secret and we all played along unintentionally. "Turn a block east of the TD mall on third street and you'll find the place!" Pierre shouted and we all leaned back.

"You lookin' for a pair of sandals kid? You don't want a pair from the dollar store they'll fall apart on ya in a day or two." He tapped Carl on the shoulder. "How many pairs of those have you gone through in the last month?" Carl thought for a moment then held up four fingers. "See! You may as well just save up and buy a pair from a real store, it'll save you in the long run. *You* work don't ya?"

"Kind of."

"Maike! You worked yestaday!"

"Yeah, I'm bad with money. Coffee and cigarettes." *And alcohol and fucking angel dust.*

"Ah well as long as you live happy." Pierre said as Lester approached bashfully with his hands in his pockets, looking at the ground. Pierre stood up and put his arm around Lester's shoulder. "Maybe you should take up an instrument like ol' Lester here and start busking." Lester smiled big and looked at Pierre with wide eyes.

"I can't start busking *yet*, are you kidding me?" Insecurity had him looking at the floor again. "I just started, I probably won't get *that* good anyway."

"With a teacher like me? You'll do great kid, why don't you grab your guitar and I'll teach you a few things."

"Nah, I already practiced for like *two hours* today." Pierre took his arm off Lester.

"Two hours!? When I started playing guitar I practiced *eight* hours every single day. I've probably practiced for over twenty thousand hours and I'm only *mediocre* compared to some of those old timers out there!"

"Really, eight hours?" Lester shuddered at the thought, but he smiled and said "Well I guess I should grab my guitar!"

He walked off to grab his guitar and Pierre looked back at me to continue the conversation he couldn't remember anything about.

"How much you make busking in a day?" I asked.

He tilted his head in both directions pondering for a few seconds.

"Depends on the day, depends on the season. Today I made seventy dollars."

"Not bad," I said, noticing Vince giving me a death glare as he walked by on his way to put the chess board away.

"For a four hour day!? That's around sixteen an hour! How much do you make in an eight hour day at your temp labor gig, Mando?"

Eighty, sometimes one hundred."

"And you're busting your back! You're getting dirty! You're wasting the good part of your day and hating every *minute* of it! That's why I feel bad for guys like you, underpaid and underappreciated!"

Waving a finger at Mando he continued, "and all those chumps out there wearing their expensive suits, going out at night, driving to work in the morning, buying their lunch!" Pierre kicked his feet up on the table. "Look at it this way; you work in a nice office, your salary's forty two thousand a year." He tilted his hand in the air. "Pretty average. Now you need to budget that so you're getting what, three thousand, thirty five hundred?" He asked Mando who shook his head like he had no clue. "You got a phone don't ya?"

Mando pulled out his phone and they worked out the math.

"Yeah, thirty five hundred a month, so divide that by thirty, what do you get?"

"One sixteen!" Mando replied.

"And that's *before* taxes! So let's say they're getting a *hundred* dollars a day! They pay seven dollars for parking, five dollars for their fancy pants coffee, ten dollars for lunch and let's say ten dollars a day on gas if they're driving."

"Eighty four." Mando answered the unspoken question.

"And then they still might need to pay for groceries, save for rent, if they smoke there's another ten dollars gone, if they drink or do any other drugs-" he laughed, with a nod and a sinister look in his eyes. "They're in trouble! Most of today's society is living cheque to cheque, if they mess up-" He kissed the air. "Good-bye Lamborghini, good-bye house!" *Life.*

"Geez."

"Me? Well I wake up in the morning same time as everyone else, but see I got some time to kill until it's my time to shine." He shrugged and leaned back in his chair even more.

"Well, I take the morning to myself; smoke a doobie, go to Tim Horton's and grab a cup of coffee, maybe read the newspaper for a couple hours."

Taking his feet off the table he leaned back in. "Then, when everyone's on their break, I go to my spot, maybe set up a milk crate or something to sit on, lay out my guitar case, crack it open, dust off the ol' guitar. Then-" He kissed his fingers and let it float into the air. "Music. Ah, well I play to about one o'clock when everyone's off their lunch break, close my guitar case, go grab a cup of coffee, maybe some lunch, smoke another doobie, go *back* out when they're all off work! By the end of the day I still have fifty dollars and I'm clean and stress free!" He proclaimed while standing and waving a fifty dollar bill at us.

Lester came back at that same time, and they walked off to practice in private. I looked at Mando and he smacked his forehead and then waved a finger in the direction Pierre had walked off in.

"He's *good.*"

"No doubt." *Gave me something to think about, that's for sure.*

"I called that number by the way;" I told him, holding up the paper he gave me. "The guy gave me a job, thanks Mando."

My intent was to leave and lay down before he could pester me, but he stood at the same time.

"You see Maike?" He said tapping the side of his head. "I wanted you to get that job and you got that job! You think good things and good things happen. I'm telling you Maike!" I waved to Carl and started walking to my room.

"Good call. I'm gonna call it an early night! Thanks again Mando."

"Maike, laundry tomorrow?"

"You gonna be there?"

"Yes." He nodded.

I don't know how long I'll be able to stand it but;

"I'll probably make an appearance." He waved me off and I laid in my bed reading a book until Mando came in and started playing around on his computer. I fell asleep with the help of a new comfortable quilt I got from laundry but was woken up abruptly around two in the morning when it was ripped off of me. I sat up just in time to see Piece leaving the room, then sat there for a full minute trying to figure out; *did he really just do that?* Leaping out of my bunk in a fit of rage, I followed Piece into the common space. There wasn't a soul around.

"Hey!" I shouted after him in a whisper.

"What!?" Piece shouted back as loud as he could.

"Come here." I whisper shouted again pointing at the ground like an angry parent, and he strolled over like an overgrown over-aged guilty child.

"I didn't do anything!"

"Bull shit you didn't do anything! Why did you rip my blankets off of me?"

"It was hanging off the side of the bed!"

"So? I was sleeping, I didn't know it was hanging over the side of the fucking bed. You don't just rip someone's blanket off like that, what the fuck is wrong with you?"

An older man I called Old Steve, because there were too many Steve's and he was the oldest, sauntered out of his room and over to us.

"Can you guys please be a little quieter? It's really late."

"Sorry." I responded before looking back at Piece.

"We'll talk about this tomorrow." The words were stern coming out of my throat while I walked back to my room.

While I laid my blanket out I thought; *either I'm a very angry person when I wake up or I'm starting to develop a spine.*

When morning arrived I awoke looking into the eyes of a middle aged African man and I noticed Mando didn't look as happy upon awakening as he did throughout the day - in fact, he seemed even more distraught than he did the first night I met him. It wasn't long until he was back to his *too* cheerful self and frustrating me to no end with never ending speculation to my character and his life changing suggestions.

By the time we made it down to laundry I was ready to call it an early night again. It was David, Jim, Mando, Ralph and I. We were working with a young Dice I'd only met a couple times; he was the part-timer who filled in for Al or Homer during the week. We folded for a little while, listening to Ralph talk about how this Dice, Gus, was *just* like Al and took advantage of him.

Then, Mando felt his pocket. He stopped folding and started pacing around nervously.

"What's up Mando?"

He rubbed the back of his head.

"I think my wallet's gone!"

Everyone stopped and looked at him.

"Did you bring it down here?" I asked.

"No, I think I left it in my pocket when I went to sleep last night!"

"Hoo hoo! Boy if you lost your wallet in the DI you can bet you'll never see that again, hyah hyah hyah hyah! You have any money in it?"

"Two hundred and eighty."

"Ew, ouch! Hyah hyah hyah!"

"Well on the plus side, we have cameras on Fifth, if someone there took it, they'll be able to find out who. I wonder if Piece took it?" I accused.

"If someone on Fifth took it, good luck getting them to pay back two *hundred* and *eighty* dollars!" Jim reinforced his point.

"Who's Piece?" David asked and I explained what happened the night before with the blanket,

Mando joined in saying he saw that. After getting myself worked up about the guy I went back to my accusation and Mando's smile came back, and he began *enlightening* me with acceptance of other people's downfalls.

"If he took your wallet are you really going to be this chill about it?"

"I don't *know* that he took my wallet, Maike!"

"Well, he's still a fucking asshole, I hate that guy."

"Maike! Why are you so angry all the time?"

"I'm not angry all the time!" I *was* angry right now though. "I guess you're right, Piece works. But I don't think Sergei would take it."

"No! Sergei would *not* take it!" *Well that leaves me.*

"It's probably still up there."

Gus came back with the thermos of coffee and Mando told him about the wallet situation. Gus asked Mando if he could wait until we went to Fifth for lunch and Mando was alright with it.

I got talking to Gus about my new job and he told me that the DI could hook me up with a program called Alberta Works to get a four hundred dollar cheque for *tools* with proof of work. Apparently all I needed to do was talk to a counselor to get the paperwork, get my boss to sign that paperwork and return it and I could have the money within a couple days. *Sounds good to me.* He made a call to the counselor and got me an appointment for two o'clock, then he gave David and me smokes with no problem, but complained when Ralph asked.

On the smoke deck he explained that he was like Homer, lived at the DI volunteering for a while and they ended up giving him a job. He was also a refugee like Ralph, only from a different country. Gus had notably similar character traits to Ralph as well and, when talking to him, I was reminded of a teenager, this man was completely enveloped in the world of video games. It was all he thought about and all he could really talk about; even to the old guys who obviously didn't care. Donald described Gus to me once as 'the annoying kid that works at the DI and never shuts up about his damn video games.' But I never met him until now.

After lunch when we were all down in laundry there was a silent air as we were giving Mando space to mourn over his lost wallet. It was gone. After a half hour I started going off about how someone could steal *Mando's* wallet, of all people. Even though he annoyed the hell out of me he was still one of the kindest people I'd met during my stay. Honestly I wasn't sure if I was actually mad about the wallet or just trying to get the point across that I didn't take it; though this situation had raised a question in me: *Would* I have taken it? *Two hundred and eighty? Now? Yeah, I would have.* I admitted to myself.

"Maike! It's okay!" Mando tried to calm me down. "It was just two hundred and eighty dollars, it's just mauney! I'll have that back in a week!" He smiled.

"Yeah but that's a week's work of temp work gone, Mando! Whoever took your wallet probably went and got fucked up with the money, *you* wouldn't have. It's just bullshit, you worked hard for that."

"It's just mauney Maike."

"Why am I more pissed off about your wallet than you are?"

"Because you're an angry pearson!"

"I'm not an angry person!" Tossing the bundle I was folding away, I decided to void my Footsink rule and grab a cup of coffee.

"Maike! Relax. It was in God's design for me to lose my wallet."

"No it wasn't."

He blinked at me a few times.

"Maike, you do not know God's design. He is testing me. You see, God would never allow *anyone* to disturb my spiritual temple." He said with a smile.

"I know! You told me that!" I started drinking the coffee and made my way over to the food table to preoccupy myself from looking in Mando's direction.

"Maike if you don't let go of your anger it will control you."

I turned around. "Why do you keep repeating all this stuff? Why do you keep trying to *teach* me things?"

"Because I love you!"

"No you don't! No one does, you don't even fucking know me Man." Everyone was watching me. "Stop it. I don't appreciate it at all." I looked at the time and it was one thirty, I turned to Gus. "I'm going to take off for my appointment if that's cool."

"Go right ahead."

Feeling like the world's biggest jerk, I left to do what I said I was going to do, but first I needed to find a smoke. I headed outside and found Brad riding a skateboard in the parking lot.

"Mikey! What's up? I missed you!" Brad claimed, rolling up holding a few smokes out for me.

I took them and lit one up.

"You remembered my name for once."

"Yeah! I've turned over a new leaf." Then he pulled out a joint. "You wanna smoke a fatty?"

Told him I had an appointment to get to but said I'd smoke weed with him some other time. After the smoke he rolled off to wherever he was going and I went inside to meet with counselor Sean again. Waiting outside his office, I caught the eye of an older man, a bit taller than me with long grey hair poking out from under his toque.

"You don't have any smokes, do ya?" He asked me.

"No, sorry man."

"Ah that's alright, that's alright." Standing beside me he scanned the lobby with me. "How long ya been here?"

"Too long," I replied trying to keep the conversation short after noticing the guy was missing both index fingers. *You don't lose those to an accident.*

"I hear ya. I've only been here for two days now; *this* stay. Just got out of jail last week." *Nice.*

"Oh yeah, what for?" He shook his head like I shouldn't be asking. "Where'd you do your time?"

"BC"

"Better out there than here?"

"No. But at least doing time here first taught me a few tricks for hard time over there."

"Like what?"

"Well for one, you tell em' you're a vegetarian."

"What's that do for you?"

"While all the other guys are eating *surprise* meat, you can count on a nice salad and a big slice of tomato to go with it. Do you know how valuable the nutrients from one slice of tomato like that in prison?"

"Pretty valuable?"

"I can tell a nice kid like you hasn't gone to jail yet. Stay out of trouble kid, or you won't be so nice." He held his hands up to show me he lost his fingers.

"Can I ask how that happened?"

"Pay your debts is how it happened." I nodded.

"I wish there were kids like you while I was in jail! Kids these days have no respect! I asked a kid your age if he could score me a couple doobies and I gave him twenty bucks and the next day at lunch he came by and dropped the doobies in my soup!" Disgust consumed his face. "It's like, 'My ID number is probably the same age as your parents, show some respect! Don't be puttin' doobies in my soup!'"

"No doubt."

Counselor Sean came out of his office following the guy he'd just been counselling and gave me a nod.

"I gotta get going, it was nice to meet you…"

"Eminem," he said shaking my hand. *Strange coincidence.* Cocking an eyebrow I gave him a funny look. *I'm not going to call you Eminem.* "Mushroom man."

I told him I'd see him around and went into the office.

When I got into counselor Sean's office I told him about the job and he gave me the paperwork promptly then asked me a few personal questions; I got the impression Gus may have told him about what went down in laundry. By the end of our conversation counselor Sean gave me a book way out of left field about spirits and the afterlife; I left the office more confused than when I went in and went upstairs to find Kelsey.

"Hey," I said sneaking up beside her.

"Hey."

A sketchy pale guy walked over and stared at Kelsey.

"Hi." She said to him.

"Mistress," he said, "What should I do now?"

She gave me a quick look then looked back over at him.

"How about you go for a walk?"

"I've already gone for two walks."

"Well how about you go for another one?"

"Do you have any smokes?"

"No," she answered, but he wasn't asking her. I held one of the two I had out to him.

"Thank you, sir!"

When he was gone I looked at Kelsey with a grin.

"He's been coming up to me all day asking me what he should do and calling me mistress!"

We both laughed.

"I keep telling him I'm not his mistress and that it doesn't mean what he thinks it means but he doesn't get it."

"Has he done this before?"

"I've never even seen him here before! He says his name is Dave." I smiled.

"There's a lot of Dave's that live here!"

"I know! And a lot of Steve's."

"A lot of Mike's."

"A lot of Andy's." We laughed.

"They're all common names though, I guess. Andy, that's the name of the kid that got hit by a train right?"

She nodded. "I think so."

"I think I met him, but I'm not sure."

"Well," she pointed to the second floor office, "why don't you go check?"

"What do you mean?"

"There's a poster over there for a funeral we're holding for people who have died here since the beginning of January to the end of March."

The poster revealed the faces of *thirteen* people who had died here in the last three months; a few that I recognized too. Andy, a young kid I'd remembered thinking was probably the youngest here.

Once my investigation was over I made my way back to Kelsey. She was talking to that weird guy again. By the time I got back she'd sent him on some other mission and was laughing to me about it.

"So you said he's been doing that all day, eh?"

"Yeah! I traded shifts with someone, I've been here since eight."

"Ah, I wish I would've known that, I spent the whole day in laundry waiting to-" *Talk to you.* "I really want to thank you."

"Thank me? Why?"

"Just now, looking at that poster I realized if it weren't for you, I could have been one of the faces on it."

"I really didn't do much, all I did was listen."

"Well it meant a lot." I looked around. "After I went broke I was planning to kill myself before I had the *genius* idea to come study the homeless. I don't know if you completely understand how hard of a time I was going through when we met, if you weren't around I might have gone crazy. I'm really thankful."

She shrugged. "Well, ya do what you can," she said with an obligatory tone.

We stared each other for a few seconds.

"I got a job!"

"You did!?" She started swaying her shoulders happily.

"Yeah, I'm starting tomorrow. I'm going to be framing again!"

"That's so great. Do you know how much you're getting?"

"We didn't talk about it. He'll probably decide after he sees me work."

"Good for you! Are you finally going to get out of here?" Her tone was hopeful.

We talked about it until it was time for her to leave and, as usual, she told me to come see her next Friday. *I'll be here.* When she left to clock out I got one of the other Dice to let me back down to laundry where Ester, Homer and Jim were chatting. Ester said something about her new landlord when I came in.

"You got a new place, Ester?"

"Oh, *yes.*"

"That happened fast!"

"Well I was browsing for places online and I found a place I could afford, I had the money so I thought 'What the Hell.'"

"Good for you!"

"Hey! Michael! How ya doin' bud? Me and Jim were just going to go for a smoke if you want to join us!" Homer invited while I quickly took the smoke he held out for me.

"Sure, thanks Homer."

"No problem bud, anytime, eh."

"Did you get a copy of your story for me by *chance*?" Ester reminded me before I got to the elevator.

"I did actually!"

It was sitting in my storage bin under my bed. Homer said it would be no problem to go up to Fifth for our smoke so I could grab it. During our smoke Jim spilled the beans that I got a job and Homer was ecstatic for me. On our way back down to laundry Homer let Jim off on the fourth floor, where I guess he stayed, and we went back down to laundry.

To my surprise Ester began reading my story from the moment it touched her fingers and didn't seem to intend on stopping until she was finished. Homer looked at the clock, then checked his watch and looked back to the clock.

"Hey bud it's almost dinner time, do you want me to let you up to Fifth?" An abundance of sheets were yet to be folded.

"It looks like you have your hands full for a change." I stated the obvious.

Frustration showed on Homer's face as he looked around at all the sheets. "I know! It's that Gus, eh? I don't know why he always does this. When me or Al work mornings we never leave it this bad. Generally I don't need to ask people to volunteer in the evening but if you're up for it, you would be a big help, eh."

"Yeah, no problem Homer. I really have nothing better to do." We started folding.

"Well you're more than welcome down here even if it's slow. A person can go nuts spending time up there on Second."

"I could imagine. There're definitely some nuts here."

"Have you ever read Dante's Inferno?"

"No, I've heard of it though."

"Do you know what it's about?"

"Descending the levels of Hell or something, right?" He nodded and laughed to himself.

"Dante has to journey through the nine circles of Hell eh, limbo, lust, gluttony, greed, anger, heresy, violence, fraud and treachery. Well when I first got here I was reading the book, eh, and I got this bizarre idea in my head that I was in purgatory. I would just sit upstairs all day trying to figure out everyone's sins." He laughed in reminiscence.

"That probably took a *long* time."

"It must have been close to a year before I spoke to anyone. I didn't trust anyone, eh, I'd just sit there with my headphones in; I hated the world, eh."

"What changed?"

"One of the staff working here noticed me around and one day asked since I wasn't doing anything if I could help set up for one of the live shows up there." He nodded a few times with a big smile.

"I really like that stuff, I think it's really neat, eh. So I started helping him with that every week and eventually he said 'Hey Homer you seem like a decent enough guy, eh, why don't you get some volunteer hours in and we'll see about getting you a bed.' I'd always just stay in Intox or on Second, I never really bothered with any of that other stuff, eh. Tried volunteering in the kitchen once and I didn't like that, so I came down to laundry and I-" Stroking his beard a few times he said "Well *actually,* I've kind of been down here ever since."

"That's pretty cool man, it sounds like he helped you out a lot."

"Great man, eh, great man. I really respect him a lot. Wouldn't be where I am today if he didn't show me the way, owe him a lot."

"You owe yourself a lot too! You couldn't have done it without *you*."

"Oh." He waved a hand in my direction. "I still have a long ways to go, bud."

"I know but it's the first steps that matter the most."

We folded for a few minutes while Ester turned through more pages.

"How did you end up here anyways, Homer, if you don't mind me asking?"

"Well, used to work as a well tester in the patch, but I got canned. Made a lot of money in my years as a well tester, but I didn't save enough to save myself from falling on my ass," he said solemnly before grabbing his imaginary stomach. "I used to have a belly, eh." He grabbed around his beard. "And I had two extra chins! Lost over ninety pounds in my first year here."

"Did you keep it off intentionally?"

"You know, I don't really know. I'd like to say *yes,* but you know, I really don't think I have an appetite for the food they serve here, eh. Oh that reminds me." He checked the clock, then his watch and the clock again. "Are you hungry bud?"

"Yeah, I could definitely eat."

"Ester?" Homer asked, she didn't answer and he waited patiently.

"Ester?" I said a bit louder.

She blinked and looked up from my story.

"Did you want something to eat before you head out?"

"No, no thank you, Homer I'm just reading Michael's story and then I'll be on my *merry* way!"

Homer went to get some food and Ester returned to the tragedy of Ben Lincoln. After a few minutes Homer came down with a plate of sloppy Joe's and insisted I eat before folding anymore. Ester finished reading around the same time I finished eating.

"*Well*!" She exclaimed.

"You like it?"

"Oh, *yes*! There's a few *hiccups* here and there, but overall what a *wonderful* story, well *done*!"

"Thank you! I'm always open to criticism."

"Perhaps we can go through it together sometime."

"Sure, that'd be great."

"The line-" She flipped through to find the page she was quoting. "'The only quality that outweighed her beauty and kindness was her wisdom.'" She touched her chest. "*Oh*! *Marvelous*!"

"Truthfully I can't completely take the credit for that particular line, I revised it from something a creepy old guy said to my ex-girlfriend one time. I also thought it was magnificent. It's very different from what he said, but I still owe it to him."

"Regardless! You have some *serious* talent. I sure hope this girl appreciates you!" Ester affirmed defensively.

"I'm seeing her on the weekend actually." *It's kind of true* I convinced myself.

"I should hope so! Anywho, I'm *off*!" She jumped up from the counter, handing my story back to me.

"You'll still come and volunteer right?" I asked.

"Absolutely!" Ester marched off with Homer while he thanked her for coming in and told her how much he appreciated her and wished her luck with her new place.

When he came back we folded in silence for only a few minutes before going out for another smoke. Because the Fifth floor was now full of occupants we went out the garage door to smoke in the parking lot instead. We lit up and started checking the environment for conversation topics.

"So during your purgatory, were you on any drugs?"

"Ehhh, I couldn't really afford em' at that time, to tell ya the truth. Could have been withdrawals, I suppose."

"What drugs have you done?"

"Oh, probably everything under the Sun by now, eh. Uh, weed of course, mushrooms, ecstasy, MDMA, cocaine, speed, meth, mescaline, oxycodone, codeine, well a whole mess of prescriptions, oh and peyote. I never did try heroin though, never liked needles."

"What was your favorite?"

"I really liked the peyote but I don't think I ingested it properly, eh. Always wanted to try it again but I'll never try it again *now*." He assured himself. "I really enjoyed my mescaline though, eh. That was probably the drug I got into the hardest."

We stomped our smokes out and went inside to finish folding the blankets.

"What's mescaline like? Like what would you do while you were on it that made it so appealing?"

"It's kind of like being drunk, eh, but you don't get all stupid like you do when you drink. *You'd* probably like it!" His eyes widened. "Don't try it though, eh, bud! I didn't mean it like that - I don't want to encourage-"

"It's cool man, go on."

"When I was on it I really liked looking at old art books."

"Like what? Picasso or something trippy like that?"

"No more like old catholic Roman art, paintings of the crucible and things like that."

"Oh you like Roman history?"

"Roman history's a passion of mine, I could probably go on for weeks."

"I used to really enjoy Roman history myself."

"Who was your favorite Emperor?"

"Ah, I'm not sure, I really don't know that many. I know the most about Augustus and Nero, most of what I know was all about the fall of the Roman Empire."

"Tiberius was my favorite, eh, but Caligula's reign was more interesting."

As much as I'd like to tell you I contributed to a phenomenal conversation, that was where Homer lost me as he dove in and out of B.C and B.C.E. and all across Europe. By the time he was done speaking I'd drawn the conclusion that Homer was quite plausibly the smartest man I ever met, even though I had no idea what he said. The way he spoke of old Rome, it was as if he was there yesterday; like he experienced every second of it first-hand.

We finished folding all of the bundles and blankets and he started going through the day's lost and found bin of clothes, throwing all the clothes in a cart and any backpacks or work equipment off to the side for people to claim. When I reached in to help him he almost had a heart attack.

"No, no, no, no, don't touch that bud!"

He reached to grab my wrist but stopped and looked at his gloves. "You can help but you need a pair of gloves if you're going to go through this stuff. You don't know what's on these clothes, eh, and you never know when you're going to find a needle in here," he said while scoring me a pair from a nearby locker.

"You find needles in the laundry?"

"More often than you'd think."

"That would be terrible to get HIV or something at work just trying to do laundry for some homeless people. People should really be more considerate." Homer shrugged.

"They don't know any better, eh."

"They should, they're grown adults."

"When you're that messed up, you're not thinkin' about that though, eh, all you're thinkin' about is finding a hot meal and a warm place to sleep, eh; and uh, your fix."

"True, I guess."

"I don't mind bud." We finished sorting everything and I followed as he pushed the cart towards the garage door.

"This job's not for everyone, eh, but I can handle it. It's relaxing."

The look on his face said he was excited to tell me a story he knew I wouldn't like.

"One time, on a Christmas morning, I shook out one of the sheets from the dirty laundry because it felt a little heavy and a turd fell out, eh." He laughed.

"Are you serious?"

"Merry Christmas to me, eh?" He continued laughing all the way to a compacter outside near the garage.

"People are ignorant, that's awful."

"It's not that bad."

"It's just the principle of it. It's Christmas, you're stuck here *working* and you have to put up with that shit?"

Homer kept giggling, I could tell he got a kick out of my spunk, so I tried to exaggerate it a little. We got to the compacter and he opened it up and started piling clothes into it.

"This is the only part of the job that bothers me, eh, throwing all the clothes out."

"Yeah that kind of sucks, a lot of people could use these."

"I know! And I just always think,'the life of a shirt, eh?'" He looked at the tag of the shirt he was holding. "Cotton shirt from Thailand. So the cotton from this shirt probably came from Africa eh, got shipped over to Thailand so some kids could sew it into a shirt for dimes, then it got packed into a box with dozens of other shirts, got shipped over here to North America to who knows where to sell it for a hundred times the price it cost them to make. Then someone either bought it so they could donate it or who knows, maybe they just bought it; all so it could be thrown in the compacter eh?" Shaking his head in disappointment he threw the shirt in.

We continued throwing them into the opening.

"That's an interesting way to look at it. Why do we throw them out, anyway?"

"If I remember correctly a volunteer stabbed themselves on something in one of the pockets and sued the DI, or tried to."

"That's bullshit!"

Homer laughed again and we finished off the load of clothes. He shut the compacter door and squished them all down, then offered me one more smoke for the night. We stopped at the garage door to light up. The old man who wore the duct tape shoes was walking in our direction but spotted us and turned away, like he meant to go somewhere else.

Homer pointed in his direction.

"I can't remember his name, but he's an interesting one, eh?"

"Yeah, I've seen him around, never had any interaction with him though." Homer nodded with a smile while puffing his smoke.

"Me either, eh, I just like observing people. We're near his spot."

"What do you mean?"

He pointed at a pile of large rocks near the compactor.

"The rocks?"

"Yeah he collects them, eh, he thinks they're really neat. We always have to get rid of them, eh, it really upsets him."

"That's what he does all day? Just finds big rocks and brings them back here?"

"Far as I know. He talks to them too, eh. He's a curious character."

The two of us watched the man as he watched us in his peripherals, changing his direction every so often so we were never out of sight.

Homer lifted up a big pylon nearby and shrugged. "This used to be a hiding spot, eh. I used to find all sorts of stuff in this pylon."

"That's awesome."

"There's stuff stashed around here everywhere, if you went out and looked hard enough I'm sure you'd find enough goods to throw a party."

He sighed and looked off into the distance and I realized I was sharing a cornerstone of his life, he'd just recently made the first big step to independence and was now taking on a more serious approach to his job as well as his life. I think our conversation was bringing it all back for him in a healthy way.

"I can't even count how many times I drove past this place without giving it a second thought. I didn't even know what it was!" The grin he was wearing became more serious. "Funny how life works eh?"

We finished our smokes and went inside. After I helped him clean up a little bit, we were done for the night. Before he let me back up to Fifth, he gave me a handful of smokes and told me I was going to do great at my new job, *eh, bud.*

When I got up to Fifth it was already lights out. Acknowledging a sad Mando with a nod of the chin as I came into the room, I climbed up onto my bunk to go to sleep, but couldn't help thinking that the day had really flown by. *Maybe if I'd just gone straight to laundry every day after temp labor I would have a lot more to show than blurry night stories.* But that didn't matter now; now I had a new job and, if I could apply the same arithmetic, perhaps I could really think about leaving the condition.

12

HEARTLESS COMPASSION

Morning came too soon, I got coffee from a thermos not unlike the one we got in laundry for the first time; normally the early risers on our floor finished it off by regular wakeup but today I happened to be one of those early risers. After a shower, I sauntered to the office and asked them to print off directions to my work site. Directions were simple enough but Google said it would take me an hour and Google is never mistaken. It was five thirty and my boss James told me to be there by seven, I had no time to lose.

When I got outside it was dark and frosty; still a fair amount of snow on the ground, but this morning it became apparent to me that the worst of the season must be over. I walked over a bridge, up a hill and straight ahead until the dawn came. When I got to the site I didn't see anyone there so decided to take a look around the house we'd be building. All the interior and exterior walls had been completed already, and it looked like today we would be starting on the second floor. There was also a guy passed out in his lap in the corner. "What's up man?" He looked up with intoxicated eyes and squinted, he must have been around my age.

"Who're you?"

"Mike, I'm supposed to be working here I think."

"Nice, I work here too man. Name's Phil."

Phil stood up and concentrated on retaining his balance, then leaned against the wall and looked at me.

"James is the boss right?"

"Yeah, yeah, James man. He's alright."

He took a deep breath and let it go, then lit up a smoke. Thought about asking him for one but he looked like he probably needed all of them.

"Fuck I've been here all night man! You know what time it is? Phone's dead."

"No phone, sorry. We probably have around a half hour until seven."

All of a sudden he started coughing and horked up something fierce before wadding it out of the empty space left for the back door.

"You've been here all night?"

"Pretty much! I got back to the Dream Centre at curfew and they said I was too fucked up to come in. Man I wasn't even fucked up so I was like 'Fucked up!? I'll show *you* fucked up!'"

You sure showed them. Before I went homeless I heard about the Dream Centre, it was at the same time I heard about the DI. Essentially it's a hotel with a zero-tolerance policy (meaning no drugs or alcohol) that provides room and board to low income individuals. Costs four hundred dollars a month, and you only have to share a decent sized room with one or two people. I considered going there a month before I left Red Deer but chose to pay my rent instead.

"Then you came here?"

"Walked all the way here, it must have taken me two hours plus I was drinkin' on the way." Phil said between his coughing and wheezing.

"You've had a girlfriend right?"

"Engaged once, actually."

"Me too!"

"Big mistake, especially at our age."

"You're tellin' me. Fuckin' whores." He spit spitefully, then told me his messy breakup story while we waited.

When James finally got there he told me to hang tight and, without a second look, told Phil to go home. Phil stuck around until the rest of the crew showed up - twin brothers and a Newfie – and he asked one of the brothers if he could crash at their house.

"You'll have to ask my bro, man, it's his house. He'd need some cash, probly."

"Shit, you want money man? I'm *made* of money," Claimed Phil.

James came over and introduced himself to me and when we got to work, Phil left. The morning went by pretty smooth, James didn't like that all I had was a hammer and tool belt but he said he liked that I paid attention to what he said and got what he told me to do done quickly. At lunch the boss and the twin brothers went off for lunch and I ate with the Newfie. He told me that James had wanted to fire Phil for some time now because he was on crack, but he was too nice of a guy to fire anyone. Once they got back we got straight at it again and by the end of the day we finished the flooring of the second floor and built and stood the exterior walls. James said I wasn't as experienced as he expected, but he would definitely keep me; we agreed on $18.00 an hour and, when we were finished, I followed him to his truck to ask him to sign my Alberta Works form.

"Oh yeah, you're one of them DI fellows eh?"

"Yeah."

"You don't drink do you?"

"No, I've been sober for months."

"Uh-huh." He already finished filling out the sheet and handed it back to me with his business card. "Don't lose that card, if you hand that in with the form you'll get your money faster. I'm really counting on you, alright? Get a lot of idiots working for me."

"I won't let you down."

After James drove off, I walked back to the DI. When I got back they were serving dinner already, I grabbed a meal ticket on Second and, after grabbing my burger and fries and small container of ice cream, I found a place on the stairs to sit and eat. Watching the Knife Lady watch people, Twitch twitch, Jib jabber, the duct tape shoe man eat dinner with his backpack full of rocks, I understood the true meaning of *too long*.

"How's it goin' kid?" Greg asked.

I looked over to see him sitting beside me on the next step up; he was drunk.

"Oh, hey Greg, I didn't even see you. How've you been?"

"Eh, still trying to get on EI."

"Brutal."

"Workin'?"

"Just started a new job today, eighteen an hour!"

"There ya go!" He patted me on the shoulder. "You're gonna do great kid." Glancing down at my plate he asked "You gonna eat your ice cream?"

"You want it?" I held my plate out to him and he grabbed the container of ice cream.

"You'll be out of here soon anyway." That was about as much as we had to say to each other before I went downstairs.

Ray came out of Intox and he gave me a friendly smile before straightening out his bushy moustache.

"Hey, uh, Michael."

"Hey Ray how ya doin'?"

"Good, just woke up an hour or so ago." He laughed and I could see his eyes were glazed, I wondered if he drank in Intox or if he went for a walk.

"Workin'?"

"Yeah, I just got a job framing, today was my first day."

"I used to be a framer! Does he need any, uh, employees?"

"I'm not sure." Pulling out James' number I wrote it down on a page of my notepad then ripped it off and gave it to Ray. "Give him a call, that's what I did. He'll like that you have experience."

"James, eh? You got a phone on you?"

"No. I'd wait to call though when you're, um, maybe a little more sober."

Ray's seemed a bit disappointed. "You can tell huh?"

"You don't *look* that drunk, you just sound a little drunk."

He put the number in his pocket. "Thanks. Maybe I'll call him when I wake up from my nap."

"Give it a shot! I called him late."

Forgetting about his disappointment he tipped his hat to me and went back to Intox and I went into counselor Sean's office. I gave him the form with James' card, and he did a few things on his computer.

"Come back tomorrow, I should have some news for you." As I stood to leave he asked "Tell me, how are you getting to work?"

"I walk."

"Is it far?"

"Takes me an hour to get there."

Counselor Sean opened his drawer and put a booklet of bus tickets on the desk.

"Can I take the whole booklet?"

"Yes, but if you can, would you mind replacing them for me when you get paid? Us counselors only get so many tickets a month to hand out."

"No problem, I really appreciate it. Thanks, Sean."

Up on Fifth, Vince was waiting to shark me for another game of chess, I told him I had some stuff I really needed to do, but all I did was watch the movie I downloaded at the somewhere motel for the billionth time. It wasn't really that great of a movie, but watching it in my room with my headphones in felt like my only privacy. That was the only time no one bothered me and this film became somewhat of a novelty to me; although I do loathe watching the same thing over and over again. Once it was over I called it a night and noticed that Sergei hadn't been there since the wallet went missing.

5:00 am wasn't as bad as 4:30 am.I showered and grabbed coffee then talked to the fifth floor office Dice for a few minutes while they figured out which bus I would need to take to get to work. I still left and arrived around the same times.

Really the day was just a repeat of the day before, except it was just James, the Newfie and me. At noon Phil came by demanding a cheque from James, saying he was leaving for Vancouver. *Guess you're not made of money after all.* James said he'd have to wait and Phil left angry because he'd already bought a bus ticket for that night. Right at the end of the day James got a call from one of the twins, apparently the other twin didn't wake up after a hard night of partying. He was found in his truck in the garage - carbon monoxide poisoning or a drug overdose were the initial theories. *Drugs will get you no matter where you are on the economic scale I suppose.*

On that depressing note we packed up and went home a little early and I bussed back reflecting on how the twins worked together the day before, the energy and good spirits; it just hit me how serious intoxication really is. Old, young, poor, rich; drugs don't discriminate; they'll take you, no matter who you are.

After that I wondered what it would be like for a twin to lose their other half, then had a vision of the potentially tragic life this loss could lead the remaining twin to live: Confused and alone due to a close life being taken far too early, finding comfort in drugs or alcohol. I embodied this vision into the term 'Wandering Twin'. Though I cannot comprehend what it would be like to lose a twin; someone you are born with a mental and sometimes physical bond to, death is still very powerful and the loss and agony that come with it is still very real. *Anyone can be a wandering twin*, I thought, *there must be billions.*

Back on the fifth floor of the DI I was reading the book counselor Sean gave me. Far as I could tell it was a manifesto of addiction advice disguised in the form of a 'true' story about a spirit quest. He made it clear that he wanted me to read it when I saw him after work, even gave me a gemstone before reinstating the importance that I read the book. Also informed me that my cheque would be ready the next day but I had to pick it up at the Alberta Works building between 3:00 and 4:00 pm.

Mando came in around nine with a takeout container of chicken wings.

"How's it going Mando?"

"Fine, you?" *Still looks upset.*

"Good." Apologizing crossed my mind but I didn't want him to get the impression I was open to more of his *wisdom* lessons. "You go out?"

"There's a pub down the street that makes the *best* chicken I have evah had!"

His eyes were notably red but I couldn't tell if he was intoxicated or if he was just tired from work. When I met him he didn't drink or anything, didn't seem the type to lie.

"Awesome." I grinned and motioned my head to Sergei's bunk. "You see Sergei there?" Mando's eyes widened.

"No! Where has he been!? You know?" He began unloading his things in his locker. "I'm beginning to get worried for him. Since I've been here he has nevah not been here. Now he's been gone for what?"

"Two days." *Since you lost your wallet.*

With a dopey smile he smacked his forehead, I returned to my reading and when he was done unpacking went back out to the sitting room to eat his wings. Two rolling papers was all I had left and I went onto the smoke deck to dig around the barrel for butts.

"Don't do that. Here, let me give you one." Garrett said.

Taking a smoke I sat down with him.

"Thanks man."

"No problem. I heard you had another run in with your roommate."

"Which one?"

"'*Pieeeeeeece of shit,*'" he mimicked.

"Yeah he ripped my blanket off of me at two in the morning."

"You're kidding!"

"I wish."

"*I* would tell staff."

"I did. They said they'd talk to him, that's all I want. I don't want him to get kicked out or anything, it's not his fault."

"Well he may have his issues, but he knows better."

We smoked for a little while longer and he told me he was fighting some kind of liver disease and the reason he lived at the DI was because he didn't want to work during that time; understandable, but terrible circumstances to go homeless over. When I got back in I went to sleep and it felt like it was time to wake up before my head hit the pillow. After my new morning routine I bussed to site. I told James when I got there that I needed to leave at noon to pick up the Alberta Works cheque he signed for and for some reason he seemed skeptical about it. The shift went well and before I left he gave me a piece of 2x4 with a new address written on it, saying to be at that place tomorrow at the same time; we had some windows to install.

There was an odd atmosphere in the Alberta Works office. Sad people waiting for aggravated employees and, besides the beeping from the on-hold lines and the telephones ringing, it was dead quiet. I managed to get my cheque with no hassle and then set off to buy the remaining tools I needed, as well as a cell phone if I could afford it. After I got the tools I decided against my plan to buy a phone and was glad I did when I found an unlocked smartphone on my bus ride.

I fought the temptation to drink with the money I had left by volunteering in laundry. It was a slow night and Homer seemed preoccupied with something. I could tell he would rather have been alone, but when I told him about my Alberta Works cheque he understood completely.

"Nothin' worse than having money in your pocket when you're feelin' thirsty, eh."

Before the day was up I grabbed a phone charger from the lost and found. *Who says nothing's free?*

***

No one was at the address James gave me the next day, but I knew I was at the right place; there were freshly installed windows. I waited at the spot smoking and listening to music that was mutual entertainment between me and the previous owner of my new phone. Reading the various messages from different numbers asking me to please return the phone, I weighed out my options, obviously choosing to be a scoundrel. Around 8:30 am I removed the SIM card and started walking towards a nearby mall I'd seen on my way to site. Waiting inside the mall until the stores opened, I found a service provider that Sergei had mentioned to me that had extremely cheap mobile phone plans for people living in major cities. Sergei was right, only forty dollars got me unlimited everything, including data.

When I checked my backpack and pockets for James' number I remembered that I left it in my locker at the DI. After all that I bussed to the site we had been working at during the rest of the week and there was no one there either, it was lunch time, though. There I sat for another hour and a half just killing time, and when no one showed up I left. Regretfully, I picked up a bottle of liquor from the nearest liquor store and wound up; you guessed it, in a bathroom stall on the third floor of the TD mall on 3rd street.

On the way back to the DI I stopped at a restaurant for a meal, eating half of it there and getting the rest to go for an alibi and then chain smoked all the way back in an attempt to hide my breath. They let me into the elevator with no problem but the Dice pulled me into the office immediately when I got up to Fifth, one woman one man. "You're drunk." The woman accused.

"No I'm not."

"Where have you been then?" The man asked. I opened my backpack and dropped the takeout container on the desk offended. They looked at each other unconvinced. "Blow on my cheek." The man ordered. I did and he looked at the woman. "I can't tell."

"I've just been smoking, honestly."

"Smoking *what*?" The woman asked.

"*Cigarettes*." I answered before dropping my smokes on the counter.

"Blow on *my* cheek." She said and I did, then she shook her head. "No, I don't know what it is. It might not be liquor but you definitely smell like *something*."

After I denied that, they made me empty my pockets and searched my bag but found nothing while I did my best to play it casual, casually offended.

They looked at each other, still unsatisfied. "I don't know," she said, then another young Dice came through the elevator, he wasn't on his way to the office, but came in when the Dice waved him over.

"What's up?" The guy asked.

"They think I'm *drunk*."

"Hm." You'll never guess what he said. "Blow on my cheek."

Again I did as I was told and he shook his head at the other two Dice. "No, he hasn't been drinking, my breath smells like that sometimes if I've been smoking heavily."

"Alright," the man said.

"So I'm good?"

"I guess so." The man answered and immediately I began packing up my things while the three of them watched me.

"I'm sorry about that whole thing with the smoke," the young Dice said.

I looked at him, puzzled, and gathered that he must have been the guy that infuriated me by giving Casey a smoke for punching me in the face all those nights ago.

"Oh that was you? I thought it was the tall guy with long hair."

"Nope, it was me."

"Oh, man that's totally cool. Thought about it after words and realized you were just trying to defuse the situation. To be honest I was just mad that I didn't have smokes." Shooting a smug smirk at the other two Dice I held my leftovers out to them. "Can you put these in the fridge for me?" The woman took them irritated and wrote my bed number on the container.

"You got smokes *now*? Well obviously."

"Yeah I'm good man. Thanks though." We left the office together.

"You workin'?"

"Yeah I just got back into residential framing for eighteen an hour!"

"What!? You're making more than *me*! That's awesome." He smiled. "A month from now you better not be living here!"

"Thanks man."

We shook hands.

"I'm glad we're cool, that's been bothering me for weeks."

The young Dice and I wished one another a good night and he went on to do whatever he originally came up for. *Thought he would have forgot about that, I didn't even think he cared to begin with.*

Sergei was in our room putting a jacket on, getting ready to go for a smoke. I asked where he'd been and when we got to talking we were told to quiet down so we made our way to the smoke deck to continue. Apparently he *found* some *liquor* and had been partying over the last couple days. He was clearly wasted; I didn't know how he made it through the brilliant screening process.

We got onto the deck and he started rolling up cigarette butts from the barrel. When I gave him one and he smiled in two directions simultaneously.

"You ever hear of the SORCe?"

"The electronics place?"

"No, the SORCe. It's a home placement program. I just did my interview today."

"Oh, yeah? How'd it go?"

"*Good,* good. I should be getting in wiffin' the next free mons, give or take. You should apply! Oh, no, but you're working right?"

"I think so." James still hadn't replied to any of the messages I sent throughout the day.

"Ah well you should still apply anyways. I'm not sure but they might take you if you're working, make sure you beef your addiction story up a little bit. Tell them you don't feel safe where you're living and they should find you a place pretty chicken Lou."

"That what you did?"

"Well." He laughed to himself. "My addiction story doesn't need any embellishing, so to speak, but you're still young, you have a lot of mistakes ahead of you yet." *I sure fucking hope not man.*

"Beef it up within reason though, right? I don't want it to sound so bad that they don't want to let me in."

"They'll let pretty much anyone in. You know Tweety?"

"No."

"She's down there somewheres." Sergei's eyes were directed at the bridge down below. "She always is." And then I knew who he was talking about; I hadn't spoken to her since I gave her the money but we'd smile at each other when I walked by. "Anyway, they gave her a room but she fucked it up."

"How?"

"She throws a wild party, let me tell you." Scratching his goatee he let out a laugh of tribute. "If they'll let her in they'll let anyone in."

He gave me directions to the place and it was right beside the library. Wasn't overly interested but he did say there was a three month waiting period; it wouldn't hurt to keep my options open. We went to bed when we got inside and I slept through my wakeup, waking up at 6:00 am with everyone else. Rushing out the door and skipping my routine I managed to make it to site on time but again there was no one there. A half hour went by before I tried calling James a few times and left discouraged when there was no answer.

Luckily my hangover still hung over me and I wasn't in the mood for alcohol. On the way to the library I saw the SORCe building and decided to go in. They did an upfront assessment and I chose not to embellish anything because I didn't think it fair to people who really needed it. The lady said I was a prime candidate and asked me to come back in the afternoon when their psychiatrist was around.

I wasted the rest of the morning at the library and went back to the SORCe at the time they asked for my interview with the psychiatrist, where we discussed my situation and my experiences with homelessness thus far. Afterward, he told me I was 'high risk acuity' and that he was going to take my name to a board within the next two weeks and he'd email me with information within the month.

Kelsey was working by the time I got back to the DI. We held each other's eyes with a smile while I walked up.

"Hey!"

"Hey."

"How was your week?"

"Oh, it was alright, you?"

"Midterms." She sighed. "How's your new job?"

After I told her about what had happened I couldn't help but notice I'd drawn my phone out of my pocket. *Don't do it man.*

"Did you try calling him?"

"No answer, I'm hoping to get ahold of him on the weekend though I hope he's still going to let me work for him."

"I hope so too, it doesn't sound like that was your fault."

"Yeah…" *She works where you live, don't be stupid.* "Do you think I could have your number? I don't mean it disrespectfully I-" Her face turned red.

"No. I mean, I can't. Not while you're living here. Or I'm working here." *Dumb stupid idiot.*

"Thought that would be the case. Sorry I just thought-"

"It's fine."

She changed the subject to something else and we talked for just a few minutes before her supervisor flagged her over. Kelsey asked me to wait a few minutes and went upstairs with him. *While I'm living here 'or' she's working here. Does that mean she wants to be with me when I get out? All I've been doing is lounging around here so I could see her, has she just been waiting for me go get out?*

Then it hit me, again. *She's not waiting, she's working. She's just doing her job, she's just concerned. She does want you to get out, but not so you can be with her. She wants you to get out because you're fucking homeless.* Though the acceptance of our dynamic was a key element to Lincoln's on Fire, it felt like I was going through it all over again. I suppose I just thought things were different.

After a few minutes of waiting a big young African-American Dice came out and stood with me. "Hey, big guy, Kelsey wanted me to let you know that she got caught up doing something on the third floor."

"Oh. Alright." *Yeah right. 'You just fucked up what you had.' Is what you mean, right?* Sick to my stomach I picked up my bag and got ready to go.

"You alright?"

"Yeah, I'm good."

"It just seemed really important to Kelsey that I let you know what was up, I just want to make sure everything's cool."

"Everything's good man."

"I'm Paul."

"Michael." Paul continued on and it stopped me from leaving.

"I just like trying to help guys like *you*, ya know? Guys that can still be helped. It makes me feel like I'm doing something here. If I didn't have to do this until next season I would say 'screw this place and all these people', you know what I'm saying?"

"You on a scholarship or something?"

"Football."

"Nice."

He talked about football for a few minutes and I began to dislike the guy, grasping the fact that he wasn't here for the right reasons at all. The antipathy evolved even more when I began to see the same flaw in myself. *We're both going to Hell, Paul.* Some guy came and asked Paul if he could let him up the elevator and when I turned to take my leave almost bumped into Brad.

"Mikey! What's up?"

"Not much you?"

"Some bum up here stole my skateboard yesterday!"

"Who stole your skateboard?"

"That guy." He said and pointed Bowser out to me.

"You're on your own man." I left and Brad followed me outside.

"You wanna smoke one?"

"Sure."

"I only have one joint, we have to train it somewhere to smoke it; I told a friend I'd meet up with him."

"Alright." We took the train to somewhere and walked a block or two from the station. Brad knocked on the door of a house and a worried woman opened the door. Brad asked for his friend and she said he was grounded, he then told her he needed his pipe back and she shut the door in his face. "Let's go to my house, it's only two blocks away, I want to get a smoke from my dad."

"I'll give you a smoke." *Just light that God damn joint.*

"I want to get a pop too."

"Alright. How old are your friends that they're getting grounded?"

"*He's* sixteen."

"That's kind of weird man."

"Well most of the group I chill with is seventeen but he's the youngest."

"You're twenty, right?"

"Yeah."

"Guess it's not *that* bad."

"Age is just a number."

"Well I don't know about that man, I haven't chilled with seventeen year olds since I was seventeen and I'll probably keep it that way."

We got to his house and his dad opened the door, there was terror in his eyes and it was very clear that Brad was not welcome.

"Daddio!" He spread his arms like he was expecting a hug but his dad just peaked at us from behind the door.

"What do you want?"

"A smoke and a pop! And one for my friend too."

"No, Bradley, you need to leave."

"This is how you're going to treat your own son!?"

Daddio attempted to shut the door and Brad threw his foot in the way.

"Dad! Listen!"

The door slammed and Brad backed up into me, pushing me off of the doorstep.

"Fuck you then! I'll fucking burn your house down, you old fuck!"

He turned and started walking. "Let's go get high Red Deer." *I wish I didn't come.*

***

While we walked to a field near his house, he sparked the joint and we stopped at a bench. He only gave me two puffs off of it then put it out halfway before asking for a cigarette.

"Sorry, I'd blaze the rest of it with you but this is all I have. We'd party all night you and me if I had a wallet full of fifties!" *A wallet full of fifties huh? Sounds familiar.*

We started walking towards the train station while he smoked, then he asked "Can I tell you something private?" *I'd rather you didn't.*

"Depends what it is I guess."

"You can keep a secret though right?"

"Again it depends." I looked at him. "You're probably better off not telling me though, I have a feeling I don't want to hear it."

"Come on! We've been through a lot together, homie!"

"Really, we haven't though."

"Haven't we?" He smiled his banana.

"Alright, what do you want to tell me?"

"Well the reason all my friends hate me is because I raped this one kid." Stopped in my tracks.

"You better be joking." He laughed.

"I'm not!"

Instead of letting the conversation continue I tried to walk away at a faster pace, Brad followed.

"It was self-defense!"

"It wasn't self-defense man, that doesn't even make sense."

"He tried to rape me first!"

Butchering him with my eyes I stopped walking again.

"Don't fucking follow me. I still can't tell if you think this is some kind of a funny joke or if you're serious, but I'm *not* dealing with this right now. Not in the fucking mood."

With his hands in his pockets he meandered along behind me while I kept my pace until he was out of sight. I got on the first train that hit the station and ended up in a part of the city I'd never been in before. After an aimless walk I got back on the train and recalculated the train route I'd have to take to get back to the DI.

Listening to music on the phone I stole, feeling more and more terrible about recent happenings, I came to the conclusion that my surroundings were transforming me into something terrible. Reading the un-replied-to text messages from friends of the owner of the phone didn't help my state of mind. After beating myself up about that I switched over to my own un-replied-to-text messages to James and wondered if it was all just a misunderstanding or if he just lost faith in me and let me go without telling me. *Too nice to fire anyone.*

I got off a few stops past the DI to go to the liquor store even though it was getting late and while I trailed down the train line to the store saw something that filled me with adrenaline; a man was gripping a woman's face with both hands and forcing her to kiss him. There I stood trying to assess the situation and figure out what I could do; trying to make sure I wasn't misinterpreting the information flowing to my brain. The woman spotted me and there was no sense of stress or disorder in her eyes but their body language was telling me the complete opposite.

I wanted to shout; I wanted to run over but was it my place? Other people were around, some looking at what I was watching and some not paying any mind at all. *Why isn't anyone doing anything!?*

The adrenaline persisted and I walked in the direction of the scene. Inches away, I felt like I was going to puke my heart out and all the blood sprinting through my body was going to spray out of my fingertips; but I just kept walking… *If something really is wrong, someone else will deal with it.*

Not ten minutes later I was drinking in spite. *What I just did is the essence of what's wrong with people in the world, fear being the key component. Some hero I am,* I thought, *I'm nobody's hero.* A nobody's hero with a pocket full of cash.

13

SCARVES & SPACEBOOTS

Walking aimlessly down a street I didn't know, I had a good think about how I wasted the last week. The weekend was spent drinking as you may have guessed, oddly enough the only productive event was passing out outside for the first time. When Monday came I didn't pay working for James any attention; he hadn't answered my calls all weekend but when my money ran out Tuesday morning I called him several times in a row until he picked up and he gave me a new address for the next day where he'd cut me a cheque. Surprisingly enough he paid me for a full week but unfortunately my tool belt was still at the other site, I think he may still have wanted me to work for him and was going through a hard time himself, however with the cheque in hand, I couldn't care less. *Tough luck.* For the remainder of the week I managed to spend most of what I had on liquor, movies and restaurants.

I bought a bottle of liquor and a pack of smokes, then sat in public sneaking drinks. For the first time I read a sign that I saw on nearly every traffic light in Calgary's downtown core that informs you that you are being monitored on CCTV cameras. George Orwell's depiction of our present never seemed so real. If Homer hadn't shared his purgatory story with me when he did, I very well may have gone into full-fledged psychosis.

While I calmed myself down on the front steps of a church, with the help of my friend Jack Daniels, just because it sounds cool, a homeless guy and his girlfriend asked if I had any change as they walked by and I gave them ten dollars. Besides the pocket full of change I had, that was the last of my money. I got on the train with the intention of seeing a cheap movie, and then got off shortly after at an unfamiliar stop when transit officers got on my car. I walked until I found a family of pine trees in front of an office building and went in the middle of them to pee. The area was fairly secluded and I decided instead to pee on the outside of it in front of passing traffic and then post up on the inside.

There I drank my bottle until I passed out.

Now it was night, it was freezing, and I was again walking aimlessly down a street I didn't know sneaking drinks from what was left of my whiskey. Spaceboots Syndrome was my working title of the phase of denial in the homeless condition, *but is it really a phase?* I'd come to see it as more of a spell. A spell that appears to come with capital. Walking around in 'space' with the mentality that things are better than they are; that they're going to get better without taking action, that you're made of money when you're not, that running will solve your problems. If you think you can rely on labor cash, spend it frivolously, your back is never going to catch up to you and you'll retire comfortably; you're wearing Spaceboots.

If you think that positive thinking alone is going to take care of you, you're wearing Spaceboots.

If you are living at a homeless shelter and calling it *home* or *the mansion*, you're wearing Spaceboots.

If you're homeless in Canada and are under the impression that Eminem and Rihanna are friends of yours that write songs about you; you're wearing Spaceboots.

Ego in denial, essentially. But could it be? *Could it truly be possible? Have I been wearing Spaceboots this entire time?* Had I become the primary subject of my own study? But things were going to get better, because I was going to make them better dammit! The question arose; *when am I going to start?*

'Scarves' was the counter-term I'd been using; nothing elegant, just something to keep you warm from your surroundings. Acceptance, though I noted right away that it was more than just acceptance of succumbing to the homeless condition; for that is inevitable, but acceptance of your place in this world. A little more defensive and safe than pro-active in my opinion, but I considered Scarves to be healthy, as everyone I considered to be wearing them made progress. Biker Mike, *most* of the laundry folk, Lester.

Then there were folks I deemed to be wearing Scarves *and* Spaceboots; explicitly Tukahoot and Mando who are able to accept where they are and make progress while refusing to let go of the dream.

This is the group I'd consigned myself in; until now. Now I came to the conclusion that in using my Scarf as a mask I only fortified my Spaceboots.

I'm a classic case I thought. *The classic case, but I'll turn into a Blink if I'm not careful.* Blink was the slightly judgemental term I'd taken to using for individuals all the way from Brad to Jib; Brad being the highest functioning Blink: Those with mental health disorders that are so far gone into medication and/or substance abuse that their life goes by in blinks. They are the ones I thought could use *extra* attention. *Damn Government.* They really didn't have control of what was going on, they'd been busted or worn out or malfunctioned and left to fend for their survival.

Besides the Wandering Twins; the rigorous addicts whose addiction is entwined, not with mental health disorders but with traumatic life events -specifically loss, everyone fit under the category of Scarves, Spaceboots and Blinks. Personally I believed anyone who didn't tally hadn't truly succumbed to the condition. *Is it possible I'm just a judgmental space cadet?* My Spaceboots wouldn't let me believe it.

My frozen fingers failed to grasp my phone, really more of a pocket watch now that the owner blacklisted it as stolen. *It must be late.* There were no people walking the sidewalk and the only vehicles in sight were parked in a parking lot I was coming up to. My idea was to look for an unlocked vehicle to warm up in and the first one I checked, a big black brand new shiny truck, was my savior. *I hoped I wouldn't meet the owner.*

As I hopped in the driver's seat I tossed my backpack in shotgun. Impulses lead me into the glove compartment and the center console. *Sue me.* All I found was a pocket knife, insurance and registration, then I drunkenly attempted to turn the knife in the ignition. *Guess that's not how you hotwire a vehicle.* I pulled out my phone charger and checked for a place to plug it in with hopes that technology had finally installed electrical outlets in new vehicles. They didn't, not this one at least. In the end I passed out then woke up to a woman freaking out on the phone; most likely with the police, as she described the situation I was involved in. It would have been stupid not to make a break for it… Right?

Sleet was falling as I stumbled up a block and, in despair, I stepped into the headlights of the vehicle that was approaching. They were close enough that they could have done serious damage if they weren't cops and they weren't already slowing down because I was the guy they were looking for. They threw me on the hood of the car and spread all my belongings out across it. When they got to my smokes, they searched through the open pack then left it open on the hood, leaving them to get soaked by the sleet. Right before I blacked out, I remember struggling and cuffs being slapped on my wrists.

Hospitals were never my scene, but that's where I woke up, in restraints nonetheless. My arms and legs were shackled to the sides of the hospital bed and a male nurse told me the reason my head was tied to the back bar was because I'd used my teeth to get out of my restraints twice. The nurse also said the cops brought me there because I was talking suicidal. Claustrophobia got the best of me as I returned from my blackout and I started howling for the nurse to let me out of the restraints. He came in with a look that told me 'shut the fuck up or you die.'

"Listen, you know what I'm doing right now? I have to go tell a woman that her four year old daughter just died in a car accident. She's sitting two rooms away." That sobered me right up.

"I'm sorry." Two long tears streamed from the corners of my eyes as he walked out of the room and I sat like stone for a few hours until they released me. They called the DI who said they'd arrange something and I sat in the hospital waiting for a group called The DOAP Team to come pick me up.

They're essentially a free taxi for Hobos in this city. Using my jacket as a pillow on the ride back home I thought about how I stepped into the headlights of that police cruiser, how, if it hadn't been a police cruiser, I could have hypothetically been responsible for the death of a four year old girl.

An old guy from the DOAP team woke me up and I piled into a van with five others, most of us were going back to the DI, some of them had McDonalds. A Native woman offered me some fries but the smell of McDonalds was already making me nauseous. They let me out at the DI and the Dice at the front turned me away until I somehow managed to explain my situation. Unfortunately there wasn't room in Intox, but they said I was welcome to sleep in the lobby for an hour before they woke everyone up.

In the end they agreed to put in a word to Daysleep, but I still had a few hours until that opened up so I found a spot on the stairs where a few people were waiting for Second floor and plunked myself into the corner. For a while I was sitting there staring at the hospital band around my wrist, half listening to the conversations around me. Someone nearby was playing music off of his phone and a song I liked came on, I started bobbing my head.

"Sup man?" The guy with the music asked.

"Not much man."

"Long night?"

I held my wrist up to show him the hospital band he probably already saw.

"Happens to the best of us!"

"Yeah. You don't have a smoke, do you?"

He nodded his head wildly and shot up and I followed him outside where he gave me a smoke.

We lit up and I realized I was very dizzy, watching this guy hop around wasn't helping.

"I just have so much energy right now! You ever feel like that?"

"Not like you."

He stopped and took a look around the parking lot before taking a big puff.

"Must be from the Jiu-Jitsu I'm taking, makes me feel like a ninja. I feel like I could run around this entire parking lot over and over and over again."

"I took martial arts."

"Oh yeah? We should spar."

"No way, man."

"Come on let's just go around the corner where there's no cameras."

"No way man, this smoke is already kicking my ass." He stopped hopping and spread his arms.

"Try to hit me!"

"No."

"Okay, just hit me. I won't move." After he stuck his face out, he just held it there awkwardly while I smoked for a few seconds. "I'm not moving until you hit me. Just a tap." I tapped his jaw and he lunged at me but didn't make any contact.

"Be careful man, I could have just destroyed you and said it was self-defense. That's fucked up, eh?"

"Yeah, man."

We went inside and waited on the stairs until Second floor opened, then found a table and I wrapped my backpack around my leg and put my head down for a while, dozing off. When I came to, the guy was still sitting with me playing a game on his phone, he saw me watching and he slid over to show me a sniper game.

"I'm so good at this game man, it's a good thing I'm a cook and not a soldier! People'd be dyin'!"

"Where do you cook?"

"Two places! I'm sous chef at my day job and kitchen manager at my night job."

"That's intense. Why are you living here?"

"Cheap rent. I'm awake most of the time anyways, I'm getting my hours in until I have my red seal and then I'll buy my own house."

"That's a pretty good plan." *Ladies and gentlemen, Scarves and Spaceboots.*

"Yeah. Oh! Vitamins!"

Like a distracted dog he shot off before coming back with horse-sized capsules of ground up herbs and a cup of green sludge that he used to wash them down.

"Get em' man! Gonna need em' if you're living here! These bad boys are the only reason I'm not sick."

"I didn't know they did that here. I'm good though."

"No, you're not! You already got the DI cough!"

"The DI cough?"

"Haven't you noticed? You got the same rickety cough everyone else has! That's *why* they give these out. If you don't want yours, go get em' and give them to me."

I did and after he gulped it all down he sprung up and pulled me up by my arm. "I need to go to work! Come with me, I'll introduce you to some people."

Luckily I remembered to grab my bag and I followed him to Bowser's table. Bowser wanted nothing to do with me and decided to have a conversation with someone facing another direction and the guy introduced me to some of the people there but I was half asleep. After the introductions he grabbed my shoulders and looked at me with crazed eyes and shouted "Remember my face!" before running off.

Breakfast at Bowser's table was uncomfortable to say the least, I ate quietly without looking at anyone and when people started lining up for Daysleep, I did too. All I knew was I wanted a bed in a corner so if anyone tried to take my stuff there'd only be one direction they could take it from.

A kick to the feet woke me up and me and another guy looked at each other. Our bunks were squished together and we were foot to foot and both of us were confused because there were tons of open beds available around us. I didn't know who got there first so I got up and went to look for another bed, but after I went to the washroom and got a drink of water I didn't feel so tired. It was around 1:00pm and I was starving. Remembering the Sunday barbecue I found myself an achievable short term goal.

Standing in line I listened to the banter between the preacher and the non-believers. "Oh lordy, lordy! Come get your ham and Jesus!" The guy in front of me said before I laughed with him. He turned around and I recognized him to be one of the guys who'd been introduced to me at Bowser's table.

"Michael right?" The short bald guy asked before smiling with whites.

"Yeah. Sorry I can't remember your name."

"Wilbur."

We shook hands and waited patiently for some hotdogs and then proceeded to the DI, he asked if I had any money.

"Nothing, sorry man."

"I just need a buck thirty and then I can get a pack of smokes."

I went through my pockets and counted out the change that I was surprised the cops let me keep, because it wasn't mine. There was a little more than enough and I handed it over to him.

"You'll give me one right?"

You wouldn't believe what I saw in the store, the store that was conveniently placed just four blocks from the DI. On display above the cigarettes this store was advertising cheap rubbing alcohol, mouthwash and cough medicine. *Do people really take advantage of the homeless like this?* Yeah, sadly they do.

Wilbur gave me four smokes and told me if I needed anything to come to him, then we smoked while we walked to the DI. "How long you been living at the mansion?"

"I've been there a while, I'm on the fifth floor now."

"What's a guy gotta do to get on Fifth?"

"Volunteer hours really, and you gotta be sober."

"Well I can definitely *volunteer*!" Seemed to be one of the highest functioning people currently at the DI.

"How long *you* been at the DI?"

"Two weeks."

"Oh weird, I thought I saw you a long time before that."

"There are a lot of fat bald guys in the world buddy."

"How long you plan on living there?"

"Hard to say, I didn't plan on going homeless!"

"Fair enough."

"Not really."

"How old are you?"

"Twenty-four but I look like I'm thirty."

Some people across the street waved to him and he went off on his own after I declined smoking a joint. Volunteering in laundry was my plan before I got to Second and ran into Kelsey.

"Where've you been?" She asked with a tilt of the head and a pitiful smile.

"I've been being really stupid again." She kept looking at me. "I might have still had that job when I last talked to you right?"

"Yeah. He didn't let you keep it?"

"No. Last night I was in the hospital, I don't know what to do anymore."

"I'll be honest, I think it's time you look for outside help besides me, I don't think I'm qualified to help you."

"I know." I told her about my high risk acuity assessment at the SORCe and that I was giving up on my book before asking her if she could let me down to laundry. We waved sadly before the elevator shut and then opened again to a different room.

Ray and Wade were the only two in there, Wade was wearing a staff vest.

"You're staff now Wade?" I asked without realizing I interrupted their conversation.

They turned to me.

"Well actually I was staff *before*. Homer replaced me."

"He didn't quit did he?"

"No, there was a death in the family. This is just temporary."

"Ah, I gotcha." Ray smiled at me. "You're volunteering again?"

"Yeah, I uh, got everything sorted out with the big guys upstairs."

"Nice! Did you call James?"

"James.. James.." He thought aloud, stroking his naked chin.

"He's the guy I was working for, framer. You said you needed a job but that was a while ago."

"Oh! James! That number that was in my pocket! That's what that was for? A job? I threw that out." He smiled. "Uh thanks anyways!"

There was still quite a bit to fold, and fold we did until dinner time came around and Wade let Ray upstairs. I asked to stay.

"I'm glad you wanted to stay! I sure as shit don't want to be stuck here all night."

We folded until dinner was served and Wade could go up to grab ours. He came back down with two plates of turkey, stuffing, mashed potatoes, vegetables and cranberries.

"What's this!?"

"Easter!"

"Shit, its Easter already?"

"Apparently!"

I grabbed a plate and sat down and he put his plate in front of me too. "You can have mine."

"No way! It's Easter."

"I'm not hungry."

For a little bit I watched him fold alone while I thought about what Ester said about his depression and story, then joined him.

"You're not eating?"

"I'm not hungry." I grinned at him and he grinned back.

"Geez you're a stubborn kid!" And we walked over to the table to eat.

"So you worked here before Homer did? Why'd you quit, or why did they need to replace you?"

"I just fell off the wagon. It's all just a bloody long story," he shrugged.

"Well, we have time don't we?"

We ate soundlessly for a few minutes, I kind of thought he was going to ask me to leave.

"You want the rest of this? It's going in the garbage if you don't." He asked. I shook my head and he walked over to the garbage, tilting his plate to it while giving me a look; proving he could be just as stubborn.

After I ate the rest of our meals I rejoined him at the folding station. "Like most people at the DI I wasn't too bad off before I got here. In fact I ran a very successful printing business for twenty odd years. With my wife."

"What happened?"

"Well-" He took a deep breath before retracting his eye contact. "Near the end of our run she was feeling sick all the time, kept getting these vicious headaches. We didn't think much of it." For a moment his mind went back a decade or two. "She was stubborn anyhow; you wouldn't catch her *dead* in a hospital. She really believed in home remedies."

Swallowing hard he fought to continue. "Then we went on a ski-trip in the mountains and she couldn't walk a kilometer without having to take a break, strange for her; she was quite the hiker. For once she let me convince her to let me take her to the hospital." With a deep breath he closed his eyes, I thought he might cry. "Brain cancer. She died five months later."

"I'm sorry Wade."

"Me too." He walked over to his backpack and grabbed something, then brought it over to me. It was a photograph of a younger Wade with hair just as long but not contained within a ponytail, and a beard; a mountain man, standing beside and holding his young wife. She was a beautiful woman with medium blond hair. They both looked very happy.

"That's her. That's Wendy."

"She was beautiful." I held the picture back to him.

"Yes she *is*." Wade said while putting the picture back before coming back over to fold.

"You really love her, eh?"

With a smile he shrugged with a tear in his eye.

"She's my soul mate."

His voice shook so I gave him a moment while we finished folding the batch we were working on, then we went over to pull more out of the dryer.

"So what happened to your business?"

"I gave it away."

"You didn't even sell it?"

"No. Money had no value to me, the printing industry was crumbling anyway, so I gave the business to a friend and over time spent every cent I had on alcohol. I had two daughters but they weren't enough for me at the time. I missed Wendy; I was going to join her." With a pause he gauged me to see if I wanted to hear the rest of the story.

"What stopped you?"

"God, the Devil, I don't know. I *tried*." He took another deep breath then exhaled. "It all got to be too much for my youngest because she got into hard drugs and by the time I realized it, it was too late to pull her out. My oldest found her dead in her room just three years after my wife died, then she killed herself the same year."

"Oh my God! How did you…?" *Bounce back.* "I mean, like, I never would have guessed. You conduct yourself so well…"

"Some friends who had been coming by ever since my wife passed got worried when I sold my house and moved to a smaller place and they wound up getting an ambulance to pick me up. Spent two years in a psych ward learning how to deal with my depression. I'd always had depression, but as you could imagine…"

"It got worse." I finished his sentence and he nodded. "You came here after with nowhere to go?"

Not quite, I got a job here in laundry first because I thought it would be an easy job where I could be by myself and after about five years into it I was drinking while I was on shift. We agreed it wasn't working out here, and once I ran out of cash, I *did* have nowhere to go."

"Wow. You seem like you're doing really good now. The DI obviously thinks so too." Indicating his vest.

I smiled at him, but he sighed and shook his head.

"I still get very depressed every so often, that's why you haven't seen me for the last month or so, the last time I was in the hospital was a few weeks ago. The DI just didn't have anyone else that could learn the job on a dime."

"Well hold onto it Wade, as a fellow alcoholic your story is really inspiring to me. You've come a long way, you should be proud of yourself."

He shrugged. "I'm not."

I reached out and grabbed his shoulder. "Well *I'm* proud of you."

When I let go I saw another tear come to his eye. By then it was almost time for Wade to close up and he said he'd let me up to fifth floor.

While the elevator door was shutting he put his arm in the way and opened it again.

"Michael, uh.." Tension left his shoulders and he forced a smile that had sincerity behind it.

"Thanks."

I waved and the door shut.

There were no staff in the office when I got onto Fifth so I went out for a smoke before I signed in and looked over the city. *It feels like a lifetime since I got here.* When I went to the office to sign in I was surprised to see Kelsey. One of the regular staff from the floor gave me a short lecture, saying that if I hadn't shown up for one more night I would have lost my bed. Once she was done I turned my attention to Kelsey.

"I didn't know you worked up here." She shrugged.

"They said they needed someone to fill in and I said I wanted to do it," she smiled. "How are you?"

"I'm alright."

"Here." She handed me a list of addresses and phone numbers with the names of addiction services and counseling agencies that she'd already handwritten for me.

"Thanks, I'll put it with these."

Kelsey looked delightfully confused as I pulled out the note she gave me along with our grade 3 picture.

"What are those?" She asked.

"The grade three picture and the note." Before I put them in my breast pocket I held them up for her to see.

"You said you didn't get the note…"

"Went back for it." We smiled at each other.

"I think it's funny you carry those." The blush returned.

"Thanks for the list of places, I can definitely use them."

"I hope you do." She stood and leaned closer to the window between us, and when she did I prayed the window protected her from the sour stench of body odor I'd developed from days without a shower.

"There's no secret that there's *something* going on. As much as I really want you to get out of here, maybe you should look into going back to rehab or possibly even get a mental health diagnoses."

"I've been thinking about going back to rehab but I don't know. There's a lot to lose." I said, trying to tell her *I want you* with my eyes.

"What about seeing a doctor about your mental health?"

"I don't want to go on medication, I really don't believe in that. Pretty sure I am bipolar anyway, I've known ever since I heard about it in health class."

She took a breath while thoughtfully thinking of ways that she could tell me to see a doctor that would speak to me.

"Look, maybe seeing a doctor and getting on meds *isn't* in your best interest, but if he can diagnose you with bipolar, or anything else if there is anything, then maybe you can start looking into some alternatives to medication that will help you."

"Yeah, maybe I'll check it out."

"For me?" She asked swaying, and I wondered if maybe she had been flirty with me, if this was even flirty, from the get-go to get me to open up to her. Whether that was the case or not, it worked.

"Yeah, I will for sure." Openly, I sniffed my arm pits. "I should really take a shower though, it's been a while."

We gave each other a playful sickly smile before I took my shower.

Once I was out of the shower and into some clean clothes I felt a lot better in almost every way. Kelsey was still there when I got out, but it looked like she was getting ready to leave. I watched her put her coat on and noticed the trace of stress and self-fulfillment from helping me, then daydreamed of what it would be like to have her come home after a long shift, taking the coat off and putting it on a rack saying 'Honey I had a long day at work'.

Finally something clicked and I understood how much of a burden I was. How wrong I had been in using her as a crutch, how much she truly supported me and how delusional I was about our relationship. *This must have been hard on her.*

"I wanted to thank you again for the information."

"You're welcome! Here!" She came out of the office and brought another piece of paper over to me and stood close beside me while pointing out what everything was. It was another list she'd handwritten, this time with tons of information on how to cope with bipolar. It meant a lot.

"Thank you Kelsey."

"You don't need to thank me, I just did a little bit of *research.*"

I pulled out the other papers and folded the new one into the pile before I put them all in my pocket again.

"I still think it's funny you carry those around."

"They all mean something to me."

Her smile was gloomy as she told me she had to go.

"Hey Kelsey?" Gravity pulled us together one more time. "Why are you doing all this? I mean I know it's your job, but this is all-"

"You might not see it, but you've taught me a lot in the time we've known each other. You're an amazing guy, I'd do anything to keep you from slipping through the cracks."

"Well thank you, Kelsey. It all means a lot to me. *You* mean a lot to me."

Misinterpretation pulled her away. Reversing towards the door, Kelsey reached a charitable hand out to me, melancholy painted on her face, and sincere devotion radiating from her eyes while looking at the sheer admiration in mine; unspoken words howling to be more, but her shift was over.

***

Lester walked up beside me while I smoked and stared out across the city. "Lester, how's the guitar coming, buddy?"

A wide smile appeared and I expected to hear that he could rip it like Jimmy Hendrix.

"I learned how to play my favorite note yesterday!"

"Right on, still a ways to go then?"

"No. I'm happy with where I'm at. When I play my note I feel like everything's right in the world. I got it so that I can play it just perfect every time."

Content, he popped a smoke in his mouth. "Now anytime I'm anxious or upset I know that all I have to do is play my note and everything will be better." *I'm not planning on wearing Spaceboots anytime soon* is what he said to me.

Mando and Sergei were already asleep when I got into the room and Piece was most likely at work, as usual. In the middle of the night I was woken up by Sergei tapping me on the shoulder with my wallet; *apparently* it fell out of my pocket while I was sleeping.

When morning wakeup came around, Sergei openly lectured me about how, if there'd been money in my wallet, I may not have been lucky enough to get it back, like *Mando*. Told me this with his arm around the guy and I couldn't tell if Mando was completely oblivious or if his spiritual temple reflected it.

The next day I decided I was going to take my laptop bag instead of my backpack and, while I transferred some of the contents, noticed a fresh charge from the police from the other night; 'theft under' for a pocket knife and phone charger. *The phone charger was mine!* Court in June.

On the way out the door I ran into Old Steve who told me he heard I was writing a book, said he'd like to talk to me about it and share some ideas; said that he's a writer too. It was almost too brief to mention and I told him we'd have to have coffee sometime.

Seeking out a counselor from Kelsey's list was my priority for the morning but unfortunately most counselors wanted money for the sessions and the ones that didn't want cash had waiting lists that were months long. During lunch I got the DI to print off a resume for me and took it to the temp agency Mando had been going to, thinking I'd get a fresh start. I sat outside the locked agency for an hour before a middle-aged red headed man stepped around the corner. He had quite a bit of muscle but it only seemed to compensate for his lack of energy.

"How ya doin' Bob!?"

"Wrong guy, my name's Mike."

"Nope, I got the right guy. I call everyone Bob."

"Alright. What's your name?"

"Bob." Bob told me all about this particular temp agency and how they were only good for four hour shifts, but I paid no mind as Mando had shown me otherwise. Once he was done complaining about the agency he got on the subject of his military career.

"How long did you serve?"

"Year and a half?"

"That's it? I thought minimum was -"

"Four back then. I pussied out if ya gotta know. Me and a buddy shot each other in the leg back when you could still get away with that."

"Honorable discharge?"

"*Dis*honorable. They knew. Fuck them though, I make a better career scavenging."

"Scavenging?"

"Dumpsters! You wouldn't believe the junk rich people throw out!" He told me a few wild stories about electronics and jewelry, valuable knick knacks and even money, that may or may not have been true.. By the time I left we'd started making plans for a day of scavenging. I had mentioned I was a writer after he told me he was a musician, and he said that dumpster diving would open up a whole other aspect of a book on the homeless. *But I need to get away from this lifestyle* was the thought that dragged me away, and for once I wasn't about to even consider it as a missed opportunity.

That night on the fifth floor I wrote out a personalized street guide for myself based on the best advice I'd come across in terms of mental health and addiction coping mechanisms as well as things I had to look forward to when I got out. After that I made an attempt to tally up the amount of money I'd *spent* in my few months homeless and it totalled to thousands of dollars. I was shocked. Reading my street guide over and over revealed rehab to be the obvious path to take. *I guess my life will have to wait.*

14

COURTESY OF THE BANK

Jonesing for a cigarette in the addictions office sounded about right

and I contemplated how I would have coped with everything that happened without the comfort of nicotine. Waiting patient hours with my laptop bag tied around my leg I eventually got in to see a woman who, while I filled out familiar paperwork, stressed that she wouldn't be my counselor, this was just a consultation and I'd have to repeat a lot of the information to the next person another day.

Once I was done filling everything out she asked "So why did you come here today?"

"Well, I was sober for a few months before I came to Calgary, then I came here to write a book on the homeless and I relapsed."

"Okay."

"Just on liquor though, kind of. I mean for the longest time I think I could have gotten out of it but I stuck around because a girl I went to elementary school with works at the shelter I've been living at-"

"And you fell in love!" She finished, cupping her hands with sparkling eyes.

"I guess." Scratching my head, annoyed, I thought *are you going to help me?* "Started drinking to make the weeks go by but now I'm just right back into the liquor."

"How do you think we can help you?"

I told her I wanted to go back to the same rehab facility I went to in the summer and she printed an application off for me. Then I asked if she knew of anyone that might be able to help me with money during the time I was in rehab because that was a problem the time previous and she told me to check with the welfare office next door.

Conveniently the welfare office was just next door on the second floor but it felt like forever before I got to see anyone, and it seemed like my request made the guy want to punch me right in the kisser; he sent me out with another application though, however he promised me it wouldn't do any good. *Figures.*

I went down the elevator and, as I went out the front door,a small dark man who had been following me thanked me for holding the door for him. He was somewhere between aged beyond his years and senior and the yellow of his teeth was sharper than a lemon, unfortunately the same couldn't be said of the smell of his breath.

"Cigarette?" He held one out to me.

"Sure, thanks." With a bit of skepticism I took the smoke and watched him suspiciously, wondering why he was going the same way I was going when I didn't know where I was going; I held my laptop closer.

"You need work?" The dark man asked me as we walked.

"Yeah, sort of. I'm thinking about going back to rehab but it'll be a few months."

"I can help you."

"Yeah?"

Grabbing my shoulder he turned me the opposite direction.

"Come with me." Pulling out a phone he made a call, holding it up to his ear before turning to me.

"You have a bank account?" I nodded my head.

"What branch?"

After I told him, whoever he was calling picked up the phone, and he began speaking in a language I didn't recognize. The way he spoke sounded pure evil as he hissed and spit. We walked for two blocks while he worked something out with the other end of the line before hanging up. "You'll have money by the end of the day."

"I don't know if I can work today man it's already past noon and I haven't eaten yet."

This new employer didn't need to know I was living at a homeless shelter, but if I was going to be shirking my first shift I had to have *some* excuse. He offered to buy me some food and a coffee and we went to a nearby Tim Horton's. Hungrily I ate my bagel while he texted on his phone and sipped at his bitter black coffee.

"Are we waiting for someone?"

"Yes, my friend is going to pick us up."

We waited for about ten minutes while he made small talk about where I came from and I told him a little bit about Red Deer. Said his name was Adam, but when I asked he stalled and I was under the impression he had made it up on the spot.

After we left the building we walked around the corner to find a rusty brown Cadillac - and that was the moment I realized this was a little sketchy. But I got in anyway and I sat in the back with a fair amount of garbage that the driver hastily tried to move out of the way before extending the same hand to me. I shook it. He looked at least twenty years younger than Adam, African-American with a goatee and a grey toque.

"Mike Jesmer!" I answered his expression.

"Mack, Yay?" The driver asked and I nodded as he turned to the wheel, adjusted his rearview mirror and took a peer at me before starting the car.

"What's your name?" I asked.

He peered at me again and like Adam, and his car, he stalled.

"Yaycob." Jacob restarted his car and we drove off while they spoke in the familiar unfamiliar language Adam was speaking earlier. Even though they were speaking the same language, Jacob didn't sound nearly as evil.

"So what are we doing?" *The jig is up* is the tone I used, though I waited until there was a small break in their conversation. Jacob looked over at Adam. Adam cleared his throat and it sounded like it did damage more than anything.

"My friend fucks her boss." He responded. *Sounds legit.*

It was a ten minute car ride before Jacob stopped on a hill in the middle of a business section of the city. Adam hopped out and told me to get in the front. Trying not to spill my coffee I got out with my laptop bag and plunked myself into the front seat before we drove off, leaving Adam behind.

The whole thing had me feeling pretty antsy, I thought about taking off, but I didn't know where we were; not to mention I wanted to see where this was all going.

Jacob stopped in a residential area and opened his center console to reveal a little bit of weed and some rolling papers. "You smoke?"

"Yeah man." My nerves were spiked, I needed to calm down. A cigarette was all I wanted but I knew Adam was the only one with smokes at the moment because earlier he handed Jacob one while they schemed. He rolled it up and looked around to make sure the coast was clear before lighting it and easing back in his seat.

"So how do you know Adam?"

"Adam?" He asked back casually while taking another puff off the joint.

When I raised an eyebrow he choked on the smoke.

"Adam. Sorry." Jacob tapped his forehead and held the joint out to me. "S'good weed. He my cousin."

Mhmm. I took a puff of the joint and passed it back.

"Where you guys from?"

"*I'm* from Montreal."

"You weren't speaking French though."

He took a puff off the joint then passed it over.

"We was speakin' Arabic."

I hit the joint and passed it back.

"Learn it through family?"

Taking a few seconds to think about it he nodded while smoking then handed it back to me, then I did the same.

"Is Adam from Montreal too?"

"No."

"Where's he from?"

"I don't know."

"He's your *cousin*!"

"Where *you* from Mack Yay?" Jacob shot back.

"Red Deer."

"Why'd you move to Calgary?"

"Didn't want to be homeless in my home city I guess." Could have been a sliver of truth there, but I figured they didn't need to know I was a writer.

"Oh," he said pitifully before passing the joint to me. "You have family there?"

I hit the joint. "You're right, this *is* good weed."

We finished the joint and he shared a half cigarette he'd saved with me. We waited for a little while until Jacob passed me his phone and told me to write my full name and social insurance number - and I did. Yeah, yeah, I know you're not supposed to give that information out, I'm not stupid.

Another half hour or so went by and Jacob began getting more and more impatient as the high wore off, but he got a call from Adam and we left to pick him up. I thought we were going to get him from the same place but we only drove a few blocks until Adam walked up to the passenger door and caught me by surprise. When I got into the back I realized I left my laptop in the front.

Jacob started driving again and I noticed the coffee had made its way through me and I started squirming a little in the back seat. Adam passed a smoke and an open envelope back to me and I pulled out the contents. There was a cheque just under two thousand dollars from a drywall company I'd never worked for with my name and social insurance number.

"You will get five hundred." Adam said extending all the fingers on his left hand while I lit my smoke.

According to the stub attached to the cheque I was a journeyman and had already made over ten thousand dollars with the company over the last few months. "We will do this for two weeks or so. By the end of it you can have your *own* apartment."

"I don't know man." Though, the cheque looked as authentic as any cheque I'd gotten before.

Adam turned to me in his seat.

"We want to help you. You need money, we need money. We all need to get by. Trust us. You're young, you're clean. People will believe you."

"I don't know if I can do it man, I'm way too nervous, I already have a criminal record; I don't want to go to jail."

"You will *not* go to jail! *Trust* us." Adam responded and put a hand on my knee for a second and then we stopped across the street from one of my branch locations.

"Trust us, Mack Yay." Jacob turned in his seat.

"Just go in and say 'I want to make a deposit.' That's *it*!"

"Alright. What if they accuse me of anything?"

"They will *not*! Just go in and say 'I want to make a deposit.'"

"I want to make a deposit," Jacob said with him as they both stared at me.

"Let *them* tear the stub."

"Alright."

They both told me to trust them one more time and I got out and walked over to the bank. When I got inside I asked the teller if there was a washroom I could use but she said they didn't have public washrooms.

"I want to make a deposit." I said, sweating and shuffling, trying not to pee my pants.

"Okay." The woman took the cheque and tore the stub off. "Did you just start working here?"

"No I've been working for these guys for a few months, I've just been taking my cheques to cash stores because I didn't want the cheque held."

While she was typing in the computer and I was imagining all the different kinds of terrible things she could be writing from noting that I was suspicious to telling the CIA I brought her a fraudulent cheque.

She smiled. "Okay I added them as your employer. I'm just waiting on my manager to see if we can bypass the hold."

"Alright." *Your manager?* If I was sweating teaspoons before I was sweating buckets now, I wiped my forehead clean. Again she began typing on the computer before giving me a more serious look.

"Do you have any ID with you?" *Yes.*

"No!" I lost my cool and started shuffling even more. *They're onto me!!*

"No problem." *She's talking to the CIA again.*

"Actually, you know what? I'm good."

"What?" She looked at me puzzled. "I was just about to-"

"No it's cool." I held my hand out for the cheque while the urine causing me to do the pee-pee dance was quite possibly dripping out of my pores and she handed the cheque and the stub to me.

"I'm sorry it was taking so long, it just takes a while to set up a new employer."

"It's fine! Thank you!"

Speed walking for the door I searched my surroundings for another exit but found only one. I watched the security guard to make sure he wasn't going to stop me but he just gave me a respectful nod and held the door open for me. The Cadillac was nowhere to be seen when I got outside so I walked up the block for less than a minute before they peeled up beside me, I hopped in. They both looked back at me with gleaming predator eyes.

"How did you do?" Adam asked.

"They asked me for ID so I left."

"Let me see the cheque." I handed the cheque and stub to him and he held them apart. "Did *they* tear this?"

"Yeah."

"Did they add this company as your employer?"

"Yeah." They looked at each other with enthusiasm and Jacob started driving again. Adam put his hand on my knee again.

"Good job."

"Good yob, Mack Yay." Jacob looked at me in the rearview mirror as he sped off.

Adam handed me back another open envelope with a cheque identical to the one before, same amount and everything but with the stub still attached. *Is this really happening?*

"We will go to another bank. You will do the same thing. Once they deposit the cheque, pull out only five hundred, and then we will take care of the rest."

"Alright."

Adam gave Jacob and I each a cigarette and Jacob cranked the music as he drove crazily, the gangster beats bumping and our heads bobbing and swaying unintentionally with the music due to Jacob's driving while we flew out of the city. It was at that moment I thought: *Okay, now I have a story.* It just occurred to me that they were preying on people at the welfare office. *How many people has this happened to?* All of it seemed so crazy to me, and my Spaceboots disguised my greed. *What a story this will be.* While we drove to Someplaceville, I daydreamed of ways to turn the event into a short story while simultaneously keeping my bladder from exploding with Jedi mind tricks.

***

Didn't know what city or town we were in when we got there but it was only twenty minutes from Calgary. We got to another bank and they gave me another briefing and words of encouragement while I freaked out again. Jacob pointed out I was shaking and Adam gave me another smoke, telling me not to do that in the bank. They waited patiently and I concluded they must have chosen to go to another city in case I chickened out or tried to run off with the cash; little did they know that having my laptop hostage in the front seat was all the loss prevention they needed; maybe if I'd had a password on it I'd be telling a different story.

When I got into the bank my back teeth were floating and to my delight *this* teller was more than happy to let me use their washroom, she even took me behind the counter and through the back. *Maybe I should just rob the joint.* What sweet relief it was as I literally felt the pressure coming off of my kidneys and in turn my mind. I took a minute to calm my nerves then walked back out into the strange real world with a little more confidence.

"I want to make a deposit." I told the teller stiffly, handing her the cheque with a confident grin.

While I entered the pin I saw her smile when she looked at the cheque. She asked if the cheque was bi-weekly or monthly and I wasn't sure if it was protocol or if she was just curious because she became quite flirty after I told her it was bi-weekly. Not five minutes later I walked out of the bank with $500, and when I failed to see the Cadillac again I thought about making a run for it. *Stupid laptop.* After less than a block of walking they drove up beside me just the same as before.

"How did you do?" Adam asked.

I handed the stub and receipt to him and he looked it all over, then held his hand out again.

"Five hundred."

Jacob started driving while he watched me wearily put the cash in Adam's hand.

"You'll get it when you're done."

"Good yob, Mack Yay."

They began speaking in Arabic again, and the conversation seemed to be getting intense as we pulled into a gas station. Adam handed Jacob a hundred bucks and Jacob filled the tank and we drove back to Calgary while they bickered. For the last ten minutes of the drive they'd settled down, Jacob was concentrating on driving and Adam sat scheming in his head; his arm perched on the center console at a ninety degree angle as he rubbed his fingers together like the dark lord Satan himself; his long sharp yellow fingernails missing each other by just millimetres.

When we got back to the city we stopped in the parking lot of a casino.

"You will go to the cash window and pull out nine hundred and eighty dollars. Get the receipt like you did at the bank. We will get the rest from an ATM later."

"Alright."

Nervously, I walked through the casino until I came upon the cash window and withdrew nine hundred and eighty dollars with the receipt, like Adam told me to. I found the same door I came in and when they weren't there I took a stroll around the parking lot until they found me. I had a big smile on my face and they smiled back before I got in, giving Adam the receipt and money.

"Good boy," he said.

We parked in the parking lot of a nearby corner store where I withdrew the last five hundred.

Once Adam counted it all out he handed me $500 as promised.

"See!?" We all laughed like tricky bank swindling hyenas.

"You was scared, wasn't you Mack Yay?" Euphoria was thick in the car.

"I've just never done anything like that before." I said shaking, though I knew it was too good to be true; this would catch up to me one day.

"We will do this for another two weeks or so." Adam reinstated. "Do you have a phone?"

"No."

Adam nodded.

"We'll get you a phone; we need you to have one." They argued in Arabic for a moment before we drove to a mall. When we got there Adam told me about the same cheap phone company I was already connected to with the stolen phone, then followed me inside the mall. I got a cheap smartphone with a forty dollar plan and it cost me $200. While we walked back to the car Adam took my number down and called to make sure it worked, then they asked if I needed anything else. Told them some weed would be nice and I gave them $60. Jacob went by himself to pick it up from a friend and I thought he either ripped me off or didn't buy the amount I gave him money for. As we drove Adam asked me to give Jacob $50 just until tomorrow; I did and then they pulled up to a motel that they said was good and cheap.

"We'll see you tomorrow, right Jesmer?"

"Yeah man."

"Good." They both shook my hand and I got out of the car. Adam passed me my laptop bag through the window and said "Call if you have any problems."

"For sure." Jacob threw up the peace sign and then they drove off.

Holy fuck. I counted out my money before I went in the motel and I had less than $200. *I hope this motel is as cheap as they said.* It was! Because they didn't have any beds available. After I bought cigarettes from a store nearby I trailed up the road aimlessly, downloading music in search of inspiration for a solution. *I'm obviously the scapegoat in this whole thing.*

A while later Adam began texting me, asking if I got a room, if I wanted a ride to a different place and so on. Obviously he didn't like not knowing where I was. *If I don't get caught during this, I'll get caught at tax time.* I needed a friend, one from my past life, but there were only two that I knew of in Calgary. I searched my emails until I found a number.

Ned was the only person I'd spoken to outside of the study since I came to Calgary, I saw him for a brief moment the first Sunday I spent at the DI. He mic'd me up and filmed a mock interview with me out of interest in what I was doing; he moved from Red Deer to go to SAIT which is where I was waiting to meet him now. Before I went homeless I could say Ned and I had similar goals, now I'm not so sure. Ned's the type of friend that upon learning upon my fall to the condition said 'I thought it would have happened sooner.'

When he pulled up in his van, Ned turned the interior light on so I could see him and gave me a wave and a friendly smile. Once I was in shotgun we shook hands.

"How's it goin' *buddy*!?" Ned shouted, excited to see me.

"Alright man, you?"

"Good!" He plugged a vaporizer pipe into his van and ground up some weed in a buster.

"I got some too."

"Nice!"

Ned looked the same as he did since grade 7; curly long hair, glasses, leather jacket, though now that he was actually a film student, he had a new confident, self-contained air about him.

"So, what's this crazy story!?"

I told him about my day, start to finish, and by the time I was done the vaporizer was hot enough to smoke out of and we passed it back and forth.

"What were they?"

"What do you mean?"

"White, Black, Mexican, Asian-"

"Arabic, well one of them was; they were cousins though, but I didn't really believe that. They were speaking in Arabic most of the day. The one guy said he was from Montreal."

"What were their names?"

"Adam and Jacob, but I didn't believe that either." Ned cackled hysterically.

"Mike, did you get scammed by Somalians?"

"Kind of - but I got five hundred dollars."

"That's still getting scammed by Somalians. They used your bank account, right?"

"Yeah."

"You got scammed by Somalians." I joined his laughter.

"Fuck, leave it to me, eh?"

"When did this all happen?"

"Today man!"

"So what happened after they dropped you off?"

"There wasn't a room at the motel they thought I was going to."

"Then you called me?"

"Yeah, man."

"Why does everyone come to me!?" He asked himself. "People *always* come to me for this kind of thing."

"Really? *This* kind of thing?"

"Not exactly, but you know what I mean, I'm always helping people."

"Brutal."

Ned packed more weed into the vaporizer and we started passing it back and forth again.

"So besides cashing fraudulent cheques, what have you been up to? Still living at the *DI*?"

"Yeah man, it's been really crazy actually."

Tried to explain the best I could the most important things I'd learned in my experiences, but I was ridiculously high and everything I was saying sounded better in my head than it did when I said it out loud.

"The books going to be epic man, you'll just have to read it."

"Definitely. Are you going to somehow *redeem* yourself at the end? Come out of it all on top nice and shiny?"

"Sure hope so."

"People love that, it makes for a good story. Like Donny Skinner when he was doing MMA before he died."

"Yeah." My heart skipped. "Wait, did you just say Donny Skinner died?"

"Yeah man," Ned laughed.

"*Donny Skinner.*"

He nodded as he reefed on the vaporizer.

"Like, *Donny* Donny?"

"Like a couple months ago." Again he laughed. "You didn't know that? Oh yeah I guess you don't have Facebook. Yeah man, he's *dead.*"

"Wow."

I told you that I was the first person from my graduating class that admitted I had a problem and did everything in my power to fix it, but Donny was the first from our grade. He had a rough childhood and was in and out of juvie, and eventually prison. The guy was the definition of gangster, but if you were on his good side, he was the best friend you could have.

"Geez, I talked to him right before I came to Calgary when he turned a year sober. We were gonna chill."

Donny was my other friend who lived in Calgary, I was very interested to see what he would think of my *project*. He was a street youth and beat all the odds, people called him a Red Deer legend, even when he was alive.

"Well, you won't be able to chill with him *now* because he's dead." *You always been this desensitized Ned? Was I like that too?*

"How did he die?"

"Brain aneurism."

"Crazy."

"People die all the time!"

Frustration changed the subject back to Adam and Jacob and I asked Ned if he would be interested in following us the next day and splitting the cheque fifty-fifty. Ned said he didn't need a thousand dollars but he'd do it anyways just so he could say he did but after we devised a few plans we decided there were too many variables for it to work, then he started his van.

"You goin' back to the DI?"

"Do you think I could crash at your place man? Just for tonight."

"I don't see why not!"

He drove to a nice area of the city and showed me the basement suite he was renting. It was spacious and even came with a theatre room. After showing me the projector that he uses to watch movies and play games, he went to sleep, leaving me in the living room. *What a day* I thought, wishing I'd gone to college.

***

I left early the next morning; early enough that I could be at the DI before 6:45am to drop my laptop off for safe keeping before they locked the doors to Fifth for the day. Adam and Jacob met me at the same place we'd met Jacob the day before around 9:45am, right before the banks opened. They seemed to both take note that I didn't have my laptop bag today but didn't give me any verbal indication.

Adam gave me my $50 back when I got in the car and I was glad that Ned and I decided against our scheme because today Adam had four separate smaller cheques for me to cash, but they all added up to around the same price. It was a long day of driving from bank to casino to bank to casino to ATM to bank and so on, but by the end of the day, Adam gave me another five hundred dollars and this time made sure I got a room at a motel before writing the suite number down on his hand.

Sitting by the door in my silent motel room, getting nervous every time the CIA walked by my door, I knew it wouldn't be long until I had some whiskey - the bottle practically appeared in my hand.

There I sat, smoking joint after cigarette after joint, until I began thinking of one of my teenage heroes; Frank Abagnale Jr., the anti-hero from the true story *Catch Me if You Can*. *What a lonely life he must have lived,* I judged while experiencing just a grain of what he lived through. Reflecting on what I really wanted to do with my life I tastelessly continued drinking and smoking until I woke up to Adam's call.

I met them a few painfully hung over blocks away from the motel, and we repeated the same process as the day before, but tension rose between them when we ran out of banks in the city and had to drive to another city nearby, presumably Someplaceville. By the time we got back to the motel they were yelling at each other, and all I knew was my name came up frequently between both of them. I assumed either Jacob had a problem with his cut or they were fighting over who had to kill me.

Adam handed me four hundred dollars this time telling me that there were *other people* involved that he had to pay. I got out of the vehicle and checked into the same motel but a different room, taking a shower before leaving for my laptop. Music wasn't really an option, as it would have stifled my awareness, but I needed some kind of distractions. *No way I'm just listening to footsteps tonight.*

***

At the DI I avoided eye contact and conversation with anyone and everyone. When the Dice that unlocked my locker asked where I'd been I told her I had been *out* and would be *out* for a while; then she reminded me if I wasn't back by Tuesday I'd lose my bed. After I grabbed my laptop bag I locked my locker, turning to see Sergei looking at me.

"So you *do* drink!" I grinned.

"Why do you say that?"

"I know booze when I smell it! Howsabout a reward for giving you your wallet back the uver night?" He laughed then slapped my shoulder. *Yeah right.*

"I'm just kidding wiff you. I'm not one of *those* assholes." With a smoke in his mouth he walked away.

"Maike!" I looked over at a confused Mando who slapped his forehead and blinked a few times.

"Where have you been!?"

"Oh, ya know, getting into all sorts of trouble." I was semi-serious, but he took it as a joke.

"You used to be here all the time, now you neva here! We always talk about you in laundry, we always say 'That *Maike*!'" he said with a big white smile. Waving a finger at me, he continued. "We have high hopes for *you* Maike. I know one day, you and me, Maike, we're going to be sitting dare laughing about the days we spent at the *DI*."

Mando went into a lecture that lasted way too long and I was getting frustrated, and the more frustrated I got the more he thought he was teaching me; he said that once.

Now he was going on about how the only reason misfortunate people are misfortunate is because they have a negative mindset. "*I* just feel bad for *them* you know what I mean? Because *I* can neva help them if they neva help themselves."

"Yeah but *who* do you want to help though, Mando?" He blinked a few times.

"*Everybody*!"

"How are you going to help *everybody*? You can't just help *everybody*, you have to know who you're helping if you say you're going to help people."

"*I* can help *everybody* Maike, if they just listen to me."

"Maybe but you can't just help people by raising awareness of the power of positive thinking, that's not going to do anything for anyone except maybe make them feel better. Yeah, I mean you'll do a lot better at life if you feel better about yourself, but there are tons of people that don't have the skills or opportunities or resources to improve their own life. Think of people in…" - I almost said *Africa* but I was staring into the eyes of a native to that land "…other countries. Victims of circumstance, man."

"Positive thinking will help them too, because you see Maike -"

"I don't want to hear it anymore Mando! Positive thinking *isn't* going to help them, not physically. If you want to help people you need to *help* them. I don't even know why we're talking about helping people, look where we're living. We can't even help ourselves." Mando stared at me discouraged for a few seconds.

"I gotta get going."

"Oh, see you, Maike."

"See ya, Mando."

I left Mando sad as a sad puppy dog and beat myself up about it all the way back to the motel; it was good vindication to drink again, though with my computer I was a little more distracted.

***

Alarms never wake me up, but I set one for early anyway so I could return my laptop to its safe locker at the DI. Adam's first call didn't wake me up but the next one did. Laying there watching my phone ring over and over I considered calling it quits, but temptation still had the best of me. I was going to call him back after I showered but I wanted to smoke a joint first but Adam knocked on the door.

"Jesmer!"

Yawning while I opened the door, I tried to pretend I just woke up.

"You're late!" he hissed.

"Am I? Sorry, my phone must have died or something."

"It's no problem." He scowled. "Take your time."

Checking out as soon as possible I got in the Cadillac and started chain smoking cigarettes as soon as we hit the road. We left Calgary as expected, but I didn't expect them to drive to Red Deer!

Looking at the streets of my home town felt more eerie than nostalgic.

We hit a few banks in Red Deer, then drove around to collect all the cash while they yelled at each other. We parked in a Wal-Mart parking lot afterward and they sent me in to the ATM to pull out my maximum limit. There was still a hundred and forty left in the account.

When I got back to the car the yelling had gotten much worse and I handed the cash to Adam. I was afraid a gun was going to get pulled out or something. Jacob's face was bright red and spit was flying out of his mouth with each word, while Adam held his ground like a rattle snake.

Jacob kept saying 'Mack Yay' while holding up five fingers, and a little relief came over me as I now knew I wasn't going to be murdered.

There was a break in their argument and Adam handed me five hundred dollars then asked if it would be okay if he took my card to *collect the rest* over the weekend. "Sure." *Nope.* I knew I had to get out. *Thank God we're in Red Deer*! The fighting continued and I began to wonder if this had all been a set up to get my bank card and information. *With the card they wouldn't need me.* Still though, the fight went on, and Adam got out of the car. Jacob looked back at me but didn't want to tell me to get out.

"Jesmer! We're going!" Adam called and I got out to follow him.

"What's up?"

"He wants more than a hundred a day for *driving." I would too, this is highly illegal.*

"Oh."

We kept walking until we were almost out of the parking lot when Jacob's vehicle soared around the corner like an eagle and charged right towards us like an angry bull; nothing short of majestic, but I almost shit myself before he drifted and came to a stop five, ten feet away.

I think Jacob was trying to bargain, but Adam waved him off then tried to leave but couldn't help but engage in another argument once Jacob got out of the Cadillac and started yelling again. While they yelled at each other I slowly backed away and out of sight behind a tree, then turned to the streetlight, frantically pressing the button so I could go the only way the law permitted. Those stupid things never work, and by the time the lights were changing, Adam was beside me. *Dammit.*

"We'll take the Greyhound back," he said. We used my expertise of the Red Deer transit system to get to the Greyhound station and he paid for our tickets. Five hours until our bus departed. I sat down across from him in the lobby and we didn't say a word to each other; he was too cross about what happened. After downloading and listening to music for a while, I eventually looked up from my phone to see him sleeping. *Is this it?*

For maybe ten minutes I stared to make sure he was asleep before I so much as took a breath. Carefully, I rose with my laptop and began tip-toeing away while maintaining my gaze; his eyes opened and I looked away as if I weren't watching him, then looked over at him as if he'd moved.

Adam just stared. *Half-asleep?*

"I'm just going out for a smoke." He didn't move. "You gonna come?"

He shook his head then slowly closed his eyes as I got out the door and ran. There's a motel across the street from the Red Deer Greyhound station and that's where I spent the most intoxicated weekend of my life. So far.

15

ARTISTIC SACRAFICE

Ned was willing to meet me at a moment's notice when I got back to Calgary on Tuesday, I was waiting for him at the same place, looking over all the messages from Adam I missed over the weekend. It was providential that my phone plan didn't come with voicemail and wasn't in service in Red Deer, but now it was time to face the music; Adam was pissed.

Ned drove up in his van and I got in. "Hey buddy!"

"Hey man."

"So you need to pick up some stuff from the DI?"

"Yeah, is that cool?"

"Yeah man, how long ya gonna be?"

"Not long, I can pay you."

"No it's fine, you'll need it." The lights exposed a grin on his face in the shadows as he drove.

"So where you gonna go?"

"I don't know yet, somewhere in BC, I think. Haven't even looked into bus tickets."

"Nice. How much do you have?"

"Two hundred and thirty bucks," I said miserably.

Ned was clearly expecting me to have a lot more, but regrettably, I'd spent a little over $400 on the motel from Friday to Monday and spent the rest on food and substances. *What a waste of money.* At the time I'd ditched Adam, I had over a thousand. Ned tried to be cool about it.

"Nice!" We drove to the DI, and since I'd never been outside Alberta, Ned told me about all the different places in B.C that would be prime to escape to. In Ned's mind, I was going to bus to a mountain town like Kamloops or Vernon and flee into the mountains, he even said he'd hook me up with survival gear he bought for summer camping. *I don't know if I'm ready for that.*

***

Rummaging, rather unsuccessfully, through my locker for anything of value or importance, I was disappointed that Mando wasn't there so I could apologize to him. I packed my laptop, some clothes, and my journals and books into my travelers backpack and quickly threw everything else into a garbage bag so the Dice wouldn't have to do it. I mournfully anticipated what I was going to do with the backpack Donald had given me. *I can't just throw it out.* Having very little of value, I found myself creating my own in anything I could - hard to say if this was learned or natural behavior.

Lester happened to walk up while I was trying to stuff it in my traveler's bag.

"Lester you want a backpack man? Zipper's broken but I fixed it with a paperclip."

"Sure!" He took the backpack from me as if it were a gift from God. "What are you doing?" Looking into his dilated pupils, I took a deep breath and exhaled.

"Lester I'm leaving buddy."

There was a slight pause, I thought his head was going to explode.

"You can't do that!"

"I have to."

"Where are you going to go?" Lester followed me over to a garbage can where I threw out all the garbage I'd accumulated.

"BC"

His eyes widened. "No no no, I don't think you should do *that*! That's a bad idea!"

"I have to!"

"Why do you have to?"

"Cause I'm in trouble man."

"*Trouble*? What kind of trouble?" His eyes got even wider.

"I don't know yet," I answered while putting on my backpack.

"Well come back!"

"Maybe to visit."

We walked over to the office.

"Do you have an email address or phone number?"

"Just Facebook," he replied.

"My bed's free now! I'm leaving!" I exclaimed to the Dice in the office.

"For good?"

"Yeah!"

"Are you sure? Once you give up your bed, it's gone."

"Don't have a choice!"

"Alright!" She called while Lester and I headed for the doors.

"I don't have Facebook, I'll try to visit. One day."

"Well good luck!"

We shook hands and Lester walked away, offended.

***

"Get everything you needed?" Ned asked while I threw my *oh-yeah-that's-heavy* backpack into the back of his van.

"Yes, sir!"

"Good."

I got into the front and we drove to his place where we sat out front smoking weed for an hour looking over different maps of places in B.C.

"So, where you gonna go, man?"

"I don't know yet."

"You have to decide."

"I don't know yet, I'll decide when I wake up, I'm baked."

"You have to decide *now*!"

"Why do I have to decide *now*?"

"The sooner you decide where you're going the sooner you can figure out how much it's going to cost and what you're going to do."

"True. Well as much as I like the idea of taking off into the bush a hundred and ten percent unprepared I think there are better options. I was thinking Vancouver, my phone would have coverage there and I could make some money and get supplies, if I *do* decide to move to the mountains." He nodded a few times.

"Vancouver's *good,* but if you go there now you'll *stay* homeless. *I* think you should make your way through the wilderness and make Vancouver your final destination, kind of like a reward. Then you'll, I don't know, actually appreciate it." *Maybe you're right.* "But it's your call."

He started typing something into his smartphone. "Well a ticket to Vancouver tonight would be a hundred seventeen."

"That's not bad."

"If you go to the mountains where would you bus to?"

"Vernon?"

"Ninety two bucks." He said before giving me a look. "So, where you gonna go!?"

I told him I still hadn't decided and we went inside where he gave me a small portable water purifier, four cans of mango juice, a few packs of noodles and a bottle of aloe pulp water. *You were going to send me into the wilderness with this?* Who knows, maybe if I actually made a decision he would have given me more.

Ned was under the impression that I was going to leave early in the morning because I told him I was going to leave early in the morning, but I slept through my alarm and woke up around noon. When I got out of the washroom he had just woken up as well. We wished each other luck and I carried myself up the stairs. *Off to the Greyhound.*

***

The ticket to Vancouver cost me $112 and I had nothing but time and brain cells to kill. A bottle of liquor and two movies later I had but two hours left until it was time to leave. Bussing near the DI I had a personal moment before staggering up and down Hobo Central a few times. *Am I going to miss it?* Reflecting on all the people at the DI that I wanted to say goodbye to, all the conversations left unspoken, all the voices unheard, all the people that still needed help. *Wow, I am going to miss this place. It's been a time.*

"You're too drunk sir." The security officer doing bag checks told me.

"I'm not drunk!"

"No, you need to go."

"Fuck you man! Do you know how much this ticket was!?"

"Yes." He waved over two more security guards.

"Come on dude I'm homeless, I spent the last of my money on this ticket."

While the other two security guards approached he looked me in the eyes and chose to believe me before he wrote something on the ticket.

"Come back tomorrow. *Sober.*"

"Thanks man."

He rolled his eyes as the other security guards escorted me outside where I paced the perimeter of the building, smoking cigarettes. *God dammit.* I called the DI and asked to speak to the fifth floor, they said my bed was already taken and I sounded too drunk anyway so I found a place behind an electrical box and tried to sleep. Unfortunately, I was sober enough that it felt like my first time sleeping outside and I couldn't manage to get comfortable, not to mention it was freezing. *Isn't it supposed to be spring?*

After a sketchy hour of people walking by me someone walked behind the electrical box and unzipped his pants, then walked away when he noticed me. *Great, I'm lying in a piss spot.* Rising out of hopefully dried up urine, I carried my giant backpack all the way to where this crazy story began.

* * *

Intox was the only place in the DI I hadn't experienced from an occupants point of view; until now. With no recollection of actually arriving at the DI I awoke on the cold floor within half an arm's reach of two other guys. There must have been a hundred of us, maybe two, laying down this way.

Most had floor mats, but I got there late.

My stomach was in knots and there were two giant bags of McDonald's that, if not for my wretched gas, I would have thought belonged to someone else. Fighting the urge to vomit from either the smell of Intox or myself was all I could do as I lay on the floor staring at the roof. Eventually I sat up and when the room stopped spinning managed to stand. I threw my bag over my shoulder and made way to leave when I ran into Ray.

"Hey Ray."

"Hey uh, Michael!" The corners of his bushy moustache raised. "How'd ya like Intox?"

"Not as bad as I thought. You want this?" I held the McDonald's out to him. "I don't know what's in there, but it doesn't smell like garbage." *Or does it?*

"Sure uh, if you don't want it I'll bring it down to laundry for breakfast. Are you coming down today?"

"Nah, I'm going to Vancouver today."

"Oh, are ya visiting?"

"No, I'm gone for good."

"Really? Well best of luck."

"Thanks. Tell everyone I wished I could have said goodbye but something came up."

After shaking his hand I went to Tim Horton's and got a coffee and a bagel, but I couldn't eat, not *that* at least. Cereal or something else is what I was craving, something that might help settle my stomach. There was only a half hour until they served breakfast at the mansion. *My last meal there.*

As you may have guessed, I was in an awful mood, not just that but my hang over was devastating. Fighting the urge to vomit, I approached the bridge beside the DI and found Tweety and her misfits loitering underneath. Tweety approached me and I almost told her to get lost.

"Are you okay?" She asked, hugging me.

I hugged her back and when we let go of the embrace she said "Everyone deserves to smile sometimes."

To be honest, that was how I remembered what I said when I was verging on my blackout the month previous.

There were still sleepers spread out in the lobby from the night before as I lined up for breakfast with Old Steve. To my surprise Steve Tower was one of them but he didn't look so good; his complexion sickly pale and his lips a light blue, chapped and crusty. Beside him was Lyle. *At least you found someone better than Brad to follow.*

While we waited in line Old Steve and I spoke a little bit about writing, and then something disturbing froze the conversation. Rod the lightening Rod, the old man that Brad introduced me to at the same time I met the now deceased Andy, was standing in the middle of the lobby bawling his eyes out, wailing unlike anything I'd ever seen. My heart sank, melted and disappeared all at once; it may have been the saddest thing I've ever seen.

Through his pain-staked eyes, I could see a life time of loss and tragedy lived at the DI. *The things he must have seen.* "Oh boo-*hoo*." Old Steve said before jumping into a fit of laughter and I understood why. *You must only feel what I just felt once.*

We got upstairs and I've never been so happy to receive a soggy bowl of Cheerios. While I ate, I scanned for familiar faces, but only came across people I'd imagined meeting. After savoring the sog and drinking the grainy milk, I came to terms that it was time to say goodbye to the DI. I put my bowl away and as I walked down the stairs to leave I saw a new face sitting in the corner of the stairs; young and scared, just staring at the floor. Standing nearby, I ripped a page out of my notepad and wrote down as much of the information I could remember from Trent. *EST, laundry… What else?* When I handed it to him it seemed like he didn't care much, but he thanked me before his eyes returned to the floor. I noticed, as I descended the next staircase, that he was reading the list.

Walking up Hobo central, I found a few Hobos outside of a lawyer's office building. *I wonder if they do consultations.* They did, and after I had what was promised to be a confidential conversation with my new lawyer, Sam Salam, about Adam and the bank fraud, he told me that he may be able to help me with the situation, but not until I'm caught however. He gave me his card and told me to turn myself in and give him a call as soon as possible so he could get me out of this sticky jam. *Yeah, I'll get right on that, bud.*

***

The rest of the day was spent watching the movies I hadn't seen in the theatre I'd been going to and buying expensive meals from a restaurant that shared the same parking lot between shows. Around 8:00 pm, after the last movie, I caved in and bought another bottle of liquor. *Stupid movie romantic interest.* Kelsey was all I could think about, it seemed the actors of every movie were scripted to play us.

I wandered around a skate park near the DI, seriously considering my options while downloading and listening to music of the 'fuck love' genre, drinking and trying to convince myself leaving was my only choice. *You could blow off your bus tonight and see Kelsey tomorrow, get out of the DI and who knows what could happen? If you leave now that's it man.*

Greyhound security was still skeptical but deemed me sober enough to get on the bus this time. There was an anxious thrill that came over me as I left my travelers backpack beside the bus for the driver to load up. As I got on the bus and seized a window seat near the back, I put my headphones in and thought; *this is really it. The end of my adventure, the beginning of a new one?* Who could know? I was still in awe of everything that happened. Scarves, Spaceboots, Blinks, Wandering Twins, stories, Hobos, Pleb's, people, liquor, drugs and oh the stupidity; what a mess I'd made in my head.

Once we started driving I began to panic. *Ned was right, man, once you go to Vancouver you're going to get stuck there, what do you know about Vancouver?*

Ned was a good friend of mine, had been for a very long time. We shared similar passions and goals, but there was always one big difference between us; my addiction. Whereas Ned would credit any action made by what some would call my 'addict self' as idiocy, the problem really laid in my inability to cope with stress.

The best way I can describe addiction to someone who hasn't experienced it first hand is having to pay rent on your body and/or mind every single day. This was something I identified when I was in rehab, but watching the buildings go by until the scenery turned to prairie and the city of Calgary scaled farther and farther behind me, I made the most fascinating observation of my study so far. What Ned and I had in common all these years was our Spaceboots. *He's got them too,* I noted. *Scarves and Spaceboots don't limit themselves to the condition; it's human nature.*

Though I wasn't sure exactly what I had just stumbled upon, it was at *that* moment I established the foundation of my study and confirmed with myself that I was on the right track to creating something meaningful. But until I did, the major contemporary difference between Ned and I is he was becoming an astronaut, and I was just pretending.

The farther we drove, the worse the weather became, until our driver made an executive decision to stop in Banff before making an announcement that there was a blizzard en route and we may have to turn around. *Good God is this ever going to end!?*

I took my jacket off and wrapped it into a make-shift pillow before I rested my head on it; just thinking. *Kelsey. Biker Mike. Everyone.* The sad truth is I would have had to say goodbye to them all sooner or later because without the struggle I would never have met them, but there was no question that every person and every story changed my life, if even just a little.

The stress of the inevitable discovery of my bank fraud kept me awake for just minutes before I calmed myself down. *Give it to the wind man, no reason to stop now.* I felt as though I could have justified crying at that moment but how could I? Everything that happened, everything that hurt me, or inconvenienced me, was brought on by none other than me. The experience was everything I dreamed of and more the night I devised my inept plan on my dirty floor in Red Deer, it was far too late to snuff it off.

Leading me through the experience was something a lot more deep rooted, and possibly more dangerous, than my addiction; my Spaceboots, and I wasn't planning on taking them off just yet. Crying *now* could only mean nothing. I arrived on the first of February and left on the first of May. *Three months sounds credible* I told myself as I dozed off.

Dreaming of better days in a better life, assuming that when I got off the bus a SWAT team would be waiting for me, I thought I may end my book with a few words of wisdom from prison followed by the line "In the end I still had all of my teeth, but fuck, were they ever yellow."

www.ingramcontent.com/pod-product-compliance
Lightning Source LLC
Chambersburg PA
CBHW051540030726
47592CB00001B/64